The

NICOLET
Corrigenda

RED BANKS

Many of the explorers who followed Columbus were more interested in finding an easy route to Asia than they were in exploring and settling this continent. In 1634 Jean Nicolet, emissary of Gov. Samuel de Champlain of New France, landed at Red Banks on the shore of Green Bay about a mile west of here. His mission was to arrange peace with the "People of the Sea" and to ally them with France. Nicolet half expected to meet Asiatics on his voyage and had with him an elaborate Oriental robe which he put on before landing. The Winnebago Indians who met him were more impressed with the "thunder" he carried in both hands as he stepped ashore firing his pistols. Nicolet reported to his superiors that he was well entertained with "sixscore beavers" being served at one banquet, but it was the pelts and not the flesh of the beaver that were to be highly prized by those who followed him.

Erected 1957

Sign Erected by the Wisconsin Historical Society in 1957 containing the popularly accepted but largely erroneous account of Nicolet's Journey of 1634. (Photograph by James Uhrinak)

The
NICOLET
Corrigenda

NEW FRANCE REVISITED

Nancy Oestreich Lurie
Milwaukee Public Museum

Patrick J. Jung
Milwaukee School of Engineering

WAVELAND

PRESS, INC.

Long Grove, Illinois

For information about this book, contact:
Waveland Press, Inc.
4180 IL Route 83, Suite 101
Long Grove, IL 60047-9580
(847) 634-0081
info@waveland.com
www.waveland.com

Cover: *The Landfall of Jean Nicolet*, E. W. Demming (a detail of the full image), 1904. (Wisconsin Historical Society. Image ID: 1870)

Maps on pp. vi–ix by Rick Regazzi.

10-digit ISBN 1-57766-606-2
13-digit ISBN 978-1-57766-606-6

Printed in the United States of America

7 6 5 4 3 2 1

Contents

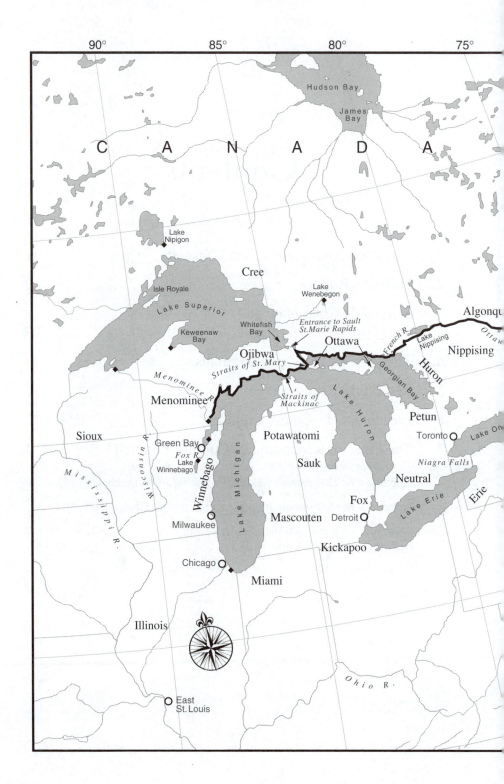

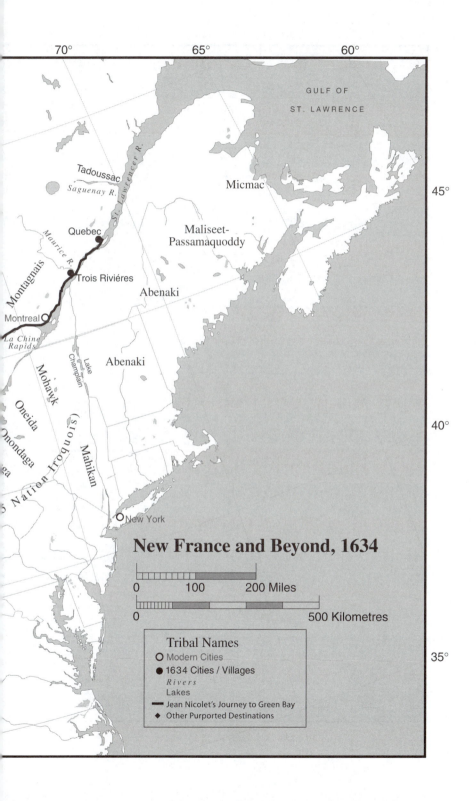

70°   65°   60°

GULF OF
ST. LAWRENCE

45°

Tadoussac
Saguenay R.
Micmac

Maliseet-
Passamaquoddy

Quebec

Trois Riviéres

Montagnais

Abenaki

Montreal

La Chine
Rapids

Abenaki

40°

Mohawk

Oneida

Onondaga

Mahikan

New York

35°

New France and Beyond, 1634

0   100   200 Miles

0   500 Kilometres

Tribal Names
○ Modern Cities
● 1634 Cities / Villages
Rivers
Lakes
— Jean Nicolet's Journey to Green Bay
◆ Other Purported Destinations

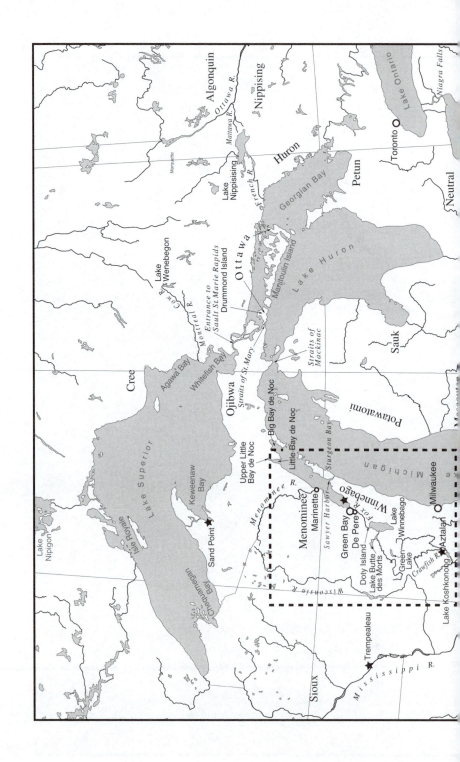

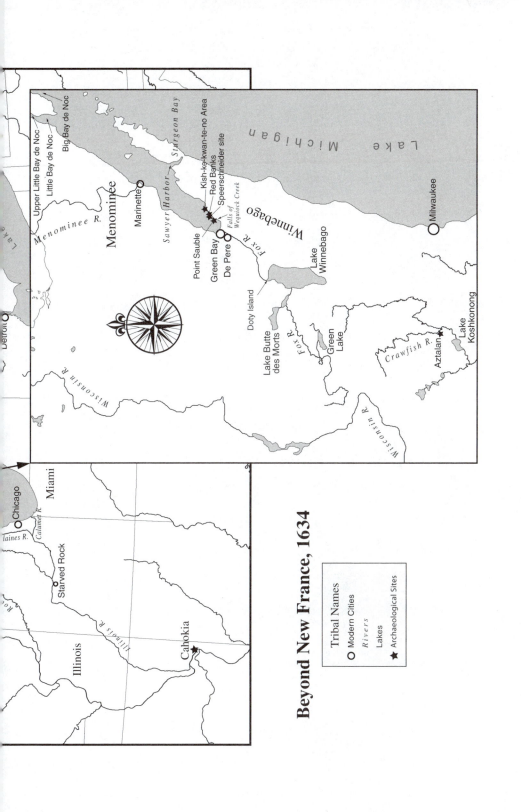

Beyond New France, 1634

Tribal Names
○ Modern Cities
Rivers
Lakes
★ Archaeological Sites

The
NICOLET
Corrigenda

Chapter 1

The Fabricated Fame
of Jean Nicolet

*W*hile Jean Nicolet is hardly a major historic figure, he is well known to American historians as well as to many history buffs and school children in Wisconsin as the first European to reach Wisconsin. His story has captured the public imagination beyond this single achievement because it is believed that he wore a gaudy Chinese robe when he met with the Winnebago Indians in the mistaken belief that they might be Chinese or, at least, had some direct connection to the Orient. The scene of Nicolet clad in a Chinese garment as envisioned by different artists is the subject of a number of large paintings hanging in public buildings in Wisconsin, which serve to reinforce the memory of a cherished but fictional incident in Wisconsin's history.

We started out accepting this familiar image of Nicolet when Lurie discovered by chance and to her astonishment that there never was a Chinese robe! Having pulled this thread, she could not resist tugging further and with Jung unraveled a whole tapestry of errors, inventions, sloppy scholarship, and passionately partisan defenses of conflicting conclusions going back well over a century regarding virtually every aspect of the Nicolet story. The corrigenda, the list of errors, introduced here will be examined in detail in the chapters to follow. Because many of the errors and controversies relate to geographical issues, the maps on pages vi–ix, "New France and Beyond, 1634" and "Beyond New France, 1634" are provided to facilitate following Nicolet's travels and supposed travels and locating all the places and peoples mentioned in our narrative.

All we really know about Nicolet's journey from the documentary record is that he set out in the summer of 1634 with seven "savages" from the Huron country around Georgian Bay of Lake Huron, having been directed by Samuel de Champlain, commandant of New France, to meet with the

1

Puant or Puan people, who had come to his attention as early as 1615. Nicolet's mission was to establish peace between them and the Huron, a term that seems to have included their Algonquian-speaking allies such as the Ottawa. The Huron spoke an Iroquoian language but were not part of the famous Five Nations League of the Iroquois. In fact, they were at odds with it; they allied with the French, while the League was allied with the Dutch and later the English.

The Puan are known today as Winnebago or by their own tribal name, Ho-Chunk, which is glossed as either "big fish" or, more commonly, "big voice," "ho" being a homonym and "chunk" signifying big in the sense of primary or ancestral. Their language is related to the Chiwere branch of Siouan that also includes Iowa, Oto, and Missouria; the Siouan language stock is totally different from Algonquian and Iroquoian. Winnebago, the standard English form of the French *Ouinepigou*, variously spelled, is what their Algonquian-speaking tribal neighbors called them. It was translated as "Puan" (or Puans or Puant) in French and "Stinkard" in English, supposedly in reference to their living or having lived near smelly water rather than to their personal hygiene. Another designation for the tribe is *Gens de Mer* or "People of the Sea." Although found in accounts going back to the seventeenth century, it is a misnomer. It was never used by the Ho-Chunk or their tribal neighbors, but it has contributed greatly over the years to enhancing the idea that the French associated the Winnebago with Asia or the fabled Northwest Passage leading to the Pacific Ocean.

We use the different names for the Winnebago interchangeably, generally favoring whichever is appropriate to the particular historical or scholarly context under discussion. In regard to different literary usages in designating Indian tribes, we use Winnebago, Potawatomi, Menominee, and so forth, as collective plurals for tribes as a whole or a single tribal member, and Winnebagos, Potawatomis, Menominees, and so forth to specify two or more members of a given tribe.

Nicolet is recorded as having met with a large conclave of Indians, some 4,000 to 5,000 people from a number of "tribes," at an undesignated location where one of the feasts in honor of the occasion included "sixscore beavers." There he delivered Champlain's message of peace, presumably to open the way to French trade farther west. Whether Nicolet explored farther or returned immediately to New France is unknown. His presence back in Quebec is not documented until December 1635, but we don't know how long he had been away. Several writers use this date to give Nicolet time to engage in extensive travel—in different directions—during the same period: that he ventured inland to Lake Winnebago and Green Lake in Wisconsin, possibly even as far as the Mississippi River, or that he followed the coast of Lake Michigan to what is now southern Cook County, Illinois.

The popular version of the story has Nicolet meeting the Winnebago Indians at their ancient stronghold, their "big village" as they still refer to it in their own language, in the Red Banks area of the Door Peninsula on the east side of Green Bay. Red Banks refers to the mile or so stretch of bluff fronting on Green Bay in the Benderville area of Brown County as well as to the major Winnebago village associated with the region. There is disagreement among historians and archaeologists, however, about the actual location of the village there, and there are strongly held differences of opinion whether or not the Ho-Chunk lived on the Door Peninsula at all at the time of Nicolet's visit. Some writers believe Nicolet did not even reach Lake Michigan but entered Lake Superior instead, necessitating the assumption that the Ho-Chunk were living outside present-day Wisconsin in 1634.

Our intention when we began this project in 2005 was simply to contribute an article concerning the landfall issue, offering what we consider persuasive evidence that Nicolet landed in Menominee rather than Ho-Chunk country, near the present city of Marinette, Wisconsin, where the great Indian council took place that would have included Ho-Chunk representatives. Our article expanded into a book and took more and more time as we returned to the primary sources and were fascinated to discover how Nicolet's journey and the people he set out to meet have been variously perceived and misrepresented in many respects besides the disputes about the site of the landfall. We also realized belatedly that it was time to pay more attention to the role of his seven anonymous fellow travelers.

It is remarkable so much has been written about Nicolet insofar as no writings in his own hand survive, and the whole documentary record of his journey consists of a few Jesuits' recollections of what he told them. We have no idea whether he kept a journal despite the mistaken claim (which refers to an actual incident in the explorations of Marquette and Joliet) that he did and it was lost "in a canoe spill" (Risjord 2001:37). The most detailed and frequently cited account is by the Jesuit Barthelmy Vimont that appeared in 1643, the year after Nicolet's death and nearly 10 years after his journey. In reviewing the skimpy entries in *The Jesuit Relations*, we were surprised to learn how they have been obscured and expanded on and how their authority as primary reference works was preempted by nineteenth-century and later secondary interpretations and assumptions.

Three other important sources are relevant to the Nicolet story, although they do not mention him. Samuel de Champlain, the founder of Quebec, learned of the Winnebago in 1615 from the Ottawa who were middlemen in the fur trade, and Champlain noted the Winnebagos' existence on a 1616 map. Gabriel Sagard, a lay brother in the Récollet branch of the Franciscan order that preceded the Jesuits in New France, recorded the existence of the Winnebago as early 1623. The third important source consists of the combined records of Nicolas Perrot and Claude Charles le Roy, Sieur de Bacqueville de la Potherie, whose own writings were based on information from Perrot; thus, the works of both men are hereafter cited simply as Perrot. These writings recount a series of calamitous events that appear to have befallen the allegedly once formidable Puan after 1634 but before Perrot journeyed to Wisconsin more than 30 years later.

Since these few primary references contain virtually all the documentation bearing on Nicolet's voyage and the Winnebago at the time, we reproduce them in full in Appendices A and B to leave no doubt as to their actual content and to obviate repetitious citations since we and other writers refer to them so frequently throughout the chapters to follow. A final appendix discusses the circumstances under which Paul Radin shared unpublished information with Lurie, cited throughout the story to follow as: (Radin, personal communication 1957).

The English versions of the historic sources contained in the appendices are derived from rather archaic French. Some of the confusion about Nicolet relates to different nuances and outright errors in English translations as well as the ways different writers have chosen to construe the same English translations. Besides that, much of the information, particularly regarding geography and native peoples, was conveyed verbally to the French in languages of the Algonquian or Iroquoian linguistic stocks, and mistranslations may have occurred.

Both the Jesuits and secular emissaries of the French government were expected to become conversant in the Indian languages as essential to their respective work. They often included more or less phonetically rendered Indian words in their writings, but there are no Indian texts to see what might have been lost, embellished, or simply misunderstood in translation. By the time Nicolet set out, the French were aware that the Winnebago language was unrelated to the native languages with which they were familiar. This fact might have influenced Champlain's decision to send Nicolet as a special envoy to open trade and military alliances among heretofore unknown tribes to the west, as France was competing with England for control of North America. We believe from the ethnographic evidence that more than linguistic distinctiveness piqued French curiosity about the Ho-Chunk; significant information has been long overlooked, as attention focused on a white explorer rather than on the indigenous people he set out to meet.

The issue of the exact site of Nicolet's landfall gradually devolved into two much broader and, to us, more interesting scholarly questions: Why has Nicolet held such fascination for professional and avocational historians and anthropologists when he accomplished nothing of historical significance apart from eventually being identified as the first European of record to reach Lake Michigan? And, why has Red Banks been neglected by archaeologists until the village site has been obliterated and its rich resource base seriously compromised by roads and other development when it offered the rare opportunity, especially in the Midwest, to connect a historically identified tribe directly and unequivocally to a precontact archaeological tradition?

By way of introduction, we can say that Nicolet's peculiar appeal derives in large part from his image, promulgated by nineteenth-century historians, as a kind of inland Columbus seeking a route to the Orient. Columbus, who was looking for an expedient route to the East Indies, mistook the people he met for natives of the East Indies; Nicolet, in his quest to reach the Orient, thought he might encounter the Chinese—at least according to the popular account (even according to the State Historical Society of Wisconsin). Nevertheless, the seventeenth-century records offer no support for many of the claims of the historical marker erected in 1957 (see frontispiece). Although both the French and British still harbored hope of finding a "Northwest Passage" across North America, by 1634 neither Nicolet nor Champlain was so geographically naïve as to think the Pacific and Asia lay just beyond the Great Lakes. As we were to discover, however, the mistaken notion persists among some writers that Champlain's knowledge of the Great Lakes was so distorted that he had no inkling of what is now designated Lake Michigan. In some cases, Champlain's supposedly flawed maps serve to bolster erroneous arguments that Nicolet's landfall and the seventeenth-century Winnebago homeland were elsewhere than on Lake Michigan.

The idea that Nicolet's journey had some kind of connection to finding a route to Asia derives almost entirely from nineteenth-century historians' interpretation of Vimont's 1643 description of Nicolet's robe. They were perhaps predisposed to make this error because Vimont embraced the poetic but erroneous name, People of the Sea, that had been misapplied to the Ho-Chunk a few years earlier by the Jesuit Paul Le Jeune.

It was much more difficult to understand why no systematic excavation was ever undertaken in such a well-publicized area as Red Banks. The mystery began to clear as we realized archaeologists have long been in mistaken agreement that the Winnebago village was located on the Albert Speerschneider farm toward the southern end of the bluff. The claim for this location began as early as 1851 and was given currency by Increase A. Lapham, the father of Wisconsin archaeology, in 1855, but the major authority rests on the egregious misreading of a handwritten 1909 report on the site by Charles E. Brown of the State Historical Society of Wisconsin. In fact, after Brown examined the available evidence, he concluded it was not the site of the famous Winnebago village and expressed the opinion that the best candidate was another site popularly believed to be the location of Red Banks village that lay somewhat to the northeast along the bluff. This site probably was the one observed more than 50 years earlier by Charles D. Robinson who described the remains of a large, fort-like enclosure, but did not associate it with the Winnebago. Although by 1909 it had been obliterated by erosion of the bank and construction of a summer resort, Brown suggested there might still be useful evidence in the environs of this location. Later writers have either ignored Robinson's description or conflated it with the nearby Speerschneider site. The modest dimensions of the Speerschneider site have been used as proof by writers who contend that Red Banks was a small, temporary refuge where the remnant of the tribe that survived the disasters described by Perrot had fled from their original stronghold—wherever that might have been.

We believe that there is evidence to suggest that their main settlement prior to moving to Red Banks and building their stockaded village was farther out on the peninsula at a heretofore ignored location, the Sawyer Harbor area on Sturgeon Bay, rather than immediately beneath the bluff at Red Banks, as is usually maintained. Besides soil and climate conditions for extensive gardening, the rich and varied array of other resources of the Door Peninsula support Ho-Chunk claims, reinforced by early historical sources, that the tribe had been populous, sedentary, and long resident in the area.

While we are confident that the stockaded village was located at Red Banks, we find no support for Nicolet having landed there and a good deal of strong, if circumstantial, evidence for the landfall and great conclave occurring in Menominee country. The Ho-Chunk tradition of having met the French at Red Banks is doubtless correct, but it was not Jean Nicolet in 1634. It was most likely Perrot, the government agent and interpreter, who arrived in 1665 and spent 15 years in Wisconsin maintaining peace among the tribes and developing the fur trade, a project that Nicolet was sent to initiate but was delayed for some 30 years by Iroquois hostilities. The Jesuit Claude Allouez entered the area about the same time as Perrot to eventually establish a mission station in the vicinity of De Pere, Wisconsin.

Archaeologically, the site Robinson described, rather than the nearly neighboring Speerschneider site, corresponds with characterizations of Red Banks in Winnebago oral traditions collected by Reuben Gold Thwaites in the nineteenth century and Paul Radin in the early twentieth century and that still have currency among the Ho-Chunk people.

While we take a certain proprietary pride in discovering new data and reaching new conclusions that we hope will stimulate further discussion and research concerning the Nicolet story and its aftermath, we gratefully acknowledge that this book could not have been written without the help, leads, encouragement, and insights of friends and colleagues. The first people we turned to were Martine Meyer, emerita Professor and Chair of the Department of French and Italian at the University of Wisconsin–Milwaukee, who responded graciously and in detail to our inquiries regarding puzzling particulars of old and modern French source materials, and her colleague at the university, Gabrielle Verdier, a specialist in seventeenth-century French. We also gratefully accepted further assistance in dealing with French sources volunteered by Helen Johnson, formerly of the University of Wisconsin–Stevens Point, who holds a doctorate in French. Leslie Weidensee, a distinguished linguist, translated two letters written by Samuel de Champlain that previously were available only in French; English translations of these documents can be found in the appendices. We owe special thanks to Ruth King and Susan Otto of the Milwaukee Public Museum Research Library and Photo Archieves Department, respectively, for their tireless efforts in responding to our many requests for reference materials of all kinds, and to Archivist Mark Thiel at the Raynor Library, Marquette University, particularly in expediting use of their Radin holdings. We also want to express our appreciation to graphics artist Rick Regazzi not only for his fine work on the maps on pages vi–ix but for his unwavering patience and good nature as we kept adding data for him to cope with.

Our work was immeasurably enriched by the contributions of James Uhrinak—forester, restoration ecologist, active participant in the Niagara Escarpment Resource Network, photographer, and all-round naturalist. His often surprising questions and gently stated critiques of earlier drafts doubtless saved us much embarrassment before going to print, as we ventured outside our own disciplines' accustomed purview without always knowing what we were getting into. We thank Lynne Goldstein and Conrad Heidenreich, who reviewed the draft manuscript and offered helpful and insightful comments. We also want to express appreciation to scholars who have explored the same territory, even those with whom we might take analytical issue, for giving direction to our research and ferreting out sources we might not have discovered so readily or at all on our own. Lurie's special debt to the Ho-Chunk people for their patient, thoughtful, and good natured acceptance of her inquiring presence among them for so many years is beyond mere words to express. Any errors in this book are, of course, our own responsibility.

We start our account, then, with Nicolet's marvelous but mythical robe. Throughout we have tried to keep the use of Ho-Chunk and other Indian words to an unavoidable minimum, retaining the spelling used in quoted sources, and otherwise using a simplified version of the International Phonetic Alphabet now adopted for language teaching by the Ho-Chunk Nation in Wisconsin. The official tribal name, Ho-Chunk, pronounced as it appears in English spelling, would be written hocank. Other vowels include: ai = "eye"; e = "ay"; i = "ee"; u = "oo"; consonants follow English sounds except r = the Spanish r in "pero"; and x = the German ch in "Bach." We trust our readers will appreciate our having managed to eschew any words with glottal stops or palatal voiced fricatives that roll off the fluent hocank tongue and are so dear to the heart of professional linguists.

Chapter 2

Nicolet's Robe

"*The* fallacy of misplaced concreteness," Alfred North Whitehead's term describing how an idea or assumption can become reified over time (1929:11), is epitomized in the story of Jean Nicolet's "grand robe of China damask all strewn with flowers and birds of many colors." Although its presumed significance, that Nicolet wore it thinking he might encounter Chinese, looms large in the various tellings of Wisconsin history, the documentary record is silent as to where he obtained the robe, why he carried it along on his journey of 1634, or its actual appearance apart from surface ornamentation. Most surprising is that in the considerable literature on Nicolet with its many disagreements about his landfall, the duration of his journey, and other matters, no one to our knowledge has ever questioned the idea that he wore a *Chinese* robe when addressing the great council of Indians described by Vimont.

Our conclusions are: (1) that it was not a Chinese robe at all; (2) that Nicolet did not take the robe along with the expectation of meeting Chinese; (3) that a nineteenth-century misidentification of the robe as Chinese led historians to surmise the search for a passage to the Orient to be an unstated purpose of his journey; and (4) that the robe can be identified as a typical outer garment a man of the seventeenth-century French bourgeoisie, such as Nicolet, would have owned and worn for more or less special occasions.

John Gilmary Shea drew attention to Nicolet in 1852 as the first European to visit Wisconsin, but Shea's major interest was in the later explorers such as Marquette, Allouez, and others who, unlike Nicolet, left firsthand records of their journeys (1852:xx–xxii). Benjamin Sulte (1876), who established the date of Nicolet's journey as 1634 rather than 1639 as reckoned by Shea, made a passing observation about the robe that was to fire the imagination of writers and artists for generations to come. In paraphrasing Vimont's well-known account he wrote:

> On dépêcha plusieurs jeunes gens au devant du Manitourininiou, l'être mérveilleux. Celui-ci qui partageait probablement la croyance que ces

9

peuples n'étaient pas loin des Chinois, ou qu'ils devaient les connaître, s'était revêtu d'une grand robe de damas de la Chine, toute parsemée de dessin de fleurs et d'oiseaux, et s'avançait vers eux déchargeant ses pistolets qu'il tenait à chaque main. (1876:430)

We are indebted to Dr. Martine Meyer for the following translation:

They sent several young men to meet the Manitouriniou, the marvelous being. The latter [Nicolet], who probably shared the belief that these people were not far from the Chinese, or that they must have known them, had put on a great robe of Chinese damask all decorated with drawings of flowers and birds, and walked toward them, unloading his pistols that he held in each hand.

Dr. Meyer added to this translation, "Note: 'n'étaient pas loin des Chinois' could mean 'were not far from the Chinese' (in distance) or 'were not far from the Chinese' (in resemblance)." In a follow-up conversation, Dr. Meyer said it would be impossible to determine which meaning Sulte had in mind without further information. This is all Sulte wrote on the matter, but successive scholars all assumed he meant distance. Sulte himself made a heretofore unquestioned assumption that the robe of *damas de la Chine* meant an entire garment imported from China.

In 1881, C. W. Butterfield published a biography of Nicolet, tracing his birth in France in 1598, his family connections, his migration to New France in 1618, his work as an interpreter (particularly among the Algonquian-speaking Nipissings), his 1634 journey, his return to Quebec (which Butterfield calculated as July 1635), and what is recorded of his life there until his death by drowning in 1642. Butterfield accepted the Jesuit Paul Le Jeune's belief that Nicolet actually visited most of the tribes whose names he provided. While this could not have been the case, as pointed out by James Clifton (1977:14) among others, Butterfield's claims of Nicolet's far-ranging explorations up the Fox River and south into the Illinois country have been reiterated by many subsequent writers.

Although Butterfield stated early in his biography that the purpose of Nicolet's journey was finding a near route to China, he admitted in a footnote, "It is nowhere stated in the *Relations* that such was the object of Champlain in dispatching Nicolet . . . nevertheless . . . [it] is fairly deducible," and Nicolet's "large garment of Chinese damask" figured heavily in clinching his case (1881:39, 58). Expanding on Sulte's musing, he raised the question, "But, why thus attired? Possibly, he had reached the far east; he was, really, in what is now the State of Wisconsin. Possibly a party of Mandarins would soon greet him and welcome him to Cathay. And this robe—this dress of ceremony—was brought all the way from Quebec, doubtless, with a view to such a contingency" (1881:58–60).

Five years later, Henri Jouan wrote an article for *Revue Manchoise,* published in Ottawa, that was translated and published in 1888 in Vol. 11 of the *Collections of the State Historical Society of Wisconsin.* This publication really launched the myth of Nicolet's Chinese robe that had been set up by Sulte and Butterfield. Jouan says without qualification, "The Chinese costume that Nicolet wore in his first encounter with the 'People of the Sea' indicates that he expected to see some mandarin come to meet him, to whom rumor might have announced his arrival" (1888:14). Grace Clark, Jouan's translator, like Butterfield, translated "*grand*" in its primary and usual French meaning as "large": "clothed in a large garment of China damask" (1881:14). (Or, a "great robe" as translated by Meyer, above). The authoritative translation of Vimont's description of the robe in *The Jesuit Relations and Allied Documents*, edited by Reuben Gold Thwaites, contributed subtly but significantly to the play of imagination about the robe. In retaining the word *grand* from the French rather than giving its more precise but prosaic English meaning, the Thwaites translation implies that the robe was "magnificent," "splendid," "sumptuous"—to cite but a few dictionary entries for the English word "grand," rather than simply "large."

The cumulative effect from Shea to Thwaites is obvious in subsequent scholarship. In 1925, Louise Phelps Kellogg says matter-of-factly in her classic work, *The French Regime in Wisconsin and the Northwest*:

> Champlain's instructions were for Nicolet to arrange a peace between all the western tribes, bringing them into the French alliance and opening the way for future trade and discovery. In pursuit of this design Nicolet carried with him "a grand robe of China damask, all strewn with flowers and birds of many colors," with the two-fold purpose of making an impression on the savage mind and being prepared in case the distant Winnebago should prove to be Asiatics instead of Indians. (p. 78)

But Kellogg adds a cautious footnote: "It seems hardly possible that Champlain with his knowledge of geography expected that his envoy would reach China on this expedition. He apparently was in doubt concerning these 'people of the sea,' and thought they might be a colony from the orient" (1925:78).

Other writers repeated this cherished piece of Wisconsin "history," including both of the authors of the present study, who, like Kellogg, wondered if Champlain really was so geographically naïve but failed to challenge the Chinese origin of the robe itself and also, like Kellogg and virtually everyone else interested in Nicolet, did not question the source of the designation of the Winnebago as the "People of the Sea" (Lurie 1960:793–794, 807, fn. 15; Jung 1997:36). Robert Hall embellished humorously on the events of 1634 while accepting the received reason for the robe as established fact: "Jean Nicolet dressed himself in a robe of Chinese damask woven with colorful flowers and birds, a garment appropriate to an ambassador to an oriental court, and so presented himself to the astonished Winnebago, firing a brace of pistols for added effect, a bearded white man dressed up in a silk robe who carried thunder in each hand" (1993:14).

James Clifton noted that while Paul Le Jeune's 1640 account of Nicolet's journey contains the first documented mention of the Potawatomi ("Pouutouatami") as among the tribes Nicolet supposedly encountered, Nicolet must have obtained information about them from other tribes, since the Potawatomi were still located in western Michigan in 1634, far from Nicolet's route to the Winnebago. The normally meticulous Clifton, like so many others, was captivated by the popular interpretation of Vimont's account of 1643 and literally added a crowning touch to Nicolet's costume: "dressed in Chinese damask robes and a mandarin's cap" (1977:12). Indeed, there is simply no mention of Nicolet wearing a cap in any primary sources.

Ronald Stiebe's book, *Mystery People of the Cove: A History of the Lake Superior Ouinipegou* (1999), is devoted primarily to proving his theory that Nicolet's landfall among the Winnebago was on the south shore of Lake Superior. He sees the documented reason for Nicolet's journey, to make peace between the French and the Winnebago and other western tribes, as a conspiratorial cover-up to hide the real reason from France's rival, England. This was, of course, to find the long-sought Northwest Passage to the Orient. According to Stiebe, French information about the distinctive language and customs of the "Ouinipegou" suggested they "were of Asian descent or may have traded with Asian people." English forces overtook Quebec in 1629 and carried Champlain off to England where he promptly took passage to France, the differences between the two countries having been settled even before the attack on Quebec; news traveled slowly in those days. Without any basis in fact, Stiebe asserts, "An Asian robe accompanied Champlain's return to New France" in 1633 so he could send out his emissary, Nicolet, with appropriate clothing (1999:92).

The story of Nicolet's geographic confusion as demonstrated by his "Chinese" robe is recounted in many books on Wisconsin history, has been enacted in many school and other pageants, and was even used on the nationally televised quiz show, *Jeopardy* (August 11, 2006) where contestants supply the questions to given answers: "Jean Nicolet entered Wisconsin wearing Chinese robes thinking this lake bordered Asia." The correct response, of course, was, "What is Lake Michigan?"

Meanwhile, a succession of artists presented their versions of Nicolet in his robe, pistols in hand, meeting the Winnebago. Full-color reproductions of five major renditions can be found in Norman K. Risjord's article, "Jean Nicolet's Search for the South Sea" (2001:34–43). While Risjord shows the range of artistic imagination concerning the robe, his title demonstrates unquestioning acceptance of the supposed reason Nicolet wore it, whatever it might have looked like. E. W. Demming's mural painted in 1904 is probably the best known and was featured on a postage stamp in 1934 commemorating the 300th anniversary of Nicolet's journey. The property of the State Historical Society of Wisconsin, it currently hangs in the Capitol Building, in the office of the state senator from the Green Bay area.

In 1910, Franz Rohrbeck, a Milwaukee artist depicted the scene in a mural for the Brown County, Wisconsin, Court House. It was criticized at the time because the assembled Indians were "pictured as short, obese persons, in sharp contrast to the well proportioned, lithe beings other artists and photographs have shown." By Rohrbeck's own admission, his models were "rather stout German burghers who were habitués of his Milwaukee studio" (*Green Bay Press Gazette*, July 18, 1934).

Hugo Ballin's depiction, completed ca. 1910, hangs in the Governor's Conference Room of the State Capitol Building. Both Rohrbeck and Ballin included a stereotypic Plains war bonnet on one of the Indians and seem to have been influenced by the Demming painting in depicting Nicolet completely covered in an ankle-length, wide-sleeved garment. All three painted a bearded Nicolet in a brimmed hat with a plume.

A rather piratical looking Nicolet was created by William A. McCloy in a mural, part of a triptych completed in 1948, in commemoration of the centennial of Wisconsin's statehood. The painting is located in the State Historical Society building and, except for the plume-bedecked hat, departs from the earlier renderings. Nicolet is shown with a mustache rather than a full beard, swashbuckler boots, and a short, yellow silk robe that is belted at the waist. McCloy's robe lacks any pattern of colorful flowers and birds, but emphasizes the Far East with sleeves suggesting a kimono and a collar and front closings that are "Chinese" in style. It is worn over a cloth jacket and knee breeches. McCloy's illustration appears to have been inspired by James M. Davidson's picture in Stiebe's book; Nicolet is wearing knee breeches and boots, the usual plumed hat, and a short, full-sleeved robe covered with rather crudely drawn flowers and birds (1999:74).

Sculptor Sydney Bedore created a larger than life-size bronze statue of Nicolet that was unveiled and dedicated on June 3, 1951, on the Red Banks bluff in Brown County, Wisconsin, overlooking Lake Michigan. Bedore shows Nicolet bare headed and wearing a long, vaguely oriental robe with sleeves. It is open down the front to reveal a fringed jacket and pants, presumably of buckskin, along with moccasin-like footgear.

So, from an unexplained robe mentioned in a single sentence we end up with a number of versions of what it looked like, the reason for Nicolet having worn it because of the expectation that the Winnebago held some kind of connection to the Far East, and that Champlain had brought it from France to Canada in 1633 for Nicolet to take along on his journey to meet the Winnebago. It was Stiebe's elaborate and outrageously unsupported explanation of how Nicolet acquired the robe that made Lurie wonder how available "Asian robes" might have been in Europe in the 1600s.

To her surprise, she discovered that not only was the Asian connection an artifact of translation of Sulte's speculative comment but the robe itself was a figment of historical imagination. A simple and reasonable explanation of the robe and what it looked like lies in the history of European clothing styles and textiles, subjects that received a great deal of attention from the 1920s through the 1960s. Francis M. Kelly and Randolph Schwabe (1925:126–127) noted the influence of military styles in men's wear of the seventeenth century but were uncertain whether any cloaks were sleeved, as

Above: Nicolet meeting the Winnebago, as imagined by George Peter, Milwaukee Public Museum artist, in a mural painted in 1917 that reflects the artist's Euro-centric bias in picturing the Winnebago as so awestruck by Nicolet as to bow down worshipfully in his presence. (Courtesy of Milwaukee Public Museum)

Opposite page: The left side of the 1917 George Peter mural was altered in the 1930s at the time of the Tercentennial of Nicolet's landing to remove the incor-rect Plains Indian warbonnet on some of the "sauvages" who accompanied him on the journey and to change the bearded European or part-European figure behind him to an Indian; the painting also was "corrected" to make Nicolet's robe appear more "Chinese." (Courtesy of Milwaukee Public Museum) details of tailoring were obscured by the way these garments were often worn draped over one shoulder in contemporary illustrations on which they relied. However, the work of a succession of researchers leaves little doubt that Nicolet's "robe" was actually a knee-, thigh-, or possibly ankle-length cape and probably circular in shape (Giafferri 1927:28; Gorsline 1952:74; Bruhn and Tilke 1955:37; Payne 1956:332–336; Laver 1963:45; Waugh 1964:16–17, 28–29; Boucher 1966:254; Hill and Bucknell 1967:90, 94). In modern French, the term robe refers primarily to a woman's dress or frock or, as in English, a dressing gown, while its earlier meaning as a seamless outer garment is seen in its use regarding the husk of a bean or a sausage casing. Its old association as a man's garment is reflected, for example, in *la robe* as a reference to the legal profession, whose once exclusively male members wore a distinctive type of courtroom garb.

Men's capes became progressively longer, from barely covering the buttocks toward the end of the sixteenth century to reaching the knees and even ankles during the first quarter of the seventeenth century, the period when Nicolet would have obtained his garment. Since there is no evidence that Champlain obtained a robe for Nicolet between 1629 and 1633, as Stiebe claims, it is likely that Nicolet had his own robe when he arrived in New France in 1618 or possibly obtained it via supplies shipped from Europe betwcen 1618 and 1634.

Opposite and this page: Drawings of gentlemen in typical garb of the seventeenth century, showing the style of robe Nicolet would have worn. (adapted from Pluvinel, 1625)

Norah Waugh, in *The Cut of Men's Clothing* (1964), provides particularly useful descriptions as well as basic tailors' patterns that illustrate how garments were constructed, noting that while ornamentation might differ regionally, temporally, or even individually, the styles of given periods can be discerned on the basis of overall silhouettes. Thus, "At the beginning of the seventeenth century a man's suit of clothes consisted of doublet, breeches, and cape or casque (cassock)." The cape was circular but for military campaigns or traveling it might be replaced by a casque also known as a mandilion. The latter was made up of separate panels that could be buttoned together to form a cape or it could be converted into a coat-like garment with the front and back panels buttoned together along the sides of the body and the shoulder panels buttoned along the length of the arms to become sleeves. By the second quarter of the century it was always worn as a coat, although "still slit centre back and sides for convenience in riding." By the end of the century, the cassock had lost any of its cape-like appearance and had been completely replaced by overcoats, that is, fitted garments with seamed sleeves set in at the shoulders; capes or mandilions were retained only for "full dress Court occasions" (Waugh 1964:14, 16).

Since capes were usually hip length but could reach the ankles (Bradley 1954:182), Vimont's word, *"grand,"* to describe Nicolet's robe in the French meaning of "large" could have had reference to the longer length or to the generously cut circular cape rather than the more coat-like, convertible mandilion. Although we must abandon the assumption that Nicolet's robe came from China, we can safely accept the assumption that it was made of silk. By the seventeenth century a great deal of silk was worn in Europe by all but the poorest classes, and virtually all of that silk fabric was produced in Europe. China, where the spinning and weaving of silk originated, was simply a metonym for silk. Crepe is a comparable example in textile terminology referring to any fabric with a distinctive crinkled surface; *crepe de Chine* refers specifically to silk crepe. *Fairchild's Textile Dictionary* defines damask as, "Originally a rich silk fabric with woven floral designs made in China and introduced into Europe through Damascus, from which it derived its name." Damask cloth can be made of almost any fiber wherein "the pattern is distinguished from the ground by contrasting luster and is reversible. . . . similar to brocade but flatter" (Wingate 1979).

The introduction of silk to Europe is attributed to two Nestorian monks sent to Asia by Emperor Justinian I of Byzantium. They returned about AD 553 with hollowed walking staffs wherein they smuggled silkworm eggs (probably *Bombyx mori*, the preferred species for silk production, that feeds on mulberry leaves) and mulberry seeds. They also brought knowledge of the long-guarded secrets of sericulture, from the care and feeding of the worms to obtaining silk by killing the larva, usually with steam, so the mature moth does not escape and damage the continuous two-ply filament making up the cocoon. Unwound intact, it is then spun ("thrown") into multi-plied threads called raw silk; a natural binding agent is washed off the raw silk after spinning in preparation for further processing (Weibel 1972:5–6; Chaiklin 2006).

Peasants Making Silk, Carrying and Spreading Cocoons, Italy; oil on canvas attributed to Giuseppe Maria Crespi (Bologna, 1665–1747). (Courtesy of The Grohmann Museum, Man at Work Collection, Milwaukee School of Engineering)

Silk remained a sparse, largely imported item in Europe until the twelfth century when production was initiated in Sicily and soon spread to southern Italy where feudalism took a new turn as landlords supplied tenants with silkworm eggs and mulberry plants to produce silk (Leggett 1949:198). Originally, weaving was one of many home crafts solely intended to meet the needs of the household, but it was among the earliest to also become a cottage industry, providing full-time employment for weavers (Weibel 1972:22). As the demand for silk cloth increased, its production diffused farther north to the Swiss Cantons, France, Germany, Holland, and other parts of Europe as a major cottage industry (Braudel 1982:316–317). Silk production lagged in England until the revocation of the Edict of Nantes in 1685 when the many Huguenot silk weavers, who had enjoyed freedom of belief since Henry IV had promulgated the edict in 1598, were forced to flee France and settled in Holland, Switzerland, and especially England (Weibel 1972:68–69).

By the mid-fifteenth century, Lyons, already ideally located as a center of trade, became a major factory producer and distributor of silk, catering to the Renaissance taste for colorful opulence both in men's and women's clothing (Varron 1938; Weibel 1972:26). Even people of lower rank wore silk for special occasions (Braudel 1982:178). The fascination with silk extended beyond secular vanity, with churchyards and cathedral grounds planted with mulberry trees, and "men of the cloth were in fact men of the silk cloth" (Feltwell 1990:100).

The finest, most elaborate European silks still came from Italy, closely followed by French silks. "This may explain why these plainer [French] silks often were enriched by embroidery worked in an overall design or in wide bands" (Waugh 1964:16). This also begins to sound more and more like Nicolet's robe strewn with colorful flowers and birds. Even Italian silk was sometimes similarly embroidered: "The tool of the highly-skilled workman traced the most varied designs, such as flowers, small crosses, foliage and little nosegays on satin, watered silk and material from Naples" (Giafferri 1927:26). Since Vimont's description of the patterning on Nicolet's robe is so vague, the strewn or sprinkled (*parsemée*) birds and flowers might have been integral to the weave of the damask itself rather than embroidered (Anonymous 1924:1–4).

Whatever the exact appearance of Nicolet's robe, it apparently conformed to the Renaissance fashion of decorative and colorful embellishment (Contini 1965:166). Paul de Giafferri's history of French men's attire from Roman times to the Second Empire notes that during the Renaissance various French monarchs tried unsuccessfully to enforce sumptuary laws in regard to decorative trim of gold and silver, jewels, and fancy buttons in order to prevent the lower classes from wearing them. However, Henry IV, whose reign extended from 1589 to 1610, excluded silks, "because they constituted an element of wealth for the industry of the country. Satin and taffeta were worn by the middle classes" (Giafferri 1927:25). During the reign of his successor, Louis XIII (1610–1642), the rising bourgeoisie, or middle classes, were so quick to copy the nobility that these style setters felt forced into almost constant innovations of details of dress to maintain their class identity (Boucher 1966:252–254). It is significant to note in this connection that while some silk was still being imported from the East in the seventeenth century, it was raw silk because "differing market demands made it more profitable than finished textiles" (Chaiklin 2006). As far as available records are concerned, if any complete garments such as "mandarin robes" had been exported out of China to Europe, they were a rare, unmentioned novelty.

In short, Nicolet was dressed appropriately for the occasion of an important meeting. Richly decorated though the robe might have been, it was not exotic, at least by European standards of the day. Yet, if the "grand robe" was no more than a fairly conventional item of gentleman's attire in the early decades of the seventeenth century, the question may then be raised why Vimont made special mention of it. Was it simply wistfulness on the part of a "black robe?" Or, has the enduring fascination with the purported China connection obscured the robe's real significance in opening trade negotiations, the only stated reason for Nicolet's journey? It might indeed have been intended to "impress the savage mind," as Kellogg suggested, but specifically in regard to what the French had to offer in the way of trade goods. At this point, they certainly had an edge over their English competitors, whose silk production was barely underway. Traps, firearms, knives, axes, kettles, and even beads and silver jewelry survive in archaeological sites and can be studied in museum collections. We tend to forget, because they are so perishable, that textiles also were an extremely important trade item. Silk, compared to wool, linen, and cotton, is particularly subject to rapid deterioration, but we know silk ribbons are listed among trade goods as early as Juan de Oñate's expeditions into the American Southwest in the service of Spain beginning in 1598 (Marriott and Rachlin 1980:23). Surviving examples of the use of silk ribbons in the Great Lakes area go back only to the early eighteenth century, preserved as trim on garments of hardier materials (Lyford 1943:131).

The style of robe Nicolet wore remained popular well into the seventeenth century as illustrated in this 1656 painting by Rembrandt. The subject, Jan Six, is wearing a circular robe over a buttoned panel robe called a mandilion, described on p. 18.

Apart from moccasins and other clearly indigenous forms of apparel, we really do not have a clear idea of how the Great Lakes Indians dressed at the inception of contact in the seventeenth century. By the time we begin to get detailed drawings and paintings at the end of the eighteenth century, aboriginal styles had been radically altered by trade goods (Conn 1980; Abbass 1980). Silk figures importantly in ribbon appliqué work, an adaptation of aboriginal decorative concepts to new material, that appears to have evolved in the Great Lakes region and diffused to surrounding areas (Horse Capture 1980). Beginning as small geometrical edgings in the early eighteenth century, by the nineteenth century ribbon appliqué developed into broad panels of splashy curvilinear patterns, as wider ribbons in many hues became available and offered the opportunity to vary appliqué techniques (Abbass 1980). As two scholars of this phenomenon note, "It is within the French sphere of strongest influence that ribbon appliqué . . . reached its highest development" (Marriott and Rachlin 1980:22).

Consigning the Chinese origin of Nicolet's robe to the realm of myth, we can appreciate its role as a harbinger of trade, an advertisement of French goods, and a stimulus to esthetic creativity among the Winnebago and their neighbors. Trade, of course, is a two-way proposition, but we tend to see complex internal political and economic ramifications of the effects of foreign trade, primarily from the European perspective, as will be shown in chapter 3. This is due, in part, to the paucity of historical records that present the Indian perspective in Indian–white relationships. In this case, however, Perrot's observations provide unusual, though long-neglected insights into native *real politik*, his account being simply glossed over as a testimonial to irrational Indian savagery and superstition. He notes that the Puan, the dominant partner in alliance with the Menominee, had subjugated the local tribes to gain control of Green Bay and "did not desire to have commerce with the French." Nevertheless, the Ottawa, by then established as middlemen in the fur trade, sent envoys whom the Puan ate. The Puans' reason is unknown, but given their demonstrated power, particularly if they derived from the elaborate cultures of the Middle Mississippian Tradition out of the Southeast (for which we will present evidence in chapter 5), they could well have seen the French as rivals for domination in the region. They also might have disdained what the Ottawa had to offer at the time, "knives, bodkins, and many other useful articles, of which they had no previous knowledge," as not worth the risk to their hegemony over neighboring tribes.

According to Perrot, "This crime incensed all the nations," but it was more than a moral outrage about killing and eating peaceful envoys that prompted them to ally with the Ottawa in making war against the Puan. The Ottawas were the conduit to French "weapons and all sorts of merchandise" that the western Great Lakes Indian nations wanted, and the Puan were as much a barrier to trade for the local Indians as they were for the French. These tribes then "made frequent expeditions against the Puans, who were giving them much trouble." Nicolet seems to have put in his appearance at this juncture, attempting to broker a peace while the Puan were still in ascendancy.

Chapter 3

Samuel de Champlain and the Mission of Jean Nicolet

The prevailing historical opinion for well over a century has been that the purpose of Nicolet's voyage was to find a route to Asia (e.g., Butterfield 1881:33–34; Kellogg 1925:78; Petersen 1960:326; Rodesch 1984:6; Hall 1993:14), a conclusion that rested largely on the misidentified "Chinese" robe. For why else would Nicolet have carried such an article of clothing if not to properly greet the ambassadors of the Ming emperor? As has been demonstrated, Nicolet did not don a Chinese robe but instead wore a French garment that was typical of the period and his official role as a diplomatic envoy. However, if Nicolet did not seek the Northwest Passage, then why did he journey westward? The answer lies in the precarious situation that New France faced in 1634.

Nicolet obviously traveled under orders from Samuel de Champlain who had founded the city of Quebec and the colony of New France in 1608 and went on to govern the colony and help explore this vast region. Early in his career, Champlain, like other North American explorers, sought the Northwest Passage: a water route through North America to the Pacific Ocean and the rich trade with Asia. Initially he hoped that such a route could be found by exploring the Great Lakes and other North American waterways (Champlain 1922–1956, vol. 1:165, 170–171, 226–230). However, it is important to stress the fact that finding a Northwest Passage was not a goal later in his career, and by 1634, the year of Nicolet's voyage, he most likely doubted that the Great Lakes provided any kind of passage to the Pacific. His concerns were primarily securing and developing New France.

The French had recently regained control of the struggling colony in 1632, after having lost it to the English in 1629, and were eager to maintain their claims in North America. The Five Nations League of the Iroquois, or

Ho-dé-no-sau-nee, in present-day upstate New York who usually allied with the English continued to threaten the security of New France from the south, as it had for most of the previous two decades. Now there were reports of a new Indian threat, the Puan or Ouinipegou, farther to the west. Champlain knew little about this powerful tribe, but reports of their hostilities against French allies such as the Huron and Ottawa posed yet another danger to the security of New France. Champlain dispatched Nicolet as an ambassador to make peace.

Champlain's published works clearly show his understanding of the geography of North America and reveal the untenableness of scholarly conjecture that Nicolet (and by extension, Champlain) believed North America was part of Asia and that by sailing west through the Great Lakes, one could eventually reach China (Sulte 1876:413–415; Lawson 1900b:1–2). Long before 1634, Champlain understood that North America was not part of Asia and was separated from it by the Pacific Ocean. Champlain was, by training, an expert cartographer intimately familiar with the discoveries of virtually all of the major European explorers who had sailed along the coasts of North and South America and confirmed that they were, indeed, continents separate from Asia (Champlain 1922–1956, vols. 1:165, 3:248, 260–301).

During the early years of his career, it is true Champlain believed that the Great Lakes might provide passage to the Pacific Ocean and thus an easy water route to the Orient. It was a long-accepted idea that his explorations helped to dispel. John Cabot, sailing in the service of England, first attempted to find such a route in 1497, asserting that a shorter passage to Asia could be accomplished by sailing west from England along the northern latitudes rather than going south toward the tropics, as Columbus and others in the service of Spain had done, because the curvature of the earth naturally shortened the distance between the continents. He was correct, but the continent that he found to be closer to Europe was North America, rather than Asia. Historians think that Cabot landed in what is today Newfoundland, but Cabot, like Columbus, believed he had reached Asia. The English, like the Spanish after Columbus's explorations, followed up on Cabot's voyages with others that confirmed the existence of North America. Magellan's circumnavigation of the world demonstrated that a South Pacific passage to Asia was hazardous, long, and not economically feasible (Morison 1971:157–209; Allen 1992:506–508; Fritze 2002:161–165). Thus, European explorers had pinned their hopes on some passage through North America that would offer an easier and shorter passage.

Champlain's explorations built on those of an earlier French explorer, Jacques Cartier, who discovered the Gulf of St. Lawrence on his first voyage in 1534 and the St. Lawrence River on his second in 1535 when he penetrated as far as present-day Montreal (Trudel 1966a; Allen 1992:512–516). Geographic information gathered by Cartier appeared throughout the late 1500s on various maps, particularly those of the Flemish mapmaker Gerard Mercator, who illustrated the St. Lawrence River as well as two of its larger tributaries: the Ottawa and Saguenay Rivers. Cartier had learned from the Indians that one could travel northwest up the Ottawa River and find a large freshwater lake. Based on this information, Mercator, with the assistance of his son, published a map in 1587 that showed the probable route of the Ottawa River, and nearby was a large freshwater lake that emptied out into a yet undiscovered northern sea. Mercator came remarkably close to understanding the true geography of the continent, for, as the French later learned, it is possible to go up the Ottawa River and enter Lake Huron via Lake Nipissing and the French River. Thus, Europeans began to develop an initial understanding of the Great Lakes chain and nascent ideas concerning Hudson Bay, although in Mercator's day, knowledge of such a saltwater body was based purely on speculation rather than exploration. However, this did not prevent Mercator from having his freshwater lake emptying into a hypothetical northern sea linked to both the Atlantic and Pacific Oceans (see Mercator Map) (Winsor 1894:64–70; Shirley 1984:179). This northern sea that Mercator and others included on their maps did much to keep alive the idea of the Northwest Passage. We do not know which maps and mapmakers Champlain consulted during the early years of his career, but his earlier writings make it clear that his ideas concerning North American geography were generally the same as those of Mercator. He believed that some sort of Northwest Passage could be found through the freshwater lake described by Cartier or through the theoretical northern sea illustrated by Mercator and other European mapmakers (Champlain 1922–1956, vol. 1:122–124; Trudel 1966c:186–187; Steuer 1984:35).

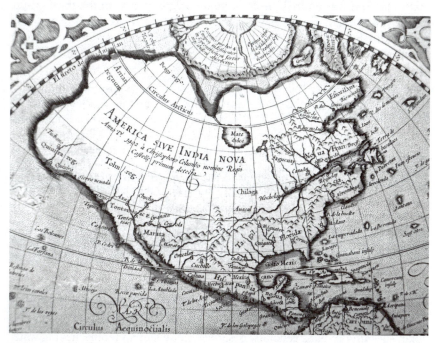

Mercator Map, 1587 (Mercator 1613).

Champlain made his first voyage to the St. Lawrence valley in 1603 as a member of an expedition led by François Gravé du Pont. He went between 30 and 40 miles up the Saguenay River with local Indians who informed him that the river actually went much farther. Champlain learned from his guides that after a 10-day journey one entered a large freshwater lake (Lac St. Jean, or, in English, Lake St. John). From there, one could travel farther north on other rivers that allegedly bordered on a saltwater "sea" (Champlain 1922–1956, vol. 1:122–124; Trudel 1966c:187–188). This body of water was, of course, Hudson Bay.

Champlain then went west up the St. Lawrence River to the Lachine Rapids at present-day Montreal where he questioned his Indian guides concerning what lay west. After leaving the Lachine Rapids, he also received information on the same topic from a group of Indians he met at the Isle of Orleans a few miles north of Quebec and with yet a third group on the northern shore of the St. Lawrence, only a few miles west of Hare Island. His informants provided quite a bit of information about the Great Lakes chain from the Lachine Rapids all the way to Lake Huron. Champlain received seemingly different information from each group, although this was probably due, in part, to faulty and imperfect translations of the Indians' testimony. From these Indians, Champlain learned of Lakes Ontario, Erie, and Huron. The Indians at the Lachine Rapids talked of Lake Erie becoming "brackish" or salty at its western extremity, while the Indians at the Island of Orleans said that Lake Erie was entirely fresh. A young Algonquin with the third group, on the other hand, said it was not the second lake (Lake Erie) that slowly turned salty but the first lake (Lake Ontario). The second group also knew of no west-flowing rivers that flowed out of Lake Erie, while the Indian guides at the Lachine Rapids insisted that such rivers existed (Champlain 1922–1956, vol. 1:153–157, 160–165). Champlain summarized the information he received from the second and third groups. He provided all distances in leagues, which averaged about 2.1 statute miles, using either the French *petit lieue* (2.03 statute miles) or the French *lieue de poste* (2.13 statute miles) (Heidenreich 1976:45–50). Champlain wrote:

> This is all I could learn from both parties, who differed but very little; except that the second who were questioned said they had not tasted the salt water... so that, according to their account, from the rapid where we had been [the Lachine Rapids], to the salt sea, which may be the South Sea [the Pacific Ocean] is some four hundred leagues [840 miles]. Without doubt, from their account, this can be nothing else than the South Sea." (Champlain 1922–1956, vol. 1:164–165)

It was the reference to "salt" that piqued Champlain's interest, for as the above passage makes clear, he still believed that the Great Lakes provided a water route to the Pacific based on the Indians' testimony. However, Algonquian-speaking Indians generally described salt water and foul smelling water (or any water that was less than pure) using the same words. Thus, the Indians whom he queried (several of whom were identified as Algonquian speakers) were not describing water that was salty but merely the declining quality or perhaps the changing composition of the fresh water as one pushed westward into the Great Lakes chain. This is not a novel discovery, for Nellis Crouse, an historian of North American exploration, first presented this idea in the 1920s (1924:35–36). However, Crouse also asserted that the young Algonquin Indian with the third group of Indians did not describe a route through the Great Lakes via Lakes Ontario, Erie, and Huron as the first two groups did but instead described the route up the Ottawa River to Lake Huron and ultimately to Green Bay, home to the Puan or Stinkards (1924:36; 1928:238–239). This is an interesting argument but almost certainly is incorrect; the editors of the two major editions of Champlain's works have suggested instead that all three groups of Indians described the former route rather than the latter (Champlain 1880:270–272nn., 274–275nn.; Champlain 1922–1956, vol. 1:153–157nn., 159–163nn.). Nevertheless, Crouse correctly asserted that what the Indians described was not saltwater but bad-smelling freshwater. Champlain, on the other hand, still believed at this time that the Great Lakes chain eventually reached the Pacific.

Champlain went back to France after his 1603 voyage and returned to the St. Lawrence in 1608, not merely as a member of an expedition, but with the official title of lieutenant, or second in command, to the expedition's leader, Pierre du Gua, Sieur de Monts, who had been commissioned by the French king, Henry IV, to establish a French settlement in North America. As a way of financing the colony, de Monts was given a monopoly on the Canadian fur trade, and this trade was already about a century old. European fishermen and whalers had been trading for furs with the Indians of the St. Lawrence and other parts of eastern North America on a steady if casual basis (Trigger and Swagerty 1996:339–361; Salisbury 1996:400–404). De Mont's monopoly began what would become a more systematic and regular fur trade between Europeans and Indians for the next two centuries. Champlain promoted the idea of establishing a permanent settlement in the St. Lawrence River valley and using the profits gained from the fur trade to finance it (Dix 1903:88–93; Champlain 1922–1956, vol. 2:5–8; Trudel 1966c:188–189). He wrote:

> So many voyages and explorations at the cost of so much effort and expense having been undertaken in vain, our Frenchmen were induced . . . to endeavor to effect a permanent settlement in those lands which we call New France. . . . But as he [de Monts] had made a report to the king of the fertility of the soil, and I had made one upon the means of discovering the passage to China . . . his Majesty commanded the Sieur de Monts to prepare a fresh expedition. (Champlain 1922–1956, vol. 1:228–231)

Obviously, in 1608 Champlain still sought the Northwest Passage, but he could not focus his energies entirely on exploration. Champlain also learned that to succeed he was obliged to assist those tribes that traded with the

French in their wars against the League of the Iroquois. This was a conflict that had been in the making for many decades. During Cartier's voyages in the 1530s, the entire St. Lawrence valley—from the village at present-day Quebec, called Stadacona, to present-day Montreal, called Hochelaga—was populated by Indians whose languages were part of the Iroquoian language family. When Champlain arrived about 70 years later, the Iroquoians who lived in the vicinity of Stadacona were replaced by the Algonquian-speaking Montagnais. In fact, the place that Cartier's Iroquoian speakers called Stadacona was, in Champlain's day, called by the Algonquian name Kêbêc (or Quebec, as Champlain wrote it), which meant "narrows" and referred to the narrowing of the St. Lawrence River at that point. The village of Hochelaga, on the other hand, had ceased to exist; the area had been completely abandoned (Douglas 1897:41–50).

What happened during the decades between Cartier and Champlain is a bit speculative, but there is enough evidence to formulate relatively sound conclusions. The Indians who resided at Hochelaga and Stadacona were definitely Iroquoian speakers, but by the time Champlain arrived in 1603, they had vanished. What prompted this demographic change in the St. Lawrence valley was warfare between various tribal alliances. In fact, the region between Quebec and present-day Montreal was largely unoccupied in Champlain's day and was a buffer zone between Algonquian tribes such as the Montagnais to the north and the Ho-dé-no-sau-nee, or Five Nations League of the Iroquois, to the south. This powerful federation of five Iroquoian speaking tribes—the Mohawk, Oneida, Onondaga, Cayuga, and Seneca—had probably already been in the process of coming together during the course of Cartier's visit, and it definitely existed in a more structured and powerful form by the time Champlain made his first voyage to the St. Lawrence. The Ho-dé-no-sau-nee fought against any and all tribes including other Iroquoians such as the Hurons. It was this fighting that had forced the Iroquoians at Stadacona and Hochelaga to abandon these and other exposed village sites in the St. Lawrence (Douglas 1897:51–54; Champlain 1922–1956, vol. 1:129; Eccles 1969:6, 30–31; Trigger and Pendergast 1978:359–361).

The Hurons were themselves a confederation that was most likely created as a defensive alliance against the Five Nations. The Indian tribes of northeastern North America did not necessarily ally with one another on the basis of linguistic or cultural affinity. Other Iroquoian speaking tribes around Lakes Ontario and Erie such as the Petun also considered the League to be their enemy. In these wars, the Hurons often allied with Algonquian-speaking tribes such as the Montagnais and the Algonquin tribe proper in their forays against the Five Nations. The Algonquian tribes tended to be more mobile hunters than the semisedentary Iroquoian tribes who practiced agriculture (Douglas 1897:51–54; Bishop 1948:49–52; Trigger and Swagerty 1996:327; Salisbury 1996:399–402). The French were immediately drawn into this conflict. In the summer of 1609, while conducting some preliminary explorations, Champlain and a party of Huron, Montagnais, and Algonquin Indians encountered a war party of the Five Nations League near present-day Crown Point, New York. Champlain fired his arquebus (an early firearm similar to a musket) at the Iroquois and killed two men, causing the Iroquois to break ranks and flee. This act began the long military alliance that usually obtained between the French and the tribes that fought against the League of the Iroquois (Trudel 1966c:190).

Over the next seven years, Champlain accompanied several Indian war parties against the Iroquois. Indeed, the Indians often made military support a precondition for assisting him on voyages of exploration. He was particularly interested in ascending the St. Maurice River so that he could see the large saltwater body he called the northern sea (Hudson Bay) that the Indians had described and then come back via the Saguenay River. While he never got the chance to make this journey, it is clear from his writings that such exploration had as its principal purpose making contact with new tribes and thus potential new trade partners (Heidenreich 1976:14–18). Champlain wrote that explorers in the interior of North America "run a thousand risks in discovering [Indian] nations and countries in order that they may keep the profits" (Champlain 1922–1956, vol. 2:218). Thus, at this point in his career, Champlain had not forgotten about finding a waterway to Asia, but he believed that exploration also had the more immediate purpose of extending the fur trade.

By 1613, he had learned about Henry Hudson's expedition in 1610 and 1611 and made an abortive journey up the Ottawa River believing that he would ultimately be able to portage into a river system that fed into this long-sought after saltwater sea known as Hudson Bay (Winsor 1894:106–107; Neatby 1966:374–375). Champlain had traveled about half the distance to Lake Huron via the Ottawa River route before he learned from local Indians that the Ottawa River did not provide easy access to Hudson Bay, contrary to spurious information he received from one of the many young Frenchmen he had sent to live among the Indians to learn their languages and bring them into France's diplomatic orbit. Nevertheless, he continued to express a great deal of interest in learning more about the country that surrounded Hudson Bay as well contacting the tribes of the region (Champlain 1922–1956, vol. 2:256–297; Heidenreich 1976:16–18). As Champlain learned more details of other explorers' voyages to Hudson Bay, he became convinced that the thick ice made any route to the Pacific via Hudson Bay either difficult or impossible. Instead, he increasingly saw the region of Hudson Bay and the tribes there as a rich, new source of furs (Champlain 1922–1956, vols. 2:218, 3:44–63, 104–105, 6:363).

This is not surprising because as Champlain's career progressed, he was given ever increasing responsibilities for matters concerning the governance of New France. The fur trade became the economic foundation of the colony, and Champlain could not justify expending resources on finding the Northwest Passage when the day-to-day management of the fur trade and requisite relations with the Indians were more immediate concerns. In 1612, King Louis XIII, who had succeeded his father Henry IV in 1610, appointed a powerful nobleman, Henry de Bourbon, Prince de Condé as the viceroy of New France, who in turn appointed Champlain the lieutenant-general of the colony. It was the viceroy's job to ensure that Sieur de Monts retained his fur trade monopoly; it was Champlain's job to ensure the arrangement was profitable (Champlain 1922–1956, vol. 2:193–194, 201–202, 209–210; Bishop 1948:185–189; Trudel 1966c:188; MacBeath 1966). Finding the Northwest Passage was not to be ignored, for Champlain's commission stated that in addition to building forts, converting the Indians to Christianity, and searching for precious metals, he was also to find "the easy route to the country of China and the East Indies" (Champlain 1922–1956, vol. 4:209–216), but this goal would eventually decline in importance.

Champlain conducted another journey of exploration in 1615 when he returned to New France with four Franciscan priests of the Récollet order. He took what later would become a virtual highway to the upper Great Lakes when he ascended the Ottawa River, made a short portage to Lake Nipissing, where the French River originates from its south shore and empties into Georgian Bay of Lake Huron. Certainly, this experience corrected his earlier view (formulated after meeting the three groups of Indians in 1603) that what we now know was Lake Huron was the saltwater body known as the Pacific Ocean, although it is likely that he learned the correct facts between 1610 and 1611 from Étienne Brûlé, one of the young men he sent to live among the Indians. The expedition was not purely exploratory but primarily military since Champlain's Huron guides and their allies expected Champlain to accompany them on a war party against the Iroquois that set out in September 1615 and descended into the Iroquois country by going through Lake Ontario. After attacking the Iroquois, he spent the winter among the Hurons (Trudel 1966c:192; Heidenreich 1976:23; Heidenreich 1997:86).

He had first queried the Hurons about the Great Lakes chain when he met a party of them at the Lachine Rapids in 1611 and learned that other large bodies of water existed west of Lake Huron (Champlain 1922–1956, vol. 2:186–191). During his stay with the tribe in 1615 and 1616, Champlain learned additional details and wrote:

> [The Hurons] have no knowledge of them [the parts of the country to the west] except for two or three hundred leagues [420 or 630 miles] or more toward the west, whence flows the said great river [the St. Lawrence] which passes . . . through a lake nearly thirty days' canoe journey in extent, namely that which we have named the Freshwater Sea [Lake Huron] . . . for it is nearly four hundred leagues [840 miles] long. (Champlain 1922–1956, vol. 3:116–119)

Champlain's estimate of Lake Huron's size was about double its actual length. Nevertheless, one can see that his understanding of the Great Lakes was slowly becoming clearer. After writing the above passage, Champlain wrote:

> Moreover, the savages . . . are at war with other tribes to the west of the said great lake [Huron], which is the reason why we could not have fuller

knowledge of it [the country to the west], except that . . . they told us that some prisoners from a hundred leagues [210 miles] off related to them that there were people there white like us and similar to us in other respects, and through their intermediary they had seen the scalp of these people which is very fair, and which they value highly because of their saying they were like us. Regarding this I can only think that those whom they say resemble us, are people more civilised than themselves. One would need to see them in order to know the truth of it. (Champlain 1922–1956, vol. 3:119–120)

This statement is very interesting and important, for it seems to indicate that there was a colony of Europeans further to the west. It is possible that the Indians were referring to the Spanish, for Francisco Vázquez de Coronado had explored the Great Plains as far north as Kansas by 1542, and Spaniards in the expedition had been killed by Indians (Winship 1904:54–63, 114, 124, 144). This passage has prompted at least a few scholars to conclude that Champlain believed the Chinese had erected a trading post or colony there, and making contact with that colony was ultimately the purpose of Nicolet's voyage (Parkman 1879:xxiii; Kellogg 1925:78). However, Champlain did not accept this information uncritically and, from his Eurocentric perspective, might have believed that if such people existed they may have been more culturally complex Indians. Certainly, Champlain had an example in mind, for as a young man he had visited Mexico and saw Mexico City, formerly the Aztec capital of Tenochtitlan, and remarked on its stunning appearance (Champlain 1922–1956, vol. 1:41–42).

The best source for understanding Champlain's geographical knowledge at this point in his career is his 1616 map, which he made when he returned to France that same year. This map was never completed or published in his lifetime, but it includes all the new geographical information that European explorers had gathered to that point, particularly knowledge of Hudson Bay and Chesapeake Bay. Also, the Great Lakes are rendered in a somewhat more accurate fashion than on Champlain's earlier maps because of the information he gained concerning Lakes Ontario and Huron during his 1615–1616 expedition. Unlike an earlier map he produced in 1612, Champlain's 1616 map correctly illustrates that it was Lake Erie (which does not have a name on the 1616 map) that connected to Lake Ontario, and that Lake Huron (called *Mer Douce*, or the Freshwater Sea on the 1616 map) came after Lake Erie in the Great Lakes chain. Champlain's map accurately illustrates the Ottawa River route to Lake Huron (see Champlain 1616 Map) (Wroth 1954).

One writer has suggested that the thin neck of land that appears in Lake Huron on Champlain's 1616 map is the Keweenaw Peninsula in Lake Superior (Stiebe 1999:59), but several pieces of evidence negate this conclusion. During the winter of 1615–1616 Champlain believed that Lake Huron was about 840 miles in length, or more than twice as long as it really is. The 1616 map illustrates why: Champlain had it simply emptying right into a gulf or estuary of the Pacific Ocean.

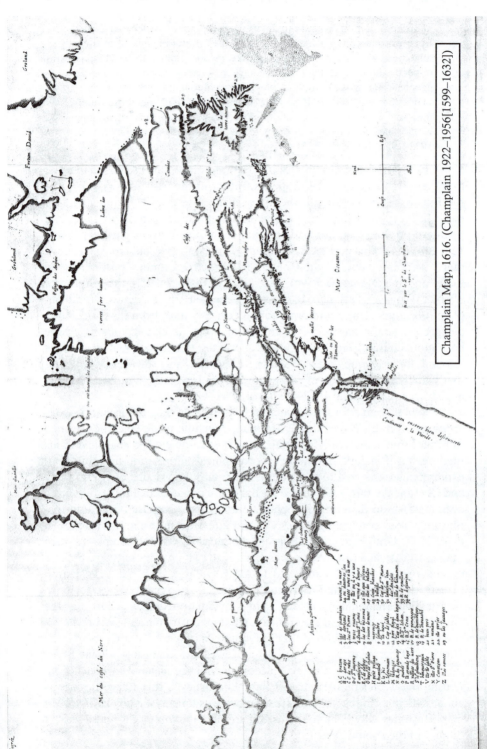

Champlain Map, 1616. (Champlain 1922–1956[1599–1632])

Made from the original in The John Carter Brown Library
for The Champlain Society, 1956

It should be noted that at this point in his career Champlain entertained a theory that the Great Lakes drained in two directions. It was based largely on information he received from the three groups of Indians in 1603, and while he eventually abandoned it as he gained more geographic evidence, it colored his thinking for some time. He initially believed that Lake Erie was some sort of gulf or estuary of the Pacific Ocean. The Indians had asserted that a third very large body of water existed beyond Lake Erie. Champlain misunderstood it to be a saltwater body and naturally (but incorrectly) assumed that Lake Huron was the Pacific. Because the Indians made it clear to him that Lake Ontario was connected to Lake Erie by Niagara Falls, Lake Erie had to drain at least some of its water into Lake Ontario. It is a fact of geography that the vast majority of lakes drain only in one direction through a single drainage channel. Indeed, there are only a small number of certain unique lakes that have dual drainages (Cabot 1946:474). However, many Frenchmen in North America during Champlain's time believed that such lakes were more common than they really are. This was due to some of the inadequately translated information they received from the Indians as well as the power of wishful thinking that the east-flowing St. Lawrence River would eventually furnish a west-flowing outlet and thus provide a water route that would serve as the Northwest Passage (Lescarbot 1911:317; Sagard 1939:43).

After seeing Lake Huron in 1615, it was no longer tenable to presume that it was the Pacific Ocean. Thus, rather than Lake Erie draining into the Pacific, Champlain shifted his geographic thinking and concluded that Lake Huron drained into the Pacific. Indeed, the 1616 map clearly shows Lake Huron draining into a large estuary that leads to the Pacific in the west, while in the east Lake Huron drains into the St. Lawrence River. The map appears to indicate that some western tide fed into the estuary, and that freshwater from the various rivers that fed into it freshened this water as it moved east. What, then, is the large peninsula that juts out into Lake Huron? Undoubtedly, it is what Champlain understood to be the Lower Peninsula of Michigan. Many early mapmakers of the Great Lakes region often portrayed this peninsula as a long, thin, sliver of land (for example, see Sanson Map). Thus, it should be no surprise that Champlain (whose information was far from perfect) would have done so as well. His 1616 map was an attempt to make his dual drainage theory of the Great Lakes chain a cartographic reality (Champlain 1922–1956, vols. 1:165, 170–171, 2:330; Karpinski 1931:11–12; Heidenreich 1976:89). In a statement to King Louis XIII in 1618, Champlain shortened the length of Lake Huron a bit from his earlier estimate of about 840 miles, but he nevertheless concluded that there existed

> the South Sea [Pacific Ocean] passage to China and to the East Indies by way of the river St. Lawrence, which traverses the lands of the said New France, and which river issues from a lake about three hundred leagues [630 miles] in length, from which lake flows a river that empties into the said South Sea, according to the account given . . . by a number of people. (Champlain 1922–1956, vol. 2:330)

Detail from Sanson Map, 1656. (Winsor 1894)

The western estuary of Lake Huron that is depicted on his 1616 map comports with his description above.

The information that Champlain used to construct this map is crucial for understanding the nature of Nicolet's journey. During his trip to Huronia in 1615, Champlain had a chance to talk with the Algonquian-speaking Ottawas who lived along Lake Huron and traveled as far as 800 to 1,000 miles to trade with other tribes. Their knowledge of what existed to the west of Lake Huron was superior to that of the more sedentary Hurons. An Ottawa chief sketched for Champlain what he knew of this country using charcoal on a piece of tree bark. It was probably this man who told Champlain about the Puan, or Ho-Chunk, first mentioned in French records on Champlain's 1616 map. The estuary into which Lake Huron emptied was Lake Michigan as Champlain understood it. The Ottawas must have related that in order to get to the Ho-Chunk, one had to travel along the northern shore of Lake Huron and pass through a strait (the Straits of Mackinac) that entered into another body of water on which the Ho-Chunk lived. They either did not mention or more probably Champlain failed to understand the eventual turn to the south that such a voyage required, and thus, Champlain simply had the route continuing westward along a hypothetical northern shore. If one turns Champlain's 1616 map 90 degrees counterclockwise, one sees the crude outline of Lake Michigan begin to emerge. The thin neck of land that Stiebe and others have mistaken as the Keweenaw Peninsula of Lake Superior more clearly becomes the Lower Peninsula of Michigan. Moreover, the Ho-Chunk are located in roughly the correct spot where they lived during this period: Green Bay (in what is now Wisconsin) (Champlain 1922–1956, vol. 3:43–44; Heidenreich 1976:23, 85–89).

The fetid water that led other tribes to bestow on the Ho-Chunk the appellation of "Stinkards" was undoubtedly the Fox River and the area of southern Green Bay near the river's mouth. Indeed, the Fox River in the era before white settlement was known to have been quite foul smelling, and the area around the mouth of the river was known to have extensive marshes of stagnant and malodorous water. There are several sources that attest to this including a 1673 description by the Jesuit explorer Jacques Marquette:

> This bay bears a Name which has a meaning not so offensive in the language of the savages; For they call it *la baye sallé* ["salt bay"] rather than Bay des Puans,—although with Them this is almost the same and this is also The name which they give to the Sea. This led us to make very careful researches to ascertain whether there were not some salt-Water springs in This quarter, As there are among the hiroquois [Iroquois], but we found none. We conclude, therefore, that This name has been given to it on account of the quantity of mire and Mud which is seen there, whence noisome vapors Constantly arise, Causing the loudest and most Continual Thunder that I have ever heard. (Thwaites 1896–1901, vol. 59:97–99)

An army surgeon posted at Green Bay in 1827 provided a similar description of the surrounding waters when he wrote that the local fort

> is now situated near the mouth of the [Fox] River . . . surrounded by swamps and prairies, with as bitter water than that of the river, which in the warm seasons, is very impure, and unfit for any other use than washing. . . . [T]he uncommon lowness of the waters and the consequent exhalations from the decaying animal and vegetable matters spread upon the adjacent swamps and prairies. . . . Diarrheas . . . have often been caused by drinking too freely of the bad water of the River, than by any other cause. Dysenteries, have generally been caused by . . . too copious draughts of bad water. (Beaumont 1827)

Marquette's writings in particular illustrate how Champlain almost certainly mistook foul-smelling water to be saltwater. Thus, early in his career it all wove together perfectly in Champlain's mind, and what was really Green Bay of Lake Michigan became the saltwater estuary of the Pacific into which Lake Huron flowed. By 1634, however, he had developed a more accurate notion of the Great Lakes chain and the location to which he sent Nicolet.

But what about Lake Superior? Champlain's 1632 map (on the following page) illustrates that whatever he knew about this body of water, he confused it with Lake Michigan. Conrad E. Heidenreich has proposed the most brilliant and definitive explanation regarding the evolution of Champlain's geographical knowledge and how it was expressed on his 1616 and 1632 maps. Heidenreich asserts that after 1616, Champlain received information about a sizeable series of rapids that connected another large body of water with Lake Huron. This, of course, referred to the Sault Ste. Marie (St. Mary's in English) Rapids and Lake Superior, but because he already had information about Lake Michigan that he almost certainly received from the Ottawa in

Champlain Map, 1632. (Champlain 1922–1956[1599–1632])

1615, he simply assumed that both stories referred to a single body of water (which Champlain called the *Grand lac*). He also received better information regarding the location of the Puan after 1616, for his 1632 map shows the river and the small lake on which they lived to be separated from the *Grand lac* by a peninsula. This, Heidenreich asserts, was Champlain's attempt to illustrate Green Bay and the Door Peninsula of Wisconsin:

> Knowing of only two large lakes, Champlain placed the *sault* between Lakes Huron and Michigan. Since the first story of the route to the *Puan* did not mention a *sault*, and the second mentioned a river and a smaller lake, Champlain chose to show that river emptying into *Mer douce* just east of the *sault*. In this way one did not have to cross a *sault* to get to the *Puan*. The route to the *Puan* was now rationalized. One traveled along the northern shore of *Mer douce* and continued along a wide river to a smaller lake where the *Puan* lived. This smaller lake lay north of the large lake (*Grand lac*), which emptied into *Mer Douce* by a *sault*. In actual fact this is a fair description of how to get to the *Puan*. One traveled along the northern shores of Lake Huron and Lake Michigan, through the long and narrow Green Bay. (Heidenreich 1976:94–96)

The 1632 map also illustrates several continuities with the 1616 map. Champlain's written comments that accompanied the 1632 map stated that traversing Lake Huron and the *Grand lac* required a canoe journey of 30 days from east to west. Hence, the 30-day canoe journey across a single lake in 1616 became a 30-day voyage across two lakes in 1632. Obviously, the length of 630 to 840 miles that he believed Lake Huron to be in 1616 also included the estuary of the Pacific Ocean that Champlain illustrated on his map that year; by 1632 this estuary became the *Grand lac*. Also, the large, slender peninsula in the 1616 map became a much smaller peninsula south of the Sault Ste. Marie Rapids (numbered as 34 on the Champlain 1632 Map). Clearly, it was still what he understood to be the Lower Peninsula of Michigan (Champlain 1922–1956, vol. 6:234; Heidenreich 1976:88–97).

However, the differences between the 1616 and 1632 maps are just as striking as the similarities, and these are largely due to information concerning Lake Superior that Champlain acquired after 1616 that he may have received as early as 1624 or as late as 1632. The person who initially acquired it was one of his young men sent to live among the Indians, Étienne Brûlé, about whom little is known. He arrived in Quebec at its founding in 1608 and lived among the Indians from 1610 onward. In 1615, he became the first European to see Lake Ontario, and that same year he went all the way to Chesapeake Bay. Although sketchy, there is enough evidence to conclude that Brûlé probably made a journey toward the Lake Superior basin between 1621 and 1623, but probably did not substantially explore Lake Superior. Nevertheless, Brûlé clearly understood its basic geography, and he communicated that to a Récollet lay brother, Gabriel Sagard (Heidenreich 1976:94). It was most likely in 1623 that Brûlé told Sagard that beyond Lake Huron was another large, freshwater lake. According to Sagard:

> The interpreter Bruslé [sic] and a number of Indians have assured us that
> beyond the *mer douce* [Lake Huron] there is another very large lake,
> which empties into the former by a waterfall, nearly two leagues [four
> miles] across, which has been called the Gaston falls [Sault Ste. Marie];
> this lake [Lake Superior], with the freshwater sea [Lake Huron], repre-
> sents about a 30-day trip by canoe according to the Indians' statement,
> and according to the interpreter [Brûlé] is 400 leagues [840 miles] long.
> (Jurgens 1966:132)

What is striking about this quotation is that it is almost exactly the same
as a passage that Champlain wrote for his 1632 map:

> Gaston Rapids [Sault Ste. Marie], nearly two leagues [four miles] in
> length, emptying into the Freshwater Sea [Lake Huron] and flowing
> from another extremely large lake [Lake Superior, or what Champlain
> called the *Grand lac*], which together with the Freshwater Sea makes a 30
> days' canoe journey, according to report of the Indians. (Champlain
> 1922–1956, vol. 6:234)

It is significant that Champlain used the name Gaston Falls, the same
appellation that Brûlé gave to what is known today as the Sault Ste. Marie
Rapids. More important, Champlain mentions nothing about the *Grand lac*
providing access to the Pacific Ocean. By calling it a lake (as opposed to a
gulf, sea, or bay) he directly implies that it was a freshwater body that drained
in a single direction eastward toward Lake Huron. Also, the shape of the
Grand lac suggests this as well. Where the 1616 map indicates an outlet to the
Pacific, *Grand lac's* shape on the 1632 map instead illustrates that it was oval
and thus an inland body of freshwater. Moreover, the Sault Ste. Marie Rapids
as well as other rapids of the Great Lakes chain on the 1632 map demonstrates that even if there were a link between the *Grand lac* and the Pacific
Ocean, such a route was essentially closed to large ships. Thus, the 1632 map
indicates that Champlain probably no longer believed that the Great Lakes
provided access to the Pacific Ocean.

Clearly, the information that Champlain received regarding Lake Superior led to this change in his thinking. He most likely received this information from Sagard, who spent a single winter among the Hurons from 1623 to
1624 (during which time he talked with Brûlé) and returned to Quebec in
July 1624. Champlain had two meetings with Brûlé; a brief one in 1623 when
Brûlé came to Quebec and another in 1629 when Champlain admonished
Brûlé for serving the English. Champlain mentions nothing in either instance
about Brûlé giving him information concerning the country west of Lake
Huron. Thus, the available evidence suggests that Champlain received his
information from Sagard, probably in 1624 (Champlain 1922–1956, vols.
5:96–97, 108, 131–32, 6:63, 98–101). According to Champlain, Sagard

> told us all that had happened during the winter he had spent with the sav-
> ages, and the bad life which most the Frenchmen had led in the country
> of the Hurons; amongst others the interpreter Brûlé, who was receiving a

hundred pistoles [gold coins] a year to incite the savages to come down and trade . . . for this man [Brûlé] was recognized as being very vicious in character, and much addicted to women. (Champlain 1922–1956, vol. 5:131–132)

While the 1632 map appears to illustrate conclusively that Champlain had abandoned the idea of a waterway to the Pacific via the Great Lakes, a petition he sent to Louis XIII in 1630 suggests that he felt it necessary to continue pandering to the expectations of his sponsors in France that such a route might exist in order to pursue his own goals of trade and colonization in New France. This same petition also anticipated and dismissed the idea that France might seek the Northwest Passage through Hudson Bay:

And moreover, if the way to China which so desired could be found, either through the rivers and lakes, some of which are three hundred leagues [630 miles] long, and if the reports of the people of the country are to be believed, some of these lakes empty into the southern and northern seas, there would be through this a great and admirable outcome, with a shortening of the way of more than three thousand leagues [6,300 miles]. That's why the Portuguese, Spanish, English, and Flemish have tried their luck through glacial seas, of Nova Zembla [Novaya Zemlya, an island archipelago in the Arctic Ocean north of Russia] as well as on the side of the Davis Strait; all these attempts with great expenses were in vain and fruitless, because the ice stopped them in the middle of their voyage; all these dangers cannot be feared in your New France where the temperature is very mild in comparison to the others. (Champlain 1922–1956, vol. 6:362–363)

New France was under English control in 1630, and Champlain wanted France to regain the colony as quickly as possible. He went to great lengths in this petition to list the many resources available in the colony that would provide the French with great wealth that could be taxed and thus put additional revenue into the king's coffers. Moreover, Champlain employed stock language that he had used in his earlier petitions concerning a water route to China via the Great Lakes. In petitions written in 1617 and 1618 he asserted that the "north and the south seas [Hudson Bay and the Pacific Ocean respectively] that one cannot doubt but that this would be the means of reaching easily to the Kingdom of China and the East Indies . . ." and that "one may hope to find a short route to China by way of the river St. Lawrence" (Champlain 1922–1956, vol. 2:326, 345). It is conceivable that Champlain believed that the Great Lakes provided a passage to the Pacific when he wrote his 1630 petition but then received information concerning Lake Superior sometime afterward and expressed this information on his 1632 map. Since both Champlain and Sagard were in France between 1630 and 1632, this is possible; however, such an assertion is speculative and not supported by any primary sources (Trudel 1966c:196; Rioux 1966).

Champlain's comments concerning the "glacial seas" in his 1630 petition as well as earlier comments confirm that he had kept abreast of the various explorations of Hudson Bay between 1612 and 1620 (Champlain 1922–1956, vol. 2:256–257). Information regarding several of these voyages was made known during Champlain's lifetime in the published works of Samuel Purchas, an English writer, who provided at least summary information concerning the voyages of Thomas Button, Robert Bylot, William Baffin, and Robert Fotherby (Purchas 1617:927; Purchas 1625:720–731, 836–843; Purchas 1626: 817–821). While it is not known if Champlain read any of Purchas's works, his 1630 petition illustrates that he knew about the expeditions of these explorers and how the treacherous, ice-clogged straits that these men navigated precluded any hope of reaching the Pacific via Hudson Bay.

The 1632 map indicates that Champlain believed that it was possible to ascend the Saguenay and St. Maurice Rivers (at Tadoussac and Trois Rivières [French for Three Rivers] respectively) and make portages to an unnamed river that fed into Hudson Bay. However, in light of the 1630 petition, it is obvious that Champlain believed at this later stage in his career that the purpose of such a journey was not to gain access to the Pacific but to make contact with the tribes of the region and acquire the furs they could provide. Champlain correctly gauged from the Indians of the St. Lawrence River valley, the Ottawa River valley, and the Lake Huron region that the area around Hudson Bay was a rich source of large animal peltries (Champlain 1922–1956, vol. 3:44–63, 101–105). Champlain asserted as much when he wrote in 1619 that there were

> others whose habitation is in those northern parts and who form a considerable division of those tribes in a country of abundant hunting and where there are many large animals. I saw several skins of these, and by their drawings of their shape I judged them to be buffaloes. (Champlain 1922–1956, vol. 3:105)

A final anomaly on the 1632 map that requires explanation is the island within the small lake on which the Ho-Chunk lived that Champlain labeled as possessing a "*mine de cuivre*" or a copper mine. The reference is probably to Lake Superior's Isle Royale, which supplied the Indians with copper for many centuries prior to the coming of the French, or possibly one of several islands in Lake Huron, or even the rich copper deposits on the south shore of Lake Superior. However, it cannot refer to Lake Michigan where the Ho-Chunk resided since the Lake Michigan basin has no significant deposits of copper. The information concerning this island undoubtedly came from Brûlé and was most likely communicated to Champlain via Sagard. In 1632, Sagard wrote that Brûlé had shown him an ingot from a mine that was 80–100 leagues (200 to 250 miles) away from the Huron country. This was a gross underestimation since Lake Superior itself was well over 200 miles from Huronia, and Isle Royale was over 500 miles away (Holmes 1901:684–696; Sagard 1939:242; Heidenreich 1976:96–97). Regardless of where this island with the copper was actually located, there is no doubt that Champlain misplaced it on his 1632 map. It is yet another example of how Champlain consistently received new information concerning both Lakes Michigan and Superior and conflated them into a single body of water.

As with the 1616 map, Champlain's 1632 map, when properly understood, records the residence of the Ho-Chunk and thus the ultimate destination of Nicolet. Misreading the 1632 map has been a major source of
confusion about the actual route taken by Nicolet, pointing several scholars
in the direction of Lake Superior rather than the proper direction of Green
Bay on Lake Michigan (Wilson 1946:216–220; Dever 1966:318–322; Trudel
1980:189–191; Stiebe 1999:59). Heidenreich's analysis is again critical, for if
one takes Champlain's 1632 map and turns it 90 degrees counterclockwise,
the small lake on which the Ho-Chunks live becomes Green Bay, the *Grand
lac* becomes Lake Michigan to the southeast, and the piece of land between
them is easily identified as the Door Peninsula. Nevertheless, while he unraveled the riddle concerning the residence of the Ho-Chunk in the early seventeenth century and the destination of Nicolet in 1634, Heidenreich, like
everyone else, did not question the popular myth that Nicolet had with him
"a robe of Chinese damask, no doubt just in case he met Chinese at his destination" (Heidenreich 1976:33, 87–88, 94–95).

Thus, Champlain clearly knew he was sending Nicolet to Green Bay,
although Champlain's incomplete and less-than-perfect understanding of
Lakes Superior and Michigan meant that he was not entirely cognizant of
Green Bay's exact location. The question of why Champlain sent Nicolet on
his journey also must be answered. It certainly was not to find the Northwest Passage, for Champlain probably no longer believed by 1634 that such
a route to the Pacific was possible via the Great Lakes. Even if he did, he
had far greater concerns in 1634, particularly ensuring the survival of the
colony of New France and extending and securing the French fur trade in
North America.

Champlain's purpose in sending Nicolet on his 1634 journey can be discerned by examining events that transpired between 1616 and 1633. Around
1618, Champlain sent petitions to King Louis XIII and the French Chamber
of Commerce. He noted that New France possessed rich soil, plentiful fisher-
ies, abundant forests, copper and iron mines, and, of course, rich harvests of
furs. He was forced to appeal to both the king and the Chamber of Commerce because he had lost his lieutenancy when the Prince de Condé was
arrested for political reasons. Champlain's plans were in turmoil, and he was
forced to spend most of the period from 1616 to 1620 in France attempting to
straighten out matters and promoting his vision for a prosperous colony. By
1620, Champlain received a commission from the new viceroy, the Duc de
Montmorency (Dix 1903:175–77; Champlain 1922–1956, vol. 2:326–345;
Trudel 1966c:193–194). He also received a letter from King Louis XIII (de
Montmorency's cousin), who stipulated that Champlain was to "keep the
said country in obedience to me, making the people who are there live as
closely in conformity with the laws of my kingdom as you can" (Champlain
1922–1956, vol. 4:370). Governance of the colony was now Champlain's
principal responsibility (Champlain 1922–1956, vols. 4:213, 5:143–146). As
one of Champlain's biographers, Marcel Trudel, has noted, from 1620

onward, "Champlain was to devote himself exclusively to the administration of the country; he was to undertake no further great voyages of discovery; his career as an explorer had ended" (1966c:194).

Champlain's journey to the Hurons from 1615 to 1616 was the last voyage of exploration that he personally undertook. Moreover, he had been prevented from conducting several voyages of exploration between 1608 and 1613 because promises made by the Indians did not materialize. Their fickleness is explained by the dynamics of the fur trade. By the early 1600s, the Indians of the St. Lawrence River valley such as the Montagnais, Algonquins, and Hurons traded European goods for furs with more distant tribes around Hudson Bay and the western Great Lakes. It was very lucrative, and they knew that if Champlain established direct ties with those tribes it would undermine their role as middlemen. Thus, they were often reluctant to provide canoes and guides to Champlain and his men. When they provided such support, the price was French military assistance against the Iroquois.

Champlain was almost certainly still interested in learning more about North American geography through exploration, but his other duties increasingly consumed his time and energy. New France, if it was to succeed, required the fur trade as its economic foundation, and Champlain needed to ensure that friendly tribes brought their furs to the French. It is telling that from 1620 to 1629 Champlain mentioned almost nothing about exploration in his writings, and when he did, he made it clear that it was now the responsibility of others. For example, Nicolet lived among the Nipissings from 1620 to 1629, and Father Joseph de la Roche Daillon spent the winter of 1626–1627 among the Neutrals. Champlain mentions neither of these men in his 1632 work, *Les Voyages de la Nouvelle France*. The reason, according to Heidenreich, is that neither man learned anything about the geography of North America that Champlain did not already know. The one exception was an unnamed explorer he sent from Quebec up the Chaudièr River to the Kennebec River via a portage to make contact with the Abenaki Indians along the Atlantic Coast: a region that Champlain had already extensively explored. His purpose for authorizing this voyage was, undoubtedly, to bring the Abenakis into the French fur trade.

Thus, expanding the trade was Champlain's new goal, and explorations conducted in the 1620s and 1630s had the expansion of this enterprise as their purpose (Hunt 1940:54–55; Eccles 1969:31–32; Heidenreich 1976:13–34; Heidenreich 1997:82–84, 87–90). Trudel sums up the situation succinctly when he writes that finding the Northwest Passage "seems to have interested Champlain less and less, or else he no longer had the leisure to concern himself with it" (Trudel 1966c:195).

Moreover, significant events occurred between 1627 and 1629. In 1627, Cardinal Armand-Jean du Plessis Richelieu became the viceroy of New France. Richelieu, the king's chief minister, was the most powerful political figure in France and was the real power behind the throne of King Louis XIII. Richelieu sought to make France the predominant power in Europe and believed that in order to accomplish this goal France had to engage in over-seas commerce. Colonies like New France were critical to such an effort. To that end, Richelieu took over the viceroyalty of New France and created the *Compagnie des Cents-Associés*, or the Company of One Hundred Associates, of which Champlain was a member. Champlain reached the zenith of his career when he received his 1629 commission, for he was now the commander of the colony of New France and the lieutenant of the most powerful figure in France (Dionne 1891:523–524; Champlain 1922–1956, vol. 6:151–152; Tru-del 1966c:195–196; Tapié 1975:253–263; Roberts 2004:513–514).

Champlain spent from 1626 to 1629 in New France supervising matters, but despite his best efforts, the little colony struggled. Prior to 1630, there were never more than 100 French persons in New France. The autumn of 1627 was typical; Champlain noted that a mere 55 men, women, and chil-dren were at Quebec. Prior to 1615, there was but one structure there known as the Habitation, comprising three cramped barracks and a storehouse with a pigeon loft. Most food was brought from France; by 1625 there were only 15 acres under cultivation in the vicinity of Quebec. The poor state of the col-ony was the principal reason that Richelieu took over as viceroy. In order to make the colony financially viable and undermine competitors who showed up each summer to trade with Indians at Tadoussac, Champlain focused his energies on developing commercial relationships with the Hurons and Algon-quins who lived up the Ottawa River (Dionne 1891:420–433; Champlain 1922–1956, vol. 5:235–236; Trudel 1966b:28). As historian W. J. Eccles notes, "By establishing direct trade relations with the Huron, one middleman could be eliminated, an assured supply maintained, costs greatly reduced, and the rival traders undersold on European fur markets" (Eccles 1969:23–24, 32).

The necessity of retaining strong relations with these two tribes was the principal reason that Champlain assisted the Hurons and Algonquins on their forays against the Five Nations League of the Iroquois. After 1615, the Iroquois expanded their hostilities and began to fight against the French and their fur trade empire. Warfare destabilized the St. Lawrence valley, and Champlain had no desire to see Quebec succumb to an attack by the Iro-quois. The situation became even more critical once the Iroquois began to secure firearms from the Dutch at Albany; the early advantage that the French and their allies enjoyed because of firearms no longer existed by the 1620s. Thus, in 1627, when a group of allied Indians asked Champlain to join them in an all-out war against the Iroquois, Champlain sought to dissuade them. He had brokered a peace between the French-allied tribes and the Iro-quois in 1622. This initial peace was successful, and the Iroquois even traded with the French in 1624. The tenuous peace held for the next three years, until 1627 when it was in jeopardy (Champlain 1922–1956, vol. 5:73–80, 117–119, 130–131, 214–223; Bishop 1948:284–288; Eccles 1969:25, 30–32).

Champlain managed that year to talk his Indian allies out of going to war, arguing that "the whole river would be closed to them, and they would neither be able to hunt nor fish without incurring great danger" (Champlain

1922–1956, vol. 5:224). Unfortunately, he was unable to convince all of them, for a few young warriors went into the Iroquois country anyway and took prisoners. Champlain worked hard to prevent this incident from destroying the fragile peace and even saved the prisoners from what would have been certain torture and execution and had them sent back to their own country, escorted by a French-allied Indian chief named Cherououny and two of his warriors, with presents for the Iroquois chiefs in order to assuage their anger over the episode. Champlain also sent along a Frenchman, who could "give more weight to their embassy" (Champlain 1922–1956, vol. 5:221–226). Nevertheless, the plan failed. An Algonquin with a personal grudge against Cherououny had told the Iroquois before the embassy arrived that Cherououny and the others were spies who intended to do them harm, and the Iroquois tortured and killed Cherououny, his warriors, and the Frenchman. For all that, this affair illustrates that Champlain sought peace (Champlain 1922–1956, vol. 5:224–231, 308–313). It is also strikingly similar to Jean Nicolet's 1634 mission, which was clearly a continuation of Champlain's efforts to encourage intertribal peace in the interests of extending French trade and hegemony in the West.

The profitability of the fur trade, however, required a strong colony to conduct that trade. One of the reasons Champlain had to spend so much time in France during his early years was that he often clashed with others over policy regarding New France. The various viceroys and companies for which he had worked were not interested in colonization but simply wanted to see profits from the fur trade, and, not surprisingly, often turned a deaf ear to Champlain's requests for additional aid and settlers. This changed with the ascension of Richelieu who wanted to see France with populous overseas colonies like those of England, Holland, and Spain. One of his goals in creating the Company of One Hundred Associates was to have 4,000 French people settled in New France within 15 years (Trudel 1966b:29; Eccles 1969:23–25; Tapié 1975:256–257).

As we have seen, these plans were disrupted in 1628 and 1629. France and England were at war, and the English issued letters of marque to seamen willing to work as privateers and plunder French ships and settlements. One of the applicants was actually a resident of Dieppe, France—David Kirke—whose father, Jarvis, had extensive commercial ties in Dieppe and London. The Company of One Hundred Associates shipped supplies for New France from Dieppe, so the Kirke family had excellent intelligence concerning the company's operations. Jarvis and a group of London merchants provided financial backing for David Kirke's expedition that set out in March 1628 and succeeded in capturing several supply ships bound for New France. The next year, Kirke departed from England with an even larger fleet and intercepted French ships sent by the Company of One Hundred Associates that carried about 400 settlers: the first of the 4,000 promised by Richelieu. With no hope of any relief arriving from France and the colony on the brink of starvation, Champlain wisely surrendered Quebec on July 19, 1629. He and the other

French residents were taken aboard the English ships and stopped at Tadoussac where Champlain met Brûlé and another interpreter who worked for the English. It was at this meeting that Champlain castigated Brûlé for his treachery (Champlain 1922–1956, vol. 6:40–61; Trudel 1966b:29–30; Trudel 1966c:196–198; Moir 1966:405–406; Eccles 1969:33).

All was not lost, for when Champlain arrived in London he learned that England and France had ended the hostilities on April 29, 1629. Thus, as noted earlier, the war had been over for almost three months when Kirke captured Quebec. Champlain met with the French ambassador in London and asked that New France be restored and then went to France and met with the stockholders of the company and Richelieu to urge that they quickly regain the colony. Nevertheless, New France was not restored to French control until 1632, and Champlain arrived back in May 1633. He immediately set about shoring up the colony's military strength with new fortifications, for he feared the English might once again try to conquer the colony, and he also sought to subdue the Iroquois, who continued to plague New France with the threat of war (Champlain 1922–1956, vol. 6:361–379; Trudel 1966c:196–198; Eccles 1969:35).

Given this information, it is certain that the mission undertaken by Jean Nicolet had nothing to do with finding the Northwest Passage to Asia but was instead a purely diplomatic undertaking. While Nicolet definitely gained new geographic knowledge as a result of his journey, this was completely incidental to its primary purpose.

Nicolet had arrived in New France most likely in 1618 and spent his first two years among the Algonquins who lived on Allumette Island near the headwaters of the Ottawa River. He even accompanied about 400 Algonquins on a peace embassy to the Iroquois sometime between 1619 and 1620, at least two years before Champlain's efforts to bring about a general peace. For eight or nine years after this assignment, he lived with the Nipissings, apparently during the time that New France was in the hands of the English. He most likely came down with a Huron trade flotilla headed to Quebec in the spring of 1633 now that the colony had been restored to France. According to Vimont, he was then promoted to the title of agent to the Indians and interpreter. Thus, from 1633 onward he was in the employ of the newly formed Company of One Hundred Associates (Sulte 1908:188–190; Hamelin 1966:516). We can deduce that both Champlain and Nicolet were at Trois Rivières in July 1634 and that during this visit Champlain delegated Nicolet, according to Vimont, "to make a journey to the nation called People of the sea [Ho-Chunk], and arrange peace between them and the Hurons from whom they are distant about three hundred leagues [630 miles] Westward." Vimont does not say who sent Nicolet, but logic indicates it was Champlain, for he was the principal representative of the company in the colony, and Nicolet was a company employee.

The second question posed at the beginning of this chapter—why Champlain sent Nicolet west—is answered in the short passage above as well as in

Champlain's own writings; Nicolet was sent to broker a peace between the Hurons and yet another hostile tribe of Indians farther to the west. Neither Vimont's writings nor those penned by his contemporaries mention anything about Nicolet searching for the Northwest Passage or going westward to meet the Chinese or any other Asiatic peoples. It also should be noted that virtually everything that is known about events in New France after 1633 comes from persons other than Champlain. The Jesuits were particularly important, for from 1632 onward they began sending regular communications to their superiors in France that became known as *The Jesuit Relations*.

We know of only two letters that Champlain wrote to Richelieu between his arrival back in New France in 1633 and his death in 1635, and neither mentions anything about Nicolet, the Northwest Passage, or exploration. His first letter in August 1633 requested that the king provide 120 soldiers to ensure that the English did not return. Champlain also stated that these same soldiers could be used to subdue the Iroquois, who, after the French left the St. Lawrence River valley in 1629, renewed their attacks against the Algonquins and the Hurons. This same argument was made in another letter written in 1633 and printed in the 1636 edition of a publication known as *Le Mercure François*. The letter was published as part of an essay by Paul Le Jeune, a French Jesuit, about events in New France; in it, Champlain gave specifics concerning the kinds of weapons and men that he believed were necessary to defeat the Iroquois. Thus, while Champlain preferred diplomacy, he was willing to use force when diplomacy with the Iroquois failed.

In his second letter, written in August 1634—about a month after Nicolet departed on his journey—Champlain told Richelieu of all his efforts to secure the colony. He had rebuilt Quebec, which had fallen into disrepair while in the hands of the English. He constructed a new fort about 30 miles upstream from Quebec in order to provide a safe place to trade as well as to command the St. Lawrence River. He also mentioned that construction had started on another fortification at Trois Rivières. He reiterated the need for 120 French soldiers. This was his last known official communication (Le Jeune 1636:841–844; Thwaites 1896–1901, vol. 5:201–211, 221–223, 247–249; Bishop 1948:330–332; Trudel 1966c:196–197; Morison 1972:213–217, 287–290).

These letters illustrate that Champlain had two priorities on arriving back in New France in 1633: ensuring the security of the St. Lawrence valley against both the English and the Iroquois and reviving the fur trade. These goals were closely intertwined, for the fur trade would not prosper if the Indians had access to English traders or if Indian convoys carrying furs were intercepted by the Iroquois. Indeed, Champlain ordered the building of a fort at Trois Rivières to provide a safe place for the Huron and Algonquins to trade with the French, and he went there in July 1634 to oversee the work. In July 1634, the Hurons departed Trois Rivières after completing their trade and took back with them three Jesuits and six other Frenchmen including Nicolet (Butterfield 1881:41–43; Thwaites 1896–1901, vols. 7:211–221, 8:73–75; Sulte 1908:191–194; Trudel 1966c:196–197).

When and how Champlain actually communicated his desires to Nicolet is another question that does not lend itself to an easy answer. *The Jesuit Relations* for 1634 notes that Champlain was at Trois Rivières in July of that year, but that he was there after the Jesuits had departed for the Huron country. However, their voyage up the Ottawa River was a tedious affair. The Indians did not have enough canoes, and the Jesuits and the Frenchmen with them were forced to travel with three different parties of Indians. The first party left on July 7, but Nicolet was not with this group. The other two parties left on July 15 and July 23, and Nicolet was with one of them (Thwaites 1896–1901, vols. 7:217, 223, 8:73, 97). The 1634 writer of *The Jesuit Relations*, Paul Le Jeune, noted that Champlain arrived at Trois Rivières after the Jesuit fathers left, but he was probably referring only to the first party. Only one historian, Marcel Trudel, has argued that Nicolet went on his voyage sometime in 1632 or 1633. While this assertion is possible, it is not likely. Benjamin Sulte has done the most detailed and convincing research into the movements of both Champlain and Nicolet during this time, and thus, historians continue to agree with Sulte's assertion that Nicolet's voyage occurred in the summer of 1634 (Sulte 1876:426–431; Sulte 1908; Trudel 1980:185–188).

Champlain, eager to maintain peace and security for the colony, must have seen that the Ho-Chunk (whom no Frenchman had ever met) now threatened New France from the west just as the Iroquois threatened the colony from the south. When this war between the Hurons and Ho-Chunk began cannot be determined, but appears to have been long-standing, for the Hurons told Champlain in 1611 that they were at war with tribes farther to the west. Also, Champlain mentioned in 1615 that the Indians with whom the French had contact (the Huron and probably the Ottawa as well) warred with western nations (Champlain 1922–1956, vols. 2:191, 3:119). Based on later information provided by Perrot, the Ho-Chunk were almost certainly the Hurons' (and the Ottawas') principal enemy in the west. Nicolet, who was fluent both in Huron and Algonquin, had spent many years with the Indians and was accustomed to the demands of living among them. He would have been an excellent candidate for such a diplomatic mission to make peace between these warring tribes. Of course, Nicolet first had to make the journey to the Ho-Chunk, and while he went into Green Bay of Lake Michigan to meet them, the precise location where the meeting took place requires yet additional historical analysis.

Chapter 4

The Various Purported Landfalls

$\mathcal{V}$imont tells us that when Nicolet and his seven companions, designated simply as "Savages" but generally believed to be Hurons,

> arrived at their destination, they fastened two sticks in the earth, and hung gifts thereon, so as to relieve these tribes from the notion of mistaking them for enemies to be massacred. When he was two days journey from his destination, he sent one of those Savages to bear tidings of the peace, which word was especially well received when they heard that it was a European who carried the message; they dispatched several young men. . . . They meet him; they escort him, and carry all his baggage. . . . The news of his coming quickly spread to the places round about, and there assembled four or five thousand men. Each of the chief men made a feast for him, and at one these banquets they served at least sixscore beavers. The peace was concluded; he returned to the Hurons.

That's it: the primary source on Nicolet's landfall that scholars and history hobbyists have analyzed, interpreted, dissected, discussed, and disputed since the nineteenth century. The fleeting effect of what was presumably Nicolet's visit is seen in Jesuit Jean de Brébeuf's report from the mission of St. Joseph at the village of Ihonatiria in the Huron country made two years later during the summer of 1636 that "the Captain of the Naiz percez, or Nation of the Beaver, which is three days journey from us," came to request that a Frenchman spend the summer with them in a fort they had made in fear of the "stinking tribe" which had "broken the treaty of peace" and killed two of their men "of whom they made a feast." Thwaites identifies the Beaver as an Algonkian-speaking group on the north shore of Georgian Bay in the Algoma district (Thwaites 1896–1901, vol. 10:322). If the stinking tribe is the Puan of Green Bay, they ranged astonishingly far afield to make war, but the fact is they first came to French notice as enemies of the Huron in the same general area, and as shall be shown, they were notorious for a propensity to eat their enemies.

Further evidence that Nicolet's role in French–Indian relations was soon forgotten is seen in the passing comment of Fr. Jean de Quen made in 1656 that we can only infer related to Nicolet: "A Frenchman once told me that he had seen, in the Country of the people of the Sea, three thousand men in an assembly held to form a treaty of peace. All those Tribes make war on other more distant Nations."

Although Nicolet was sent to make peace with the Puan people, his "destination" is ambiguous and the passage is confusing because Vimont does not present the events in chronological order. He leads off with Nicolet's arrival at some unknown locale. Wherever it was, it was not necessarily in Puan territory, nor was the meeting held exclusively with the Puan tribe since he later notes a large gathering was attended by "tribes" from "places round about." Then Vimont backtracks to Nicolet sending news of his presence two days before arrival at his "destination" and the reaction to it. Nicolet might have been the first white man in the territory, but the passage indicates the Indians knew about "European" people. Trade goods probably already had been filtering in via other tribes prior to actual contact with Europeans, as we know archaeologically was sometimes the case.

Carol L. Mason had already pointed out in 1994 what we later discovered, "that much of what I had taken as Nicolet's landing place was fiction," the speculations of early historians being accepted as fact by later writers. While we differ with her reasoning as to where Nicolet might have landed, we are grateful for her well-documented identification of the gifts hung on two sticks as a calumet ceremony—tobacco and the pipe itself, especially the stem, being integral to diplomacy among tribes of the Great Lakes and beyond (Mason 1994:39–40).

Nicolet's meeting with a great gathering of Indians is commonly believed to have been in the Green Bay area, but there are differences of opinion as to precisely where it occurred. The most publicized is Red Banks, the known site of a seventeenth-century Winnebago settlement on the Door Peninsula some 12 miles northeast of the present city of Green Bay, distinguished by historic markers and Nicolet's statue, but the exact location of this village is disputed. Another contender proclaimed with a historic marker is upstream from Green Bay on the Fox River at Doty Island in the Neenah-Menasha area at the north end of Lake Winnebago (Lawson 1900a:206, 1900b, 1907a). Butterfield implies the landfall among the Winnebago occurred at the mouth of the Fox River and then has Nicolet journeying upstream to visit Lake Winnebago and turning south to Green Lake County and visiting the Illinois and other tribes (1881:63–72). Carol L. Mason rejects these sites in favor of an unspecified place on the south shore of Lake Superior that might be in Michigan or the Chequamegon Bay area of Wisconsin. Others have argued for locations definitely outside Wisconsin: Lake Superior (Gagnon 1996); specifically Whitefish Bay at the east end of Lake Superior (Wilson 1946; McCafferty 2004); north of Lake Superior (Dever 1966; Trudel 1980); Keweenaw Bay, known as the "cove," on the south shore of Lake Superior (Stiebe 1999); and on Lake Michigan south of Chicago (Hall 1993, 1995, 2003). Whatever the differences of opinion about the location of the meeting, it is presumed to have been on Winnebago turf, although Harry Dever and Marcel Trudel give a special twist to the definition of Winnebago.

We believe the meeting actually took place in Menominee country in the vicinity of Marinette, Wisconsin, about halfway up the west coast of Green Bay at the mouth of the Menominee River that marks the boundary between Wisconsin and the Upper Peninsula of Michigan. Butterfield sees this as Nicolet's first stop where he sent news to the Winnebago of his impending visit (1881:57). The area has long been identified as the location of a major Menominee village, although the exact site has yet to be determined (Mason 1997:81–83). Winnebago delegates could well have been present at the gathering as one of Vimont's "tribes." We will review and evaluate the arguments for alternative sites on Lake Superior and Lake Michigan to lay them to rest and help clarify the lay of the land. The merits of the case for the Marinette location will then be considered in a separate chapter.

There is general agreement that Nicolet's journey from Trois Rivières was via the Ottawa River to Lake Nipissing and from there along the French River to Lake Huron where he most likely followed the northern shoreline of Georgian Bay to the St. Mary's River. Here disagreement begins. Did he keep on going west past the Sault Ste. Marie Rapids and enter Lake Superior? Or, did he turn southeast and then west, following the coast of Michigan's Upper Peninsula through the Straits of Mackinac to enter Lake Michigan? The debate hinges in large part on the French term *au delá*, "beyond," as used by the Jesuit Father Paul Le Jeune in his 1640 account of Nicolet's journey. Those who hold the former position insist that "beyond" means he went *through* the rapids into Lake Superior. Supporters of the latter position construe "beyond" to mean Nicolet went *past* the entrance to the rapids to eventually enter Lake Michigan (see Map: Beyond New France, 1634).

In either case, there is the problem of the Winnebago supposedly living on a "little lake," mentioned by Le Jeune. It often is equated with a little lake "des Puans" shown on Champlain's map of 1632 that appears to lie to the north, between Lake Huron and another Great Lake, thought by many to represent Lake Superior. Of course, there is no little lake in this location. Proponents of different sites on Lake Superior as the place of Nicolet's landfall make allowances for confusion about Indian information obtained by the French and even manage to find candidates for what was meant by the little lake. Actually, as was discussed in chapter 3, Champlain was made aware of what we now know as Lake Michigan through Indian information and tried to depict it rather than Lake Superior in his 1616 and 1632 maps. Thus, the little lake on which he placed the Puan most likely referred to the whole of Green Bay at the northern end of Lake Michigan. It might possibly have been Big Bay de Noc at the head of Green Bay or, just beyond it, Little Bay de Noc. On

the other hand, since we know this western side of Green Bay was not Winnebago country, Champlain's informants may have had reference to a little
lake on the east side of Green Bay adverted to by Spoon Decorah as the location of the tribe prior to their occupation at Red Banks (1895:147). Publius V.
Lawson (1900b) identified Champlain's lac des Puans as Lake Winnebago.

Clifford P. Wilson admits that "[old] maps are sometimes misleading,"
and argues that the French confused north with west or northwest and that
the "little lake" where the Puan were located is really Whitefish Bay at the
east end of Lake Superior (1946). After emerging from the Sault Rapids,
according to Wilson, Nicolet would have encountered this constricted body
of water that forms the eastern entrance to Lake Superior. There is a certain
logic to this identification of the "little lake," but Wilson makes a far less persuasive case in dealing with a second problem. All accounts and maps subsequent to Nicolet's journey consistently place the Menominee and Winnebago
in the Green Bay area (Tucker 1942:Plates I–IV). Wilson rejects this evidence, pointing out that these records were made some 20–30 years after
Nicolet's journey because further French exploration had been delayed by a
period of protracted hostilities with the Iroquois. He says of the Winnebago
and Menominee: "It so happens that these tribes without exception, were
nomadic, and in 1634 could easily have been living on the shores of Lake
Superior, instead of Lake Michigan" (Wilson 1946:217–218).

In addition to embracing a discredited concept of nomadism as simply
wandering to new destinations rather than following a seasonal round to different resources, Wilson is dead wrong about the Menominee and particularly the Winnebago. All the ethnographic and historical evidence indicates
the Winnebago were sedentary, village-oriented people known for their large
gardens (Radin 1923:51, 77, 184–189; Lurie 1978:692). Albert E. Jenks,
whose classic study of wild rice (1900) concentrates on the Algonquian
speakers, particularly the Ojibwa, lumps the Winnebago with the wild rice
people because some of their villages were located where wild rice flourished.
However, that was from the late eighteenth through the early nineteenth centuries when the tribe dispersed along the Fox-Wisconsin and Rock River systems, forming smaller settlements in response to the fur trade. Their choice of
village sites appears to have been determined by climate for gardening far
more than the presence of wild rice. The historic villages in Wisconsin as
mapped by Lawson (1907b:88) can be seen to have stayed within the con-
tours of the zone of 120 consecutive frost-free days required for Indian corn.
This was hardly the climate along the north shore of Lake Superior where
Wilson places them, or even the south shore during most years, although
wild rice flourishes this far north.

As for the Menominee, it is generally thought they are the state's oldest
known continuous residents and were well established there at the time of
European contact, but the precise antiquity of their residence has not been
determined (Mason 1997). According to some Ho-Chunk accounts, they preceded the Menominee in the area. The Menominee, whose very name means

"wild rice," were "basically hunters and gatherers," but also raised squash, beans, and corn in contrast to their more northerly Algonquian-speaking neighbors (Spindler 1978:708).

Dever made the same interpretation of *au delá* as Wilson and also has Nicolet entering Lake Superior via the Sault Ste. Marie Rapids. He also accepts the 1632 map as showing the Puans' little lake north of Lake Superior. More anthropologically and linguistically sophisticated than Wilson, he concluded that Nicolet landed by mistake among people living somewhere north of Lake Superior who were called Winnebago but were not *the* Winnebago he was seeking whose residence on Green Bay is well documented. Whether or not we agree with this conclusion, Dever provides a very useful review of the etymology of the word Winnebago and its widespread application in various spellings not only to the people who, as Dever notes, call themselves Ho-Chunk, but to other people and places as well. Winnebago means water that is nasty in the sense of bad smelling, fetid, turbid, even salty or sulfurous. It can describe inland or ocean waters when appropriate, but it does not mean seawater specifically. Employing the linguistic distinction between Algonquin, the tribe, and Algonquian, the family of related languages (including Algonquin, Ojibwa, Cree, Ottawa, Menominee, and others), Dever offers the following analysis, showing that Le Jeune came to the erroneous conclusion that the word Winnebago meant or referred to a sea:

> The explanation is that the French of that time, not nearly so familiar with the native languages as historians would have us believe, misunderstood the meaning of *Ouinipigou*. They thought it meant "salt water," hence, "the sea," whereas the term actually meant "nasty water." Sometimes, it is true, Algonquians called the sea "nasty water," but they also called some other places by this name, such as Green Bay, Lake Winnipeg, and Wenebegon Lake (Sudbury County, Ontario). The last might reasonably be reached after three days journey up the Montreal by portage to the Cow River. One map of Nicolet's time shows a small *Lac des Puants* up a river east of the Sault, which must be the Mississagi and its continuation, the Wenebegon River. (Dever 1966:320)

Dever contends that the Winnebago Nicolet met were an Algonquian-speaking group and builds his case on what he calls the "nickname" the Winnebago supposedly used to greet Nicolet, *Manitouiriniou*, "the wonderful man or being," according to Vimont. This has puzzled many scholars. The word is patently Algonquian while Winnebago is a Siouan language. *Manitou* generally means spirit in the various Algonquian languages, and it occurs in about as many place names as the changes rung on Winnebago: Manitowoc, Manitoulin, Manitoba, and so on. The French were aware that the Winnebago who call themselves Ho-Chunk spoke a language unknown to them; yet, according to Vimont, Nicolet successfully conveyed his message to the Winnebago. How else, Dever reasons, could Nicolet have addressed them if not in something closely approximating their native tongue, that is, Algonquin in which he was fluent? Dever further supports his contention by noting that Nicolas Perrot and other later visitors to Wisconsin make no mention of Nicolet.

The eminent French Canadian historian, Marcel Trudel, reviewed the Nicolet story and discovered new evidence in French archives that Nicolet probably migrated to Canada in 1619 rather than 1618 as is commonly believed and that his famous journey, given the paucity and uncertainty of the documentary evidence, might have been during the period 1633–1634 instead of 1634–1635. These minor issues aside, he ascribes the claims that Nicolet was the first European to reach Michigan and Wisconsin as nothing but an inflation of Canadian national pride and takes the same position as Dever, whom he cites, that Nicolet entered Lake Superior and ended up among an Algonquian-speaking group in Canada called Winnebago, not the Siouan-speaking Winnebago on Green Bay (Trudel 1980:183–196).

Jacques Gagnon, without specific reference to the phrase *au delá*, clearly took it to mean through the rapids of Saint Mary's River rather than past its mouth, claiming in his opening sentence that Nicolet was one of the first Europeans to shoot the rapids and travel on Lake Superior: *"l'un des premiers Européens à franchir le Sault Sainte-Marie et à naviguer sur le lac Supérieur"* (p. 95). Despite the title, "Jean Nicolet au Lac Michigan: Histoire d'une Erreur Historique" (Jean Nicolet at Lake Michigan: History of a Historical Error), Gagnon's brief article actually concerns nine errors he found in Shea's account of Nicolet, six of which have nothing to do with the controversy of whether Nicolet reached Lake Michigan rather than Lake Superior and three that are only tangentially related to it. He traces the errors largely to Shea's cribbing from and unsupported "corrections" of historian Edmund Bailey O'Callaghan's 1847 publication regarding *The Jesuit Relations* and the history of Canada and the American Old Northwest.

A related thesis is put forth by Lucien Campeau, who claims that Nicolet met the Winnebago at Lake Nipigon, north of Lake Superior. This is another example of misinterpretation of Champlain's 1632 map (which has been discussed in greater detail in chapter 3), that the large lake shown on the left edge of the map is Lake Superior and the Lake of the Puants lay north of it. Given this reasoning, Lake Nipigon is easily mistaken for the latter lake although there is no evidence of the Winnebago ever having lived in this area (Campeau 1987:73).

Ronald Stiebe cites both Wilson and Dever and follows their reasoning that Nicolet went through the Sault Ste. Marie Rapids into Lake Superior rather than past the entrance and on into Lake Michigan. His book, *The Mystery People of the Cove*, is subtitled *A History of the Lake Superior Ouinipegou*, with a self-serving teaser on the cover page, "Who were the Sea People that have eluded historians for 145 years and archaeologists for almost 30?" Stiebe consistently violates his own guiding principle in arguing his case: "It is most essential for any serious historical researcher to retain the highest degree of objectivity possible in the course of establishing factual information" (Stiebe 1999:9).

Dismissing all the evidence placing the Winnebago on Green Bay as simply biased and using a version of the French spelling throughout his book as somehow more authentic than the standard English spelling, he says, "They were called Ouinipegou (pronounced Wee-Knee-pea-goo) [sic] by the Algonkin [sic] people, from which the name Winnebago is derived. The French called them Puans, but their proper name was the Sea People." Stiebe rejects Dever's perceptive realization that *Gens de Mer* was simply Le Jeune's personal take on "ouinipeg":

> Some of the French call them the "Nation of the Stinkards," because the Algonquin word "ouinipeg" signifies 'bad smelling water,' and they apply this name to the water of the salt sea,—so, that these peoples are called Ouinipigou because they come from the shore of a sea about which we have no knowledge; and hence they ought not to be called the nation of Stinkards, but the nation of the sea.

In fairness to Stiebe, he is far from alone in using Le Jeune's flawed reasoning as if it were proven fact. Even Vimont accepted Le Jeune's conjecture without qualification that Nicolet "was delegated to make a journey to the nation called People of the sea." Jesuit Paul Ragueneau, in the *Relation* of 1648–1649, paraphrased and embroidered on Le Jeune's phrase, or perhaps Vimont's repetition of it, so that it sounds as if the Ho-Chunk themselves actually claimed to have lived not only on a sea, but a distant northern one, at that: "These peoples are called Puants, not because of any bad odor that is peculiar to them; but, because they say they come from the shores of a far distant sea toward the North." Le Jeune at least had admitted the French heretofore had "no knowledge of" this sea.

In believing that Ragueneau's statement confirmed Le Jeune, Stiebe recognizes the added details raise a question as to Ragueneau's source of information since, as far as anyone knows, no French explorers visited the Ho-Chunk between 1634 and 1648. Ragueneau, Stiebe reasons, must have had access to information from unrecorded French exploration after Nicolet but before recorded history resumes. As proof, he offers the "Bentzen Stone," named for the farmer who found it in 1905 on the east side of Keweenaw Bay across from Sand Point. It looks like a ground stone celt in the accompanying photographs, although Stiebe calls it a pestle. The stone is inscribed with what appear to be a series of initials, a face that Stiebe identifies as female, and the numbers 1647 that Stiebe points out correspond to the year before Ragueneau's account was written. While Stiebe goes to great effort to find candidates in *The Jesuit Relations* whose names match the initials, he offers no information as to the stone's present whereabouts for independent examination by other researchers (Stiebe 1999:149–151).

Challenging Dever, Stiebe claims the first recorded reference to the "Sea People" was made in 1636 by Jean de Brébeuf, the Jesuit missionary to the Huron who called the Winnebago *Aweatsewaenrrhonon*. Brébeuf supplied no etymological information, but Stiebe cites later Jesuit sources where a Cree group is called by this name and that it means people "who inhabit the coast of the Sea" (Stiebe 1999:117, 149–150). We are indebted to linguists Ives Goddard of the Smithsonian Institution and Blair Rudes, an Iroquoian specialist at the University of North Carolina at Charlotte. Rudes writes in answer to Lurie's inquiry forwarded to him by Goddard (Goddard to Lurie, March 24, 2005), "The short answer is that the Huron name means roughly the same as 'Winnebago,'" for which Goddard had supplied the Algonquian Meskwaki version and the meaning, "filthy water." Rudes continues that the Huron name is more correctly written *awentsiwaenronon*; the first four letters referring to water, the last two syllables to people of, and the middle syllables signifying "to be bitter." It also encompasses "things salty, astringent, bad tasting, so it is pretty close in meaning to 'foul water.'" In short, it might be used to describe sea water, but it does not mean sea water per se, nor does it have anything to do with living on a sea coast.

Ho-Chunk, the Winnebagos' own name, offers no clues. There are arguments whether "*ho*" should be glossed as "voice" or "fish," but phonetically it has absolutely nothing to do with water, let alone salty or sea water. The fact that the documentary record is silent about any other reason for Nicolet's journey than to make peace with the "Ouinipegou" is evidence, in Stiebe's view, of a cover-up to keep the real reason secret from competing nations, the "quest for a route to the South Sea that was thought to lead to China and Japan" (Stiebe 1999:9). This is easily proven false, for Champlain himself gave a map of New France to the English in 1629 in order to show them the various explorations that the other French explorers had made in the interior of North America. He did this because the English had recently conquered Quebec, and Champlain believed France's superior claims to sovereignty were largely founded on these explorations (Champlain 1922–1956, vol. 6:147; Heidenreich 1997:90).

Stiebe rejects Dever's idea of a northern Algonquian-speaking group known as Winnebago and is convinced that Nicolet visited the "real" Winnebago at their village on Keweenaw Bay, his nominee for the "little lake," albeit on the south shore of Lake Superior rather than north of it (Stiebe 1999:81). In view of the fact that Green Bay and Keweenaw Bay are about the same distance from the Sault Ste. Marie Rapids and both fall short, according to Stiebe's calculations, of the 300 leagues (630 miles) cited as the distance Nicolet traveled from the Sault to the Winnebago, Stiebe argues that Nicolet took the long way around Lake Superior. Starting at the northeast end, he supposedly circumnavigated about three fourths of Superior's 1,800-mile coastline to enter Keweenaw Bay from the west to "arrive at the doorstep of Sand Point" on the south shore (Stiebe 1999:94). As Stiebe notes, wave and weather conditions make it easier to go west along the north shore of Lake Superior and east along the south shore, still the preferred route of canoeists and kyakers.

Stiebe pinpoints Nicolet's landfall at Sand Point on the west side of L'Anse Bay that forms the foot of Keweenaw Bay because of an archaeological site there, and it is where, as Stiebe reads the cartographic evidence, Champlain's 1616 and 1632 maps appear to show the Puan. As was demonstrated in chapter 3, the spit of land on Champlain's map that often is identified as the Keweenaw Peninsula really is evidence of Champlain's knowledge, albeit sketchy, of the Lower Peninsula of Michigan.

The accidental discovery of human remains in what appeared to have been burial mounds at Sand Point in the summer of 1967 led the Michigan Archaeological Society to call for the site's scientific excavation. After contacting archaeologists at Michigan State University and the University of Michigan who dismissed the mounds as natural dunes, they finally interested a young faculty member at Western Michigan University in Kalamazoo, Winston Moore, who organized a field school and dug the site with students and volunteers during the summers of 1970 and 1971. To Stiebe's justified indignation, records were mishandled and some artifacts disappeared, including surface finds of a purported musket ball and gunflint. Although the site is clearly prehistoric, to Stiebe, the "mere presence" of these historic artifacts is "more than just coincidental," and he concludes:

> This would highly suggest that there is a strong probability that it may have been the very round that was fired from the hand of Nicolet himself! It is especially significant that the round ball and gun flint would both be found in the same area, indicating that the musket ball was fired and not dropped by some intruder. The flint could have come loose from the firing mechanism of the pistol, either in the course of discharging it, or become entangled in his clothing. Remember he was wearing a loose fitting Asian robe that was to complement the purpose of his mission. (Stiebe 1999:97–98)

It should be stressed that while the presence of a gun flint and musket ball at the Sand Point site is evidence of the presence of Europeans, it is impossible, despite Stiebe's certitude, to link such objects specifically to Jean Nicolet. Indeed, there was a strong French presence in the Keweenaw Bay from the late 1650s onward. Sieur des Groseilliers and his brother-in-law, Pierre-Esprit Radisson, were known to have portaged at the site, most likely in 1658, and the Jesuits established a mission in the area in 1660. Moreover, sites in Wisconsin that were occupied by the French during the late seventeenth and early eighteenth centuries often turn up gun flints similar to those used decades earlier by Frenchmen like Nicolet (Kellogg 1925:109, 146–149; Tanner 1987:36; *Milwaukee Journal Sentinel* 1996). Thus, the gun flint that Stiebe describes was most likely left behind by a Frenchman, but it is naïve to think it can be linked to any specific person, let alone attribute its loss to Nicolet's nonexistent "Asian robe."

The conclusions of Wilson, Dever, Trudel, Mason, and Stiebe all derive from the misreading of Champlain's map of 1632, confusing Lake Michigan with Lake Superior, and from the gloss of *au delá*, "beyond," as meaning through the stretch of rapids at Sault Ste. Marie. We can now turn to writers with whom we agree that the correct interpretation of "beyond" in this context is that Nicolet bypassed the mouth of the Sault Ste. Marie Rapids to eventually enter Lake Michigan, but among whom there are conflicting opinions as to the location of the Ho-Chunk and the place of Nicolet's landfall on Lake Michigan.

By the beginning of the twentieth century, the stretch of bluff a mile or so in length about 12 miles east of the city of Green Bay known as Red Banks was generally accepted as the location of a large Winnebago village. It first came to public attention in 1856 when Charles D. Robinson published his then recent observations of fort-like archaeological remains there. His primary interest was in collecting legends about an intertribal battle that supposedly occurred at Red Banks, and he did not identify the site with the Ho-Chunk. One side fronted on a precipice overlooking Green Bay while the other three sides were surrounded by earthwork "walls" and a moat or ditch. To the south and east lay hundreds of acres of old garden beds, overgrown with trees, but the regular furrows were easily recognized (Robinson 1856).

A half-century later, Arthur C. Neville verified Robinson's observations, writing that his description "corresponds exactly to my own recollection of the ground when visited by me a few years later" (Neville 1906:148–149). Neville must have been very young at the time, as he was only five years old when Robinson presented his findings, but apparently he made subsequent visits as he states, "In the fifty years since Mr. Robinson wrote, the erosion of the cliff has been so great that all traces of these ancient works have disappeared." Neville leaves no doubt that he considered it the site of the Ho-Chunk village of Red Banks.

At the end of the nineteenth century, most people interested in Wisconsin history simply accepted that Nicolet met the Winnebago at Red Banks on Green Bay. However, at the annual meeting of the State Historical Society of Wisconsin held in the city of Green Bay in 1899, papers given by Herbert B. Tanner and Publius V. Lawson made passing reference to Nicolet ascending the Fox River from Green Bay and meeting the Ho-Chunk at Doty Island in Lake Winnebago. This claim set off a controversy between Neville, cited above, and Lawson that was to go on for many years (Tanner 1900:212; Lawson 1900a:206). It was shaped as much by Lawson's and Neville's personalities as by their supporting data. Though much alike, they were natural antagonists. Neville was born in 1850, Lawson in 1853, and both had been brought from eastern states as small children to settle in Wisconsin. By the time of the Green Bay–Doty Island rivalry, both were successful businessmen able to indulge their avocational interests in Wisconsin history and both were politicians and lawyers. Neville, a Democrat, had served a term as mayor of Green Bay and Lawson, a Republican, had served six terms as mayor of Menasha. They had constituencies they could rally in the intercity contest, and their arguments smacked of the courtroom as much as the academy.

It began with Neville's paper presented at the 1905 meeting of the Society, "Historic Sites on Green Bay," quoted above. Neville reviewed the possible locations of Father Claude Allouez's mission before it was established at

1634 · 1909 · COMMEMORATING THE DISCOVERY OF WISCONSIN IN 1634 BY JEAN NICOLET, EMISSARY OF GOVERNOR CHAMPLAIN OF NEW FRANCE. IN THIS VICINITY NICOLET FIRST MET THE WINNEBAGO INDIANS. UNVEILED AUGUST 12, 1909, BY MEMBERS OF THE STATE HISTORICAL SOCIETY OF WISCONSIN AND THE GREEN BAY HISTORICAL SOCIETY.

Historic markers at Red Banks on Green Bay and Doty Island, Lake Winnebago, both claiming to be the site where Nicolet met with the Winnebago Indians. (Photographs by James Uhrinak)

NEAR THIS SPOT LANDED
1634
FIRST WHITE MAN IN WISCONSIN
JEAN NICOLET
MET THE WINNEBAGO TRIBE
HELD EARLIEST WHITE COUNCIL

ERECTED BY
WOMEN'S CLUBS OF MENASHA
1906

De Pere in 1670 near the present city of Green Bay, but the paper was primarily a defense of Red Banks as the site of the major settlement of the Winnebago and "*ipso facto,* the place of Nicolet's visit" (Neville 1906:144). He marshaled his evidence from personal observations of Red Banks, his familiarity with Green Bay as an avid boater, reference to the Champlain map of 1632, data from Henry Rowe Schoolcraft citing the Winnebagos' insistence that they originated at Red Banks and had built a stockaded village there, the narrative of Ho-Chunk elder Spoon Decorah describing Red Banks as the tribe's residence at the time of European contact, and *The Jesuit Relations.* He relied heavily on Allouez who was in actual contact with the Winnebago in the Green Bay region. By that time, the Potawatomi tribe had expanded into Wisconsin and established a large village at Point Sable (sometimes spelled Sauble) just south of the Red Banks bluff. Neville dismissed Lawson's 1899 statement about Doty Island, that he could find "neither reason nor authority" for it (Neville 1906:147).

Apparently, he had not seen or chose to ignore the reasons Lawson had set forth in a pamphlet, *The Winnebago Village on Doty Island*, published by the *Menasha Evening Breeze*, September 11, 1900 (Lawson 1900b). Lawson interpreted the Champlain map as showing Lake Winnebago, Doty Island, and the Fox River flowing into Lake Michigan. Quoting Vimont that when Nicolet was two days' journey from his destination he sent a man ahead and several men returned to "escort him" and "carry all his baggage" (Thwaites 1896–1901, vol. 23:279), Lawson reasoned that Nicolet reached the mouth of the Fox River and ascended it with Winnebago assistance, particularly in portaging around the series of eight steep rapids to reach Lake Winnebago.

This remained Lawson's argument in a paper, "Habitat of the Winnebago, 1632–1832," that he gave at the Wisconsin Historical Society meeting in 1906 and that was published in the society's proceedings the following year (1907a). A footnote by the editor explains that it was in opposition to Neville's 1905 paper, and that the society took a neutral position, merely acting as the medium for the full presentation of both sides of a controversy, adding that, "Adopting Mr. Lawson's view, the Women's Clubs of Menasha have erected a monument to Nicolet on Doty's Island." A photograph of the monument, unveiled September 3, 1906, accompanies the article. The editor's footnote continues that the Green Bay Historical Society, "acting on Mr. Neville's view," contemplated a monument "of similar import" at Red Banks (Lawson 1907a:144). That monument was erected in 1909.

Lawson set about discrediting Neville's "witnesses." References in Schoolcraft to a palisaded village really meant Aztalan in southeastern Wisconsin but were cobbled together with other Schoolcraft data supplied by Jonathan Fletcher to support Winnebago claims that they had a palisaded village at Red Banks; Spoon Decorah himself had apologized that he was old and his memory wasn't what it used to be; there was no proof the Winnebago had built the earthworks at Red Banks, even if they said they did—after all, Henry S. Baird, a prominent Wisconsin settler, politician, and early officer of the State Historical Society, said of the Winnebago that "their lying propensities were proverbial," and, anyway, Red Banks wasn't much of a site. Furthermore, Lawson argued, there was evidence of a palisaded village at Doty Island, too (Lawson 1907a).

In 1670 Allouez, the first Jesuit to ascend the Fox River and reach Lake Winnebago, had found that although the lake abounded in fish, the area was uninhabited, a circumstance he attributed to fear of the Sioux. Lawson pounced on this information to mean that the Ho-Chunk Allouez said he ministered to in the Green Bay area had simply taken temporary refuge there during the calamitous period noted by Perrot and were not regular residents as Neville claimed. The Ho-Chunks' real stronghold, Lawson maintained, had always been Doty Island to which they returned after Allouez's visit and where all subsequent visitors found them until they abandoned the site when the land was ceded to the United States by treaty in 1832.

Once Lawson gets beyond his obsession with the primacy of Doty Island over Red Banks, he is a useful source, particularly regarding the role of the Winnebago in the struggles of the French, English, and Americans for supremacy in North America. In 1907, the same year his "Habitat" paper appeared in the Historical Society's proceedings, Lawson published an 85-page article, "The Winnebago Tribe," in the *Wisconsin Archeologist*. Besides creditable historical research, Lawson collected valuable ethnographic information directly from tribal members (now finding them trustworthy, despite Baird's opinion), documenting, among other things, the dispersal of the tribe into small settlements along the Rock, upper Fox, and Wisconsin Rivers during the eighteenth century (Lawson 1907b).

Neville continued his historical interests, publishing a number of scholarly papers and serving as the moving force in founding the museum at Green Bay that bears his name. While the accumulating weight of historical and ethnological evidence favors Red Banks over other contenders as the major Ho-Chunk settlement at the time of European contact, the triumph of Red Banks over Doty Island and other locales as the officially declared site of Nicolet's landfall rests largely on Neville's "ipso facto," reinforced by vigorous publicizing out of Green Bay even after Lawson died in 1920.

Following World War I, Green Bay planned a homecoming for its veterans that evolved into a historical Pageant of Progress held August 4–5, 1921. Beginning with a bit of romantic nonsense about the resident Indians and a totally fictitious battle between the Menominee and Winnebago at the village of Red Banks, Nicolet appears on the scene to rescue a Menominee captive and restore peace between the tribes (Hall 1993:15–17).

In 1934, the 300th anniversary of Nicolet's landing, a more seriously historical pageant was held at Bay Beach Park showing Nicolet clad in a Chinese robe. A group of Winnebago who formed part of the cast camped at the park and a baby girl was born there, named Jean Nicolet in honor of the occasion by her parents Mr. and Mrs. Archie Elk. The Demming painting of Nicolet was featured on a first-class postage stamp, then worth three cents,

Larger than life-size bronze statue of Nicolet by Sydney Bedore. Commissioned after the 1934 Tercentenary, it was to be erected on the lawn of the State Capitol building, but after storage in a university building in Madison during World War II, it was erected at Red Banks on Green Bay in 1951. (Photograph by James Uhrinak)

with Green Bay chosen for its first day of issue; President Franklin Roosevelt, the nation's foremost philatelist, gave an address at the gathering. Shortly after this celebration it was decided to erect a statue of Nicolet to stand on the lawn of the State Capitol. A commission was appointed to arrange for the statue to be done by Sydney Bedore, a Wisconsin sculptor whose work graces a number of public buildings in the state. Funds were collected from school children throughout Wisconsin in 1939 and 1940. For unknown reasons the statue disappeared until about 1950 when it was discovered in the basement of a building at the University of Wisconsin in Madison and was erected at the Red Banks bluff in 1951, thereby serving to reinforce the idea that it was the site of Nicolet's landfall. The unveiling was in the hands of two young women, Jean Nicolet Elk and Catherine Gibbons of Milwaukee, who had given the first nickel to the project in 1939 (*Green Bay Press-Gazette* 1976). Meanwhile, the original bronze plaque erected by Neville's supporters in 1909 had disappeared during World War II and was replaced after the war.

In the 1950s, the story became further muddled as archaeological opinion centered on the Speerschneider site as the location of the palisaded Winnebago village of Red Banks. It is so close to the village site described by Robinson and Neville that the two are frequently conflated. This issue is discussed in a later chapter.

Yet another Nicolet landfall outside the Green Bay area and even outside Wisconsin has been proposed by Robert L. Hall. His essay, "Rethinking Jean Nicolet's Route to the Ho-Chunks in 1634" (2003), locates both the Ho-Chunk and Nicolet's visit in southern Cook County, Illinois. This account must be read in conjunction with two of his earlier publications (1993, 1995) in which he develops his provocative premises that Nicolet never visited Green Bay and that the Ho-Chunk did not take up residence there until about 1640–1650.

Although not presented in the following order, Hall's several publications boil down to: (1) Nicolet reached Lake Michigan but bypassed the entrance to Green Bay and continued down "the shore" all the way to Illinois. (2) At the beginning of the seventeenth century the Ho-Chunk were a large, widely scattered tribe numbering 20,000 or more with their stronghold in present Cook County, Illinois, south of Chicago where "the particular Ho-Chunk villages visited by Jean Nicolet in 1634 were located" (2003:249). (3) By historic times this area was inhabited by the Illinois Confederacy (a collective term covering the Miamis, Weas, Piankashaws, and other related groups), but it was a recent occupation. (4) Devastating warfare, famine, and plague reported by Perrot occurred in Illinois a few years after Nicolet's visit, not at Red Banks as is usually described. (5) The Illinois filled into the area vacated by the fleeing Ho-Chunk who then took refuge at Red Banks. (6) The Ho-Chunk had "completely ceased to exist" as a tribe for a generation or so before the French returned (1995:23). (7) When Father Allouez established his mission near Green Bay in 1670 and reported ministering to the Ho-Chunk, among others, the formidable tribe that had excited French interest in the 1630s was reduced to perhaps 750 people, counting many spouses from other tribes. (8) The remnants reconstituted themselves culturally at Red Banks along the lines of their neighbors, particularly the Menominee, their longtime friends and allies. (9) The Ho-Chunk myths placing their origin at Red Banks refer to the genesis of what was, in effect, a new tribe, Ho-Chunk in name (and language) only.

We think not.

Neither Lawson nor Hall give any grounds for disregarding Father Claude Dablon's 1672 report on the history of tribal succession in the Green Bay area when they dismiss the Red Banks area as a mere refuge occupied briefly by the Ho-Chunk after fleeing their "real" homeland where they were allegedly visited by Nicolet. This would have been Doty Island according to Lawson, or southern Cook County, Illinois, according to Hall, following the disasters described by Perrot. Dablon's account is consistent with other seventeenth-century references and Indian oral tradition. Writing from the mission of St. François Xavier near De Pere, Wisconsin, Dablon stated, "This Mission embraces eight different Nations, or even more, if we include some unsettled tribes which sustain relations to it" (Thwaites 1896–1901, vol. 55:183). Narrowing down to the groups closest to the mission, he explained that "Four Nations make their abode here,—to wit, the people named Puans [Stinkards], who have always lived here as in their own country, and who have been reduced to nothing from their very flourishing and populous state in the past, having been exterminated by the Illinois, their enemies; the Pouteouatami, the Ousaki, and the nation of the Fork also live here, but as foreigners, driven by their fear of the Iroquois from their own territories." He added a "fifth Nation" in the vicinity, the Menominee, living "15 or 20 leagues away" on the Fox River (Thwaites 1896–1901, vol. 55:183, 185).

Hall bases his contention that Nicolet bypassed Wisconsin to land in Illinois on the interpretation that the "little lake" meant "a combination of Green Bay and Bay de Noc." He cites Le Jeune's information from Nicolet: "Passing this smaller lake we enter the second fresh-water sea [Lake Michigan] on the shores of which are the Maroumine [Menominee] and still further on the same banks, dwell the Ouinipigou" [Winnebago]. Hall goes on to say:

> So, the Ho-Chunks are described as living not on Green Bay but on the
> shore of Lake Michigan to the south of the Menominee. This is the point
> at which I feel that all past interpreters of Nicolet's route went astray.
> Nicolet went straight south along the Lake Michigan shore, where he
> encountered the Menominees and, farther on, the Ho-Chunks. (Hall
> 2003:245–246)

A glance at any map of Lake Michigan, including Hall's own map (2003:246) illustrating "Routes of Jean Nicolet's Travels in 1634 as Interpreted by Various Writers," provides clear visual evidence against his case. There is no way Nicolet could have found the Winnebago south of the Menominee except by following the shore of Green Bay. Hall is saying either the shore of Green Bay is not also part of the shore of Lake Michigan, which defies logic, or the Menominee did not live on Green Bay in the Marinette area in the seventeenth century (which no one has ever disputed) but on the east side of the Door Peninsula (which no one has ever claimed). Even with the maddening gaps in the record of Nicolet's journey, it is still hard to imagine him simply reporting that he followed the shore south from the Menominee to the Winnebago when that "shore," according to Hall's route, necessarily would have included crossing the mouth of Green Bay. This would entail traversing stretches of famously treacherous waters between the islands from the tip of the peninsula framing the east side of Big Bay de Noc to the tip of the Door Peninsula where unbroken shoreline then continues to the southern end of Lake Michigan.

An alternative explanation of Hall's route is that Nicolet met the Menominee at Marinette. He then crossed Green Bay diagonally southwest to enter Sturgeon Bay on the west side of the Door County Peninsula, re-entered Lake Michigan on the east coast of the Door County Peninsula via a short portage (now a canal), and continued on down the coast to the southern Cook County area in Illinois. However, this, too, involves a discontinuous "shore" and crossing open water.

Hall arrives at the large Ho-Chunk population in the early seventeenth century by interpreting Perrot's estimate of 4,000 to 5,000 "men" to mean only warriors. Applying the historians' conventional multiplier of four or five yields a total population of 16,000 to 25,000, including women, children, and old men. Given the full context, Perrot's 4,000 to 5,000 could have referred to the entire population. The dictionary definition of "men" in French (*hommes*), as in English, can mean all humankind or people, including both sexes, or male as compared with female. That Perrot had the first meaning in mind seems borne out by the fact that in discussing the disasters that resulted in terrible loss of life among the Ho-Chunk by the end of the seventeenth century, he specifies they were reduced to 150 "warriors," not just men, which would justify multiplying by four or five to yield a total of about 600 to 750 survivors altogether.

Hall's contention that the Winnebago ceased to exist as a people for a generation or so following the disasters after Nicolet's visit (Hall 1995:23; 2003:251) and re-emerged Algonquianized in virtually all respects but language ignores the persistence of deeply rooted cultural attributes coupled with social resilience that so impressed Radin: "Entirely uninfluenced by these simpler [Algonquian-speaking] tribes they did not remain but what they borrowed was unimportant," by which Radin means largely material culture. He commented on "the manner in which the basic older structure remained intact and yet new elements were freely adopted that is so characteristic of the Winnebago civilization" (Radin 1945:50–55).

Hall also ignores the weight of oral tradition and even some documentary information that Red Banks was a large, well-established settlement. From the available records, we don't know if Nicolet actually visited Red Banks or any Ho-Chunk village, let alone "villages." Hall bases their location in Cook County, south of Chicago, on archaeological grounds and tautological reasoning:

> There is a consensus among archaeologists that the Puants or Ho-Chunks of the Late Prehistoric and Contact periods should have been carriers of a late variant of the so-called Oneota culture. The problem is that there is no major Oneota presence anywhere in eastern Wisconsin after around AD 1450 corresponding to the territory usually attributed to the Ho-Chunks. On the other hand, there is for that time period a significant Oneota (Huber phase) presence in the Calumet River drainage south of Chicago. If the Ho-Chunk numbered many thousands, as La Potherie (1722) describes them for Nicolet's day [i.e., as Hall reads La Potherie's figures], they would just about have to have been carriers of a Huber variant of Oneota culture found in more than a dozen Late Precontact and Contact period archaeological sites in southern Cook County, Illinois. (Hall 2003:249)

Consensus does not constitute proof; there is absolutely no evidence showing a clear continuum linking any prehistoric Oneota manifestation (defined largely by ceramic and lithic materials) to any historically documented Ho-Chunk occupation. While this could mean, as Hall says, the Ho-Chunk weren't in "the territory usually ascribed to them" it could also mean that they simply were not carriers of Oneota culture. Hall's own discussion of the Illinois would make them the more likely carriers of the Huber variant of Oneota since he notes there is continuity from prehistoric materials to European trade items in the area. In fact, he subscribed to this idea at one time, ascribing the Huber variant of Oneota to the Miamis but changed his mind (Hall 1995:27).

Hall supports his contention that the Ho-Chunk were not living at Red Banks when the hostilities described by Perrot occurred because O-kee-wah, an elderly woman quoted by Charles D. Robinson, claimed that the "defenders of the fort," suffering desperately from thirst, tried to lower vessels to the water but their enemies on the beach cut the cords (Robinson 1856:491–494). According to Hall, the Red Banks bluff was not steep enough for this tactic, but Hall subscribes to the Speerschneider farm as the site of the Red Banks village rather than the once steep but now eroded bluff Robinson described. Hall furthermore contends that O-kee-wah's narrative really refers to an incident during a late eighteenth-century siege of the Illinois by the Potawatomi at Starved Rock, Illinois, on the Illinois River. In effect, Hall throws out the Red Banks baby with the O-kee-wah bathwater. Augustin Grignon, who knew O-kee-wah, discredited her as an authority on Red Banks or the Winnebago while offering other data upholding the history of a battle having occurred at Red Banks (Grignon 1857:203). Whatever O-kee-wah's historical confusion, however, something on the order of the incident she described seems to have occurred with the Ho-Chunk in the seventeenth century, perhaps in regard to a single settlement:

> They were living at a place near Red Banks. The enemy had shut off all the water and the only way they could get any was to tie their pack straps

to their pails and let down these pails in a deep canyon. However, this
was also discovered after a while and the enemy cut the pack straps.
(Radin 1923:57)

This sounds like a familiar location along the Niagara Escarpment that
forms the spine of the Door Peninsula, just below the Wequiock Falls on
Wequiock Creek.

Hall (1995:20) seeks further support for the Ho-Chunk being located in
Illinois in paraphrasing a passage from Le Jeune: "[Nicolet] returned saying
that he had also journeyed far enough on a 'great river' which issues from the
second lake of the Hurons to be within three days' travel of the sea." "Would
a Frenchman," Hall asks, "who lived on the St. Lawrence describe the Fox
River at Green Bay as a great river? Hardly, and besides, the Fox River flows
into Green Bay and thence into Lake Michigan and not from it." Hall is right
that the passage has nothing to do with the Fox River. As will be demonstrated in chapter 7, the river to which Nicolet referred was the St. Mary's
River, which is truly a great river that flows from a freshwater "sea"—Lake
Superior. The case that Hall makes for an Illinois location based on this passage from Le Jeune strains credulity:

> The only river of any description that could be said to issue from Lake
> Michigan is the Illinois because its tributary the Desplaines comes within
> the distance of a short portage of the Chicago River. During periods of
> high water it was possible to canoe from Lake Michigan up the south
> branch of the Chicago River and into the Desplaines with scarcely a
> break for portaging. Nicolet could then have traveled far enough upon the
> Illinois, a "great river," to be within three days of the Michigamea, one of
> the several tribes of the Illinois, whose name does translate as "big lake"
> or "sea." (Hall 1995:21)

In further support of an Illinois homeland, Hall claims that the Ho-
Chunk made important use of wild rice in historic times and that it "must
have been known" to their precontact ancestors. He notes that "wild rice
(*Zizania aquatica L.*) is said to have been a common plant in the Calumet
River drainage of Cook County, Illinois," implying this resource would have
been conducive to Ho-Chunk settlement (Hall 2003:247). He shores up this
claim by reference to his archaeological research at Carcajou Point on the
northeastern shore of Lake Koshkonong in Jefferson County, Wisconsin
(Hall 1962). There, an early nineteenth-century Winnebago village overlay a
large, prehistoric village, the two occupations separated by a gap of 300 years.
Hall identified certain pits in the older component as probably used to hull
wild rice by treading on it. Despite the discontinuity between the two occupations and because of certain Oneota traits in the older one, Hall suggested
that it "may be an expression of Winnebago culture at the time." By 2003, he
unqualifiedly refers to "the Precontact Ho-Chunks" at the Carcajou site, noting that Lake Koshkonong holds more than 1,000 acres of wild rice beds but
offers no evidence of its use in the historic Ho-Chunk village (Hall 2003:247).

Literally and figuratively, wild rice is a weak reed to lean on to establish a Ho-Chunk presence anywhere. Although, as noted, Jenks included the Winnebago with neighboring tribes such as the Ojibwa and Menominee as primarily dependent on wild rice, there is virtually no evidence to support this categorization. Juliette Kinzie (1930:45–46) is sometimes cited as having observed the Winnebago harvesting wild rice on Lake Butte des Morts in 1830, but she merely mentions "Indian women." Given the location of the lake on the boundary between the two tribes, they might just as easily have been and probably were Menominees. Similarly, it is not clear if the reference is to the Ho-Chunk or Ojibwa in an entry from Indian agent Jonathan Fletcher: "Wild rice is the most important article for food that grows spontaneously" (Schoolcraft 1860, vol. 4:57–58).

Wild rice was not an important Ho-Chunk resource. Radin's only reference to it that he apparently collected himself concerns a Bear clan person's account of the yearly round of activities (Radin 1923:124–125). Otherwise, he relies on two paragraphs of a newspaper article by Jenks describing some Winnebagos gathering wild rice, in the sloughs of the Mississippi near La Crosse. This differs markedly from Radin's list of other wild plants and domesticated crops where he gives the Ho-Chunk names along with data on harvesting and processing (Radin 1923:114–118, 319). Radin didn't even bother to provide the Ho-Chunk word for wild rice, which, interestingly, is *wankshik zin*, Indian rice. Store-bought white rice (*Oryza sativa*) is just *zin*. One would expect wild rice to be called *zin*, as it probably was called originally, and white rice to be called *maixetezin*, white people's rice. The willingness of the Ho-Chunk to give priority to the European introduction seems to reflect the lack of importance they attached to the native product. Compare this to the Ojibwa who call wild rice *manomin*: good or nutritious seed. White rice is *wabinanomin*, the latter referring to color but also connoting its having come from the white people (Roger Thomas, Ojibwa, personal communication 2007; see also Baraga 1966:213, 289; Vennum 1988:5).

The harvesting and processing of wild rice, referred to colloquially as "ricing," doubtless occurred opportunistically, but it is not a cherished cultural focus among the Ho-Chunk. While it is always risky to rely on negative evidence, the fact that Radin, whose primary interests were in myth and ritual, is silent in regard to wild rice in these contexts certainly offers a strong indication of its unimportance. Compare this to its pivotal place in legend and ceremony among the Ojibwa, for example (Vennum 1988:58–80). The Ho-Chunk focus was and is on the familiar corn, beans, and squash, particularly a range of varieties of corn, with traditions of gardens in the Lake Winnebago–Green Bay area being several arrow shots in length and breadth (Lurie 1960). Five of the 12 Ho-Chunk lunar months or moons concern gardening: "drying of the earth [in expectation of the growing season], digging the ground or planting corn, hoeing, corn tasseling, and corn popping or harvest time" (Schoolcraft 1860, vol. 4:239–240). Radin collected essentially the same list, and it is still known today (Radin 1923:124–125). By contrast, the moons of the Ojibwa make no reference to any gardening but include a rice harvesting moon (Vennum 1988:157–158), while the Ottawa, Menominee, and Potawatomi give prominence to wild rice in the month names of the fall harvesting period, but not corn, and wild rice figures importantly in their mythology (Griffin 1960:816–817). Even during the Ho-Chunks' repeated removals in the nineteenth century when they faced starvation, they managed to save their seed corn. Ho-Chunk families still raise their old strains of corn and dry it according to traditional techniques. Boiled with meat, dried Indian corn is an essential ingredient for religious feasts and special secular occasions. Both ricing and corn harvesting and processing are labor intensive, usually at about the same time; the Ho-Chunk have opted for corn.

In his effort to refute an old Ho-Chunk association with Red Banks, Hall anticipates the question why they were called Winnebago by their tribal neighbors if not for their location on Green Bay with its odorous estuary marshes and spring die-offs of fish. His explanation is the presence of sulfurous springs in northern Illinois where he conveniently places the Ho-Chunk, with no supporting data, prior to their Cook County location. Then he adds for good measure, that the name also might have something to do with Chicago, the first two syllables in many Algonquian languages being the root word for skunk or skunk cabbage (Hall 1995:27). His 2003 article contains a long disquisition on "The Lakes of the Stinkings" showing how many places were so designated besides Green Bay (Hall 2003:247–248), a matter recognized by Dever in 1966. A visitor to the sulfur springs, noted above, reports in a personal communication that they are not excessively offensive to the nose in contrast to the estuarial odors of the Fox River that have long evoked comment. As noted, these "exhalations," for example, were even held responsible for illness at the American military post at Green Bay in the 1820s (Beaumont 1827).

Our final chapter will present the case for Nicolet's landfall having occurred in Menominee territory near the mouth of the Menominee River that forms the boundary between present-day Wisconsin and the Upper Peninsula of Michigan. We also will consider the unsettled questions of the duration of his journey and return to New France. Before taking up these issues, however, it is necessary to sort out the conflicting opinions that clutter the Nicolet story in regard to Red Banks and what we can discern of Ho-Chunk history, culture, and social organization preceding and following European contact.

Chapter 5

Red Banks Reconsidered

*T*his chapter offers new interpretations of familiar data and some heretofore overlooked information relevant to the Ho-Chunks' presence in the Red Banks region about the time of European contact there. The basic premise is that the people who became known as the Winnebago migrated to the Door Peninsula from Aztalan, the stockaded village in Jefferson County that was established about AD 1000 and abandoned about 200 years later. This idea was first set forth by Lurie in 1973 in an unpublished but widely circulated paper in an unsuccessful attempt to encourage systematic archaeological work in the Red Banks area while there was still time to test the premise in the face of accelerating destruction of the terrain from road construction and other development.

It is generally accepted that Aztalan was a colony out of Cahokia, the huge site in southeastern Illinois that also was abandoned about the same time as Aztalan, in either case, the reasons being subject to debate (Birmingham and Goldstein 2005:101–102). One possibility in the case of Aztalan, besides the usual reasons of soil exhaustion and depletion of nearby supplies of firewood, could have been accelerated population expansion by natural increase and further immigration from the south requiring a search for *Lebensraum.* The Aztalan population within the enclosing walls has been estimated at no more than 500 people in the twelfth century. Assuming these were ancestral Ho-chunk, some 500 years later Perrot estimated their numbers at the time of European contact as 4,000 to 5,000 "men," roughly a tenfold increase if men means people in general. As noted earlier, Hall infers what would be a more dramatic increase by assuming "men" stands for warriors to give a total population of as much as 25,000 (2003:239).

Alice Kehoe's perceptive comparison of Cahokia data with sacred texts collected by Francis La Flesche in the early twentieth century from the Dhegiha Siouan speaking Osage leaves no doubt as to the strong Mississippian and Middle American influences that persisted with this historic Plains tribe whose language stock is closely related to Chiwere Siouan with which

Ho-Chunk is affiliated (Kehoe 2007). A similar persistence of southern traits seems to have been at work among the Ho-Chunk, distinguishing them from other tribes in the area of the western Great Lakes where they had settled well before European contact.

We propose that over a period of about 400 years, the ancestral Ho-Chunk migrated north from Aztalan, spreading out from their formerly restricted habitation to occupy the Door Peninsula where their primary settlement was initially in the vicinity of Sawyer Harbor on Sturgeon Bay. They may have been there on the eve of contact when Perrot notes that, "They did not desire to have commerce with the French. The Outaouks [Ottawas], notwithstanding, sent to them envoys whom they had the cruelty to eat." The encounter may have prompted the Ho-Chunks' move to Red Banks where they established a stockaded village as a defensive measure in the face of retaliatory hostilities by the Ottawa and their allies.

Warfare, internal dissension, disease, and famine greatly reduced the Ho-Chunk population, and they rebuilt their strength by intermarrying extensively with neighboring tribes, incorporating many of their economic and social patterns that were adapted to the white presence in the upper Midwest, particularly in relation to the fur trade. By the time Europeans were interacting with the Ho-Chunk as trading partners and potential allies in the struggle for control of North America, they seemed to be cast in the same cultural mold as their Algonquian-speaking neighbors, but this was largely a veneer of material culture.

When the people identified here as Ho-Chunk or proto-Ho-Chunk (possibly still including what would become Iowa, Oto, and Missouria) were at Aztalan, known archaeologically as a Middle Mississippian site, they appear to have succeeded people who are archaeologically termed Woodland. The nature of the temporal relationship between the two groups is unclear, but this Woodland manifestation at Aztalan differed significantly, for example in pottery styles, from other Woodland sites in the area that were contemporary with Aztalan (Birmingham and Goldstein 2005:52–53; Goldstein, personal communication 2008). In all probability these latter Woodland peoples were Algonquian-speaking and if some neighborly intermixing occurred, as might be expected in such circumstances, it could account for the fact that in addition to Mississippian antecedents Ho-Chunk oral history suggests Woodland ancestors. Very old ties to the region are hinted at in some family stories of ice-age mammoth hunting. In historic times, there is ample evidence of admixture with Algonquian-speaking peoples to explain different tribal recollections. The Ho-Chunk people are aware that different families and clans have particular stories or include special details in common stories indicative of mixed ancestry from the early contact period when population loss obliged them to seek spouses among neighboring tribes.

The interpretation of Ho-chunk history offered here rests in discerning and distinguishing between two major ancestral lines: tenuous but enduring attributes of the precontact cultures of the American Southeast manifested at

Aztalan in Wisconsin and the more recent Algonquian-influenced lifestyle. A full understanding of this scenario requires an initial review and assessment of the various scholarly views regarding the location and nature of Red Banks.

By the 1950s, when public opinion had pretty well settled in favor of Neville's claim that the seventeenth-century Ho-Chunk stronghold was at Red Banks on Green Bay rather than Doty Island on Lake Winnebago as Lawson had argued, a new complication developed as to the exact location of the Ho-Chunk village in the Red Banks area. The choice was and is between the now obliterated site first described by Robinson in 1856 that Neville championed and another site less than a half mile to the southwest that was first described in 1851 by Morgan Lewis Martin and cited by Increase A. Lapham, the founding father of Wisconsin archaeology. It is named for the owner of the property, Albert Speerschneider, at the time it was described in 1909 by Charles E. Brown of the State Historical Society of Wisconsin. The misreading of Brown's four pages of unpublished, scribbled field notes has become accepted archaeological fact that the Speerschneider farm was the location of the stockaded Ho-Chunk village at Red Banks.

Without public fanfare like the Neville–Lawson debate, there has been a kind of insidious replacement of the Robinson–Neville location with Speerschneider and sometimes conflation of the two sites (Hall 1993:22).

The Speerschneider site is of interest less for its own sake than its role in forwarding other issues. It serves Hall's theory, as discussed in connection with Nicolet's purported landfalls, that Red Banks was a late, insignificant refuge for the remnant Ho-Chunk. Much earlier, simply under the name of Red Banks, it served to bolster nineteenth-century theories justifying the dispossession of the Indians. It is useful to review Lapham's work to appreciate its importance and lasting impact on the development of archaeology in Wisconsin, even in this rare instance regarding Red Banks when he was in error.

Lapham, a civil engineer who had worked on the development of canals in the eastern states, came to Wisconsin in 1836, but the canal project that brought him to Milwaukee failed and resulted in a career change that would have profound effects on the growth of scientific knowledge and the development of educational institutions in the region. His avocation as a naturalist became his life's work. Self-trained, he was extraordinarily gifted and methodologically rigorous and seems to have taken similar qualities for granted in associates whose data he used. His pioneering research and publications dealt with botany, geology, zoology, climatology, and archaeology. He was particularly intrigued with the effigy mounds that are more abundant in Wisconsin than anywhere else in the country. They are distributed as part of a complex including conical and linear mounds in the southern half of the state with the heaviest concentration in the southeastern quarter where the earliest and increasingly destructive effects of white settlement occurred during the nineteenth century. Lapham's major opus, *The Antiquities of Wisconsin as Surveyed and Described*, published in 1855, represents a prodigious amount of work accomplished in the space of a few years under conditions of utmost urgency

(Hayes 1995:10–15; Lapham 2001:vii–iv). Most of the mounds he mapped are now gone—some of them being destroyed even before his *Antiquities* volume was published. Thanks to Lapham, however, we at least have a record of their specific shapes, dimensions, and geographic distribution and, in some cases, test excavations to reveal suggestions of construction and contents.

One set of earthworks differed markedly and dramatically from the rest, "Aztalan," on the west bank of the Crawfish River, a tributary of the Rock River, some 50 miles west of Milwaukee. Nathaniel F. Hyer was among the first to observe the site and brought it to public attention in a newspaper article in 1837. He chose the name Aztalan believing the site might be the mythical northern homeland of the Aztecs of Mexico. Although this association is fanciful, Aztalan bears definite relationships to Cahokia, the huge complex of earthworks in southern Illinois, which, in turn, shows influences out of Middle America (Birmingham and Goldstein 2005:20–36). Aztalan was already imperiled by farm operations when Lapham mapped it in 1850 and did some preliminary archaeological excavation. His work revealed the remains of a stockaded settlement, rectangular in shape, enclosing about 20 acres of dwellings, plazas, and flat topped, pyramidal mounds. Called temple mounds in the early literature because of evidence that structures once stood on them, they now are known by the more neutral term of platform mounds since we cannot be sure if they supported civil or religious buildings. Round mounds some distance outside the walls might have served as lookouts. Lapham took an active role in preserving the site.

Perhaps constraints of his own publishing schedule and the less imminent threat of destructive settlement explain why Lapham did not visit the northern part of the state although he included available information about the region. Along with noting the locations of native copper mining on Lake Superior, he cited reports of mounds in the region that he deemed similar to those at Aztalan, in particular a "temple mound," 15 feet square and about 10 feet high. Although its appearance and location were precisely described, later researchers have been unable to find it.

Lapham appears to have been completely unaware of a group of platform mounds near Trempealeau, Wisconsin, on the Mississippi River north of La Crosse that are clearly out of the same tradition as Aztalan although they appear to have no association with a village like Aztalan. Even after G. H. Squier published a description of them (Squier 1905), they evoked little archaeological interest until nearly the end of the twentieth century. This is in striking contrast to the amount of work devoted to Aztalan, particularly since the 1920s when Samuel A. Barrett, Director of the Milwaukee Public Museum, undertook the first systematic study of the site, laying the foundation for successive generations of professional archaeologists who would work there (Barrett 1933).

It is almost as if sites required Lapham's imprimatur to qualify for future archaeological attention, but highly contentious political and intellectual issues of the nineteenth century that are nearly forgotten today also underlie

Reconstruction of Aztalan based on Samuel A. Barrett's archaeological research as envisioned by artist George Peter. (Courtesy of Milwaukee Public Museum)

the short shrift Red Banks has received. Faulty scholarship in the twentieth century gave respectability to the politically motivated errors promulgated in the nineteenth century regarding the location and size of the Red Banks village. Besides relying on other observers where he could not investigate sites himself, Lapham apparently used such information to help him decide what did or did not merit his personal attention. His entry regarding Red Banks reduces the site to an acre or two enclosed by an "embankment" adjacent to several hundred acres of garden beds that had been abandoned for 500 years (Lapham 2001:60). His source was an address Morgan Martin delivered before the State Historical Society of Wisconsin on January 21, 1851. Martin was typical of the nineteenth-century frontier elite. A lawyer, politician, and land speculator, he left New York State to settle at Green Bay in 1827. He served in the successive legislatures of the Michigan and Wisconsin Territories, the Wisconsin Constitutional Convention in preparation for statehood in 1848, and the State Assembly and State Senate. As a community leader, he supported cultural and educational endeavors and was among the founders and early officers of the State Historical Society that was established in 1846.

The society did not begin issuing publications until 1854, so Martin's 48-page address was privately printed and is now quite rare (Martin 1851). References to Martin's data are usually cribbed from Lapham's citation of it rather than the original publication. Martin devoted most of his address to the history of white exploration and settlement of Wisconsin, which, it should be emphasized, at that time did not include knowledge of Nicolet or his journey that sparked so much public interest in Red Banks by the turn of the twentieth century. His few pages dealing with the aboriginal residents show the influence of Ephraim G. Squier and E. H. Davis whose essay, "Ancient Monuments of the Mississippi Valley," was published by the Smithsonian Institution in 1848. The authors subscribed to the theory that the impressive earthworks were beyond the capability of the Indians and must have been made by an earlier, superior race that had been wiped out by the ancestors of the contemporary tribes. The idea had gained special currency during Andrew Jackson's presidency, 1829–1837, as a justification of his Indian removal policy announced to both houses of Congress, December 7, 1830. Robert Bieder offers a telling analysis of the Jacksonian position: "by interpreting the mound builders as an advanced civilization and attributing their downfall to 'savage hordes,' civilization was justified in warring against the Indian tribes. The white race in the name of civilization would do to the Indians what the Indians had once done to the mound builders" (Bieder 1986:112).

Lapham stood apart from the political issues. As a scientist he was convinced by the growing weight of comparative skeletal studies and emerging stratigraphic data that there was no support for the theory of a pre-Indian, mound-building population (Lapham 2001:viii). Martin acknowledged that there were two points of view on the matter, but he was not persuaded the Indians he knew or their ancestors had the capacity to create monumental earthworks. As a politician with a constituency of land-hungry white settlers, he probably had a reflexive inclination if not a calculated stake in pushing earthworks far into the past to dissociate them from possible ancestry to any living Indians and in pushing the living Indians out of Wisconsin. At the time Martin presented his paper, Jackson's policy of moving the eastern Indians to one great Indian Territory west of the Mississippi River was under reconsideration in favor of establishing small reservations for the tribes in the homelands they had ceded. Since the discovery of gold in California in 1848, the resident tribes of the Great Plains were beginning to pose enough of a threat to wagon trains moving through their country without adding more hostiles to the situation. Furthermore, indoctrination into the ways of the white world could be more easily managed with the tribes confined to small, isolated reservations and less able to make common cause against the whites.

Historically and geographically, Wisconsin was on the cusp of this policy change. By 1848, the year Wisconsin became a state, the resident tribes had ceded all their land to the United States through a series of treaties with the federal government and were scheduled for removal. Only the Oneidas, Stockbridge-Munsees, and Brothertowns, who had moved to Wisconsin in the 1820s and were known collectively as the New York Indians, were to be allowed to remain. The Santee Sioux had already decamped to what is now Minnesota, remaining bands of Potawatomi and Winnebago were in the process of being moved, sometimes by force, and the half dozen Wisconsin Ojibwa bands and the Menominee were living on ceded land waiting for reservations to be assigned to them west of the Mississippi. As it turned out, more than 500,000 acres of Wisconsin land were set aside under the new policy in 1854 for the Ojibwa and Menominee reservations rather than being thrown open to white settlement (Lurie 2002:6, 7, 15–33).

After preliminary remarks regarding the occasion of his address, Martin devoted three pages to the prehistoric occupants of the state: "All, all alike are buried in oblivion, and we are driven to the conflicting theories from time to time put forth by ethnolograns [sic] to determine the origin, language, character and destiny of the races, now no more whose place we have supplied." For the most part, he went on, evidence of these former residents' habitations that lay in the path of white settlement had been obliterated, but some survived.

> The most remarkable of these which have fallen under my observation, are found at the "Red Banks" in Town 25 N., Range 22 E., on the eastern shore of Green Bay. The furrow is still distinct as if made with the plow in modern use, over a tract of several hundred acres, now overgrown with forest-trees of large size, the product, according to usual computation, of five centuries. The remains of a parapet, enclosing some acre or two of ground, occupies an elevated position in the immediate vicinity, bearing incontrovertible evidence that it had been either the large plantation of a single family, who must have known some of the arts of civilized life, or the rude cultivation of a village of untutored sons of the forest, who had erected a temporary breastwork in time of war for defence. *The former supposition is much easier sustained than the latter.* (Martin 1851:6) [Italics supplied]

Martin doubted that any contemporary Indians could shed light on the "scattered remains" of ancient earthworks and garden beds, evidently unaware that the very name Red Banks was a direct translation of the Winnebago name for the area they claimed as a former stronghold. Lapham disregarded Martin's politically motivated discourse, and simply paraphrased his few words of descriptive data, substituting the word embankment for parapet, without noting the absence of a section number in Martin's description to establish the exact location of the site. Nor did he question Martin's "usual computation" to arrive at the age of trees that were not identified as to species, height, girth or growing conditions.

The year Lapham's *Antiquities* appeared, Charles D. Robinson gave his account of his recent visit to another, nearby earthworks also located on the Red Banks bluff that was published the following year in the *Collections of the State Historical Society of Wisconsin*, although, as noted, Robinson does not identify it with the Ho-Chunk tribe. A newspaper man from Marcellus, New York, Robinson arrived in Green Bay in 1846 where he established the *Green Bay Advocate* and remained editor-in-chief until his death in 1886. One can only wonder if Lapham would have chosen to visit this site (or at least have looked at Martin's work more critically) if Robinson's description had been available to him before he went to press with his *Antiquities*. Robinson obviously is not describing the same site Martin described despite assumptions to the contrary (e.g., Hall 1993:22; Speth 2000:4).

Upon a high bank, on the eastern shore of Green Bay about twelve miles north of the town [Green Bay], is an interesting earth-work, bearing a singular resemblance to military defences [sic] of modern times. Its walls, at one time, must have been some seven feet in height or thereabouts, having a ditch or moat on the outside, and provided on its three exposed sides with regular bastions. Its fourth side fronts on a precipice of perhaps one hundred feet in height, whose base is washed by the waters of Green Bay; and leading down this steep bank impassable at any other immediate point, is what seems to have once been a protected passage of steps cut into the clay, and perhaps covered with boughs of trees. This was the communication from the fort to the water. . . .

In, or near the centre, are two parallel walls, about twenty-five feet long which were probably united at the ends, as there is some appearance of it now. It is very difficult to imagine the use of this part of the structure, unless it was to protect valuables, or such inmates of the fort as were incapable of aiding in its defence. . . . A few rods to the north, outside the walls, and on the very brink of the precipice, is what was once apparently, a look-out—a high mound of earth, a few feet high, now half carried off by wearing away of the cliff. To the southward and eastward of the fort, occupying some hundreds of acres, were the planting grounds of the people who inhabited the place. Large trees now over-grow the ground, yet the furrows are as distinctly marked as if made but last year, and are surprisingly regular. (Robinson 1856:491–494)

We have no idea if Lapham ever learned of Robinson's description. Given his familiarity and fascination with Aztalan, one can only guess what he would have made of this account of earthworks 25 feet long *within* the main enclosure and the remains of a mound that appeared to Robinson as a lookout outside the walls, also reminiscent of Aztalan, although Janet Speth thinks it might have been a burial mound (Speth 2000:4). As discussed in the review of the purported Nicolet landfalls, Hall questioned Robinson's credibility because of his inclusion of O-kee-wah's narrative among accounts he collected about the Battle of Red Banks. However, if Robinson was a poor ethnographer in his choice of informants, it is hard to argue with the testimony of his own eyes, especially when Arthur C. Neville who observed the site a few years after Robinson's visit verified his description and noted that in the ensuing 50 years, "the erosion of the cliff has been so great that all traces of these ancient works have disappeared" (Neville 1906:148–149).

The earliest reference to earthworks and gardens on the Door Peninsula was made in 1831 by Samuel Stambaugh, U.S. Indian Agent at Green Bay, but it is not clear from his wording whether it is an eyewitness account or based on information from local settlers. His manuscript, "Report on the Quality and Condition of Wisconsin Territory," was filed with the War Department but it was not published until more than 60 years later. It concerns land ceded in 1831 by the Menominee, including the entire Door Peninsula, to assess its suitability for the location of small reservations for the New York Indians. He noted:

About twelve miles below the Fort [Howard, predecessor of the city of Green Bay, downstream on the lake current that runs from the mouth of the Fox River along the east shore of the peninsula] there is a very conspicuous promontory, called the *Red Banks*—they are, at the highest point, about a hundred feet above the level of the Bay. The ground on these banks presents the appearance of once having been under cultivation, probably by the early French settlers; and one place evidently bears vestiges of fortifications of some kind. I have not heard these appearances accounted for by the Indians or the present French settlers. (Stambaugh 1900:425; see also Royce and Thomas 1899:726–730, Wisconsin, Map 1)

Stambaugh was not the only government official to report on these earthworks prior to Robinson. The Army Corps of Engineers was busy studying navigable waters in what was still territorial land in the 1840s and is doubtless the source of a map showing soundings of depths in Green Bay and shoreline features that was reproduced by Neville and identified simply as "U.S. Chart, 1844" in an article titled "Historic Sites About Green Bay" (Neville 1926:11). A rectangular outline labeled "Ruins" clearly refers to the remains of the Red Banks village but is probably noted as a matter of local knowledge rather than actual mapping. Although its shape is tantalizingly suggestive of Aztalan (and much larger in scale), it may be no more than a standard printer's symbol such as those used elsewhere on the chart. It is too far away from the bank and extends too far northeast to be a precise depiction of either of the contested village sites. This map came to our attention shortly before going to press, and we have not yet located the journal in the scattered records of the Army Corps of Engineers that usually accompanied such charts and might contain further information.

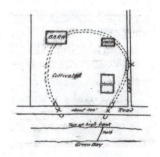

Charles E. Brown's 1909 sketch of earthworks at the Speerschneider farm, Brown County, as described to him from memory by old settlers who had played at the site as children. (Wisconsin Historical Society, Archives Box 17, Folder 1879–1944)

Stambaugh's commentary about the lack of Indian knowledge of the earthworks and his attribution of cultivation to French settlers reflect the party line of an Indian agent appointed during Jackson's administration. The fact that he specified the highest elevation and that his information antedated Robinson by some 25 years when the "fortifications" would have been even less eroded suggests that his reference is to the Robinson site and not the Martin site. It is safe to conclude that the latter is one and the same with the Speerschneider farm visited by Charles E. Brown on August 15, 1909.

Brown went with a local resident to investigate some garden beds "about a half mile south of the supposed site of the early Indian stockade at the Red Banks (Benderville) on Green Bay." It appears from his four pages of unpublished field notes that he only expected to record information about the garden beds that were south of the beds near the Robinson-Neville site. These are drawn with some precision on squared paper with the description of details written on a sheet of lined loose-leaf paper.

When Brown was apprised of earthworks in the vicinity of the garden beds, he evidently was out of paper and made do with what he happened to have at hand to record information volunteered by some old settlers: the 1908 program of a joint meeting of the Wisconsin Archeological Society and the Sauk County Historical Society. The writing on the back and front of this smaller sheet is barely readable, especially the last page that is scribbled over the printed program. The writing is further obscured by the fact that the ink has bled through both sides of the poor-quality paper. Researchers, from the anonymous writer of the Wisconsin Historical Society's marker erected in 1957 to Hall and others up to the present time, have guessed that these nearly illegible pages establish the Speerschneider farm as the site of the Winnebago village at Red Banks, a guess that now has become settled archaeological doctrine: "In 1909 three short segments of an enclosure were mapped by Charles E. Brown on the Albert Speerschneider farm just south of Benderville. Brown's (1909) map shows a roughly circular enclosure about 500 feet in diameter" (Hall 1993:22). As a matter of fact, Brown did not "map" anything and categorically denied his informants' contention that this had been an "enclosure," let alone the site of the Red Banks village.

This is what Brown really said:

> According to Mr. J. P. Schumacher, the early Indian village thought to have been the place where the envoy Jean Nicolet encountered the Winnebago appears not to have been at the present summer resort known as the Red Banks but about a quarter of a mile to the south of it on the farm now owned by Mr. Albert Speerschneider.

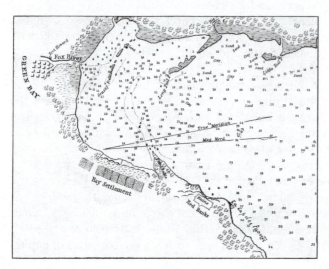

"1844 Government Chart" showing water depth soundings at the end of Green Bay and presence of "Ruins" in the Red Banks area (Neville 1926:11).

Mr. Carl [illegible] and Matt and Tom Gibson and Eli Martin, old settlers in this neighborhood, whom Mr. Schumacher had interviewed all state that the embankment that previously enclosed the village was on the Speerschneider place. Some of these men claim to have played within the embankment as boys and all remember it well.

The sketch is according to their memory of its location and shape. Its obliteration by cultivation was begun about 30 years ago and some supposed remnants of the embankment can still be seen along the road and farmyard lane (see X). The enclosure was not of very large size, about twice as long as wide and of a horseshoe shape. The [the words "walls were" are scratched out] embankment was about 2-1/2 feet high and possibly [continues on back of page] fifteen feet wide. The small portions which remain actually resemble portions of linear mounds.

If such an enclosure was ever located on the present site of the Red Banks resort, some remnants of it must remain in the undisturbed remnants of woodland about it.

The question has often arisen in the writer's mind whether the so-called embankment at the Red Banks is not a myth.

Morgan L. Martin on whose early communication nearly all of the scattered and fragmentary literature on the subject is based, very probably mistook the linear, effigy and conical mounds (especially the former) for the remains of the fortification, a common error of early and some later writers on local archaeology. The old settlers who state that the embankment was on the present Speerschneider place also probably mistook a number of linear mounds for an embankment. The remnants shown to me on Aug. 15, 1909 are suggestive of partly destroyed linear mounds. Some indications of the [writing ends here]. (Brown:1909)

The misunderstanding of Brown's manuscript as endorsing the Speerschneider site as the location of the Red Banks village is understandable insofar as the first paragraph suggests just that, but careful reading of the whole account makes clear he rejects this idea and opts for the "summer resort" area as the more likely location—the general area Neville designated to erect a historic marker in 1909 where most of the bluff that once held the village had eroded away. Brown's sketch and dimensions at the Speerschneider farm bring to mind Martin's estimate of an acre or two comprising what he believed was a dwelling area surrounded by a "parapet" and related to the sizeable garden beds nearby. Brown evidently thought so, too. His use of the term embankment rather than parapet suggests his source was Lapham's précis of Martin rather than Martin's original publication.

Brown was personally familiar with the summer resort location. Although surface features were nearly obliterated, he had discerned traces of ancient gardens and earthworks there (Brown 1906:295–296). Since Brown was associated with the State Historical Society, he must have been aware of the content of Neville's 1906 paper and the Neville–Lawson dispute leading to the erection of a historical marker at Doty Island prior to Neville's supporters' placement of the marker at Red Banks. Speth, among the few people who seem to have really read the Brown manuscript in its entirety, nevertheless accepted the Speerschneider farm as the location of the Red Banks village. She believed Brown was mistaken in identifying the remains of earthworks on the Speerschneider farm as linear mounds because they are outside the usually accepted distribution of such mounds (Speth 2000:14). The important point is that there are two practically adjacent but distinct sites. Although confusion has arisen from writings that combine the two, the archaeological community has generally accepted the Speerschneider site over the summer resort area as the location of the Ho-Chunks' seventeenth-century Red Banks village.

Robinson, Neville, the 1844 Army Corps of Engineers map, Ho-Chunk oral tradition, and hints from the documentary record favor the summer resort vicinity. The resort was named Kish-ke-kwan-te-no by Louis Bender who built it as a clubhouse in about 1900 for people who rented cottages from him. According to Stambaugh, in the Menominee Indian language it is supposed to mean "sloping to the cedars" in reference to a cedar swamp "in the rear of the cliff" (Kuhm 1952:44). As the homesites were sold, the resort evolved into a home owners' association. The clubhouse changed hands and became a supper club that was closed after a fire in 1973 and was totally destroyed by fire in 1982. In 2004, Marion Sickel, who owned the property since its sale after the fire, presented it to the Brown County Historical Society.

When the Society made plans to build a parking lot and gazebo on the old clubhouse property, Speth and a Neville Museum intern did five shovel tests of the area but uncovered mostly bits of twentieth-century debris—glass, aluminum, plastic, and nothing of archaeological significance. Although unproductive because of disturbance of the soil from building and bulldozing, it was a commendable precautionary preservation effort, especially given Speth's skepticism about the area's association with the village site (Speth and Schneider 2004). There remain some "undisturbed remnants of woodland" in the vicinity that Brown thought worth investigating that the Ho-Chunk Nation is working to protect and preserve.

A marble plaque proclaiming it the site of Nicolet's landfall that stood at the entrance to the former Sickel property has been relocated to the gazebo. This is a replacement of the original bronze plaque erected by Neville and his supporters that was stolen during World War II (Hall 1993:17). Bedore's statue of Nicolet has also been moved because of road rerouting and now stands on the Red Banks section of the Niagara escarpment near Highway 57 about a mile east of its original location. It is about equidistant from the Speerschneider site and the Brown County Historical Society land. Nearby is the Wisconsin Historical Society's 1957 marker that says Nicolet landed about a mile to the west, thus indicating, though not naming, the Speerschneider site.

While Robinson does not give overall dimensions, he clearly is talking about a much larger area than an acre or two and more complex earthworks than described by Brown in 1909 and much earlier by Martin. Neville reported that evidence of the village had all but eroded away in the 50-some years since Robinson and he had first visited the place, so the plaque he was instrumental in having installed near the summer resort property in 1909 apparently was not intended to mark the actual village site but simply its general vicinity and immediate resource base.

It might seem strange that Martin missed seeing a landmark as impressive as that reported by Robinson and Neville, but we do not know when he actually visited the site he described in 1851. It could simply have been more accessible at the time than what became the summer resort area. When Martin arrived at Green Bay in 1827, virtually all of Wisconsin was still Indian land; the area in question was not ceded until 1831 by the Menominee who had succeeded the Ho-Chunk in the area. What became Wisconsin was still part of Michigan Territory. It was not until statehood, barely three years before Martin presented his paper, that systematic exploration, surveying, and development of roads to expedite settlement by whites got underway.

The mystery of the archaeological neglect of Red Banks begins to lift. If a mere acre or two on the Speerschneider farm was the site of the stockaded village of Red Banks it is thus easily characterized as a short-lived "refuge" for the greatly reduced Ho-Chunk tribe following the period of disasters recounted by Perrot. Since historic sources and Indian oral tradition indicate the Ho-Chunk were once sedentary, populous, and a formidable threat to their neighbors, archaeologists have fastened on the widespread and regionally varied Oneota archaeological tradition as their prehistoric forebears and have looked for them in their glory days in such disparate locations as south of Chicago, Lake Koshkonong southwest of Milwaukee, and west of Lake Winnebago near the city of Winneconne. Many publications, including two large anthologies (Overstreet 1993; Green 1995), are devoted to possible Oneota connections with the Ho-Chunk.

For most nonarchaeologists, it is tough and tedious to read the literature that archaeologists write for each other in their own jargon with common understanding of how it evolved. Yet, a brief introduction to the terminology is necessary because of its relevance to the questions of Nicolet's landfall and why Champlain really sent Nicolet on a special mission to visit the Ouinepigou/Puan.

As archaeological work progressed in Wisconsin and surrounding states, the arbitrary naming of sites and their features tended to obscure similarities and differences for comparative study. In 1939, Will C. McKern, head of the Anthropology Department at the Milwaukee Public Museum and Barrett's successor as museum director from 1943 to 1958, proposed his Midwest Taxonomic System, using the terms "Pattern, Phase, Aspect, and Focus" to represent wider to narrower expressions of cultural relationships (McKern 1939). These are based on styles of stoneware including chipped stone projectile points (the layman's "arrowheads") and ground stone objects; pottery (including shapes, sizes, temper, and ornamentation); various artifacts of bone, shell, or copper; variations in colors of the earth giving evidence of hearths, posts, and the like showing dwelling and settlement patterns; and treatment of the dead (buried in flexed or extended positions or reburied as bundles of bones after the flesh decayed in the ground). McKern's attempt at a hierarchical classification influenced by the biological sciences proved untenable but provided archaeologists with terms of reference on which they are generally agreed for the succession and nature of major cultural traditions shown in the charts below. Some dates overlap because some traditions or stages started earlier or lasted longer in different areas, and details of dates are subject to modification as more data are unearthed. The charts below are derived from a number of sources (Ritzenthaler 1985:11; Goldstein and Osborn 1988; Birmingham and Eisenberg 2000:55; Birmingham and Goldstein 2005:xi, 11).

Tradition	*Stage*
Paleo-Indian	
Early	10,000–8000 BC (probably older)
Late	8000–6000/5000 BC
Archaic	
Early	8000–4000 BC
Middle	6000–1200 BC
Late	1200–100 BC
Woodland	
Early	500 BC–AD 100 (pottery appears)
Middle	100 BC–AD 500 (gardening)
Late AD	AD 400–1200 (to historic period in northern Wisc.)
	(500–1100 effigy mounds period)
Middle Mississippian	AD 1000–1250
Upper Mississippian (Oneota)	AD 1000–historic period

Of special interest for present purposes is what McKern originally designated the Mississippian Pattern with Middle and Upper Phases. The Oneota Aspect of the Upper Mississippian Phase has now become simply Oneota and is synonymous with the former Upper Mississippian. Named, localized variations of Oneota—Orr, Huber, Lake Winnebago, and so forth—are referred to rather informally as expressions, variations, or even focuses. Upper and Middle Mississippian refer to each tradition's presumed place of origin along the length of the Mississippi River, with the Middle Mississippian deriving from Cahokia and the Upper Mississippian or Oneota originating in Wisconsin. As noted, Aztalan showed extensive influence from Woodland people, particularly in ceramic styles, who may actually have been coresidents at Aztalan. Oneota pottery, however, is totally lacking at Aztalan (Overstreet 1995:39). Each year more information is revealed through archaeology—distinctive lithics, ceramics, stockaded villages, and other hallmarks—of the chronology and routes taken along the Mississippi north out of Cahokia (Birmingham and Goldstein 2005:46).

Although it was initially believed that Upper Mississippian or Oneota evolved directly out of Middle Mississippian, current thinking on the subject generally sees Oneota to have been influenced by Middle Mississippian but grafted onto an old Woodland base, while Woodland per se continued as a separate, parallel tradition; ongoing studies and publications tussle with the fine points of these relationships. What is significant here is that the attribution of Oneota ancestry to the Ho-Chunk is based in large part on the dismissal of Red Banks as a major Ho-Chunk settlement but simply a refuge area of a small remnant of the tribe after contact and not worth intensive archaeological study. As to a village site in the old summer resort area, perhaps so much has washed away into Green Bay that even underwater archaeology forays for stray artifacts on the lake bottom are a forlorn hope in settling the issue. It is, however, worth considering.

The ethnographic and ethnohistorical data point at least as strongly in the direction of Middle Mississippian, namely Cahokia-Aztalan, rather than Oneota precontact origins for the Ho-Chunk, whatever influence the later admixture with peoples descended from Woodland and Upper Mississippian Oneota traditions may have had on them. The lists below are greatly simplified and intended only to indicate major differences. As noted, for a long time all we knew about the Middle Mississippians in Wisconsin was what had been discovered at Aztalan; data on other sites are in process of discovery.

Middle Mississippian	*Upper Mississippian—Oneota*
Permanent stockaded villages	Permanent villages—longhouses
Pyramidal platform mounds	Burial mounds
Shell temper ceramics with incised designs, variety of shapes	Shell temper ceramics, plain surfaces, broad trailing or flared rims
Maize, beans, squash gardens	Maize gardens but hunting, fishing predominate
Large towns with villages, hamlets	Villages 70–90 people
Wattle and daub construction	
Distinctive side-notched triangular points	Plain triangular points, although not exclusive to the Oneota
Large, chipped stone hoes or spades	Ground stone celts, axe heads
Fragments of human remains in Aztalan refuse pits (cannibalism?)	

Giving voice to an opinion generally shared by his fellow archaeologists as well as many historians, James Griffin commented, "Many new tools have become available through the advancement of scientific discoveries and have been more successful in interpreting America's prehistory than tribal memories" (Griffin 1995:10).

However, no serious archaeological research has been undertaken in regard to possible proto-historic and historic Ho-Chunk occupation of the Door Peninsula, including the Red Banks area. Perhaps this is not surprising insofar as the limited cadre of archaeologists in the state have been occupied with other, broader questions than trying to pin down evidence of a particular historic group, but it is hard to escape the impression in discussion with archaeological colleagues that they see nothing worth bothering about because of entrenched acceptance of the Speerschneider site as the location of the Red Banks village. With a few exceptions, the archaeological literature on occupations in the Green Bay area that go back for millennia and cover virtually all of the Midwest prehistoric traditions is confined to surface surveys and shovel testing or analyses of often imprecisely provenienced specimens in museum collections. Moreover, it often is difficult to tell from the occasional mention of Red Banks and even maps whether the references are to Speerschneider, Kish-ke-kwan-te-no, or simply the stretch of bluff known as Red Banks (Overstreet 1980; Benchley et al. 1995; Speth 2000, 2001, [2004?], 2007; Richards and Richards 2003; Speth and Schneider 2004; Overstreet 2005). This is not to discredit the importance of these studies, but to point out that in regard to the Ho-Chunk in particular there is little but ethnohistorical sources and tribal memory about Red Banks to help identify their precontact origins. Review of information derived from the Ho-Chunk people might lead to new interpretations and even archaeological initiatives where no one has thought to look.

Lapham had traveled as far as Lake Winnebago and Little Lake Butte des Morts to the west of Green Bay where he observed the large "hill of the dead," supposedly the burial place of Fox Indians after a war with the French but actually antedating European contact by some two millennia (Birmingham and Eisenberg 2000:33). He noted, "Among the articles discovered in the field nearby, was some burnt clay in irregular fragments, with impressions of the leaves and stems of grass, precisely like those found at Aztalan" (Lapham: 2001:61). We now know these so-called brickettes are broken chunks of walls constructed of wattle and daub, small branches woven together and plastered over with clay, fortuitously preserved by fire. Lapham did not dwell on possible relationships between these examples and Aztalan.

While diffusion through trade cannot be ruled out, some intriguing surface finds in Green Lake County may offer further possible evidence of a northerly migration route out of Aztalan. These consist of two copper disks, each no more than an inch in diameter, that are unmistakably Middle Mississippian in decorative motifs of equal-armed crosses and repoussé method of manufacture. Surface-found potsherds in the same area show Aztalan affiliations (Pasco and McKern 1947:72–75; Pasco and Ritzenthaler 1949:63–64).

Lapham's additional comments, based on Martin's data, indicate that he considered the Green Bay area barren of archaeological potentiality worth his time to investigate: "No other aboriginal works about Green Bay have come to my knowledge, though they may have existed and been long since destroyed; for settlements have existed there since a period nearly or quite as far back as the year 1665" (2001:60). Lapham's opinion applied to the city of Green Bay and its more immediate environs to the west and south, long a busy gateway to the interior of the continent. His comments did not apply, however, to the then still largely unsettled Door Peninsula extending many miles northeast beyond the city of Green Bay and especially beyond the geographic feature known as Red Banks.

One of many still unanswered questions about Aztalan is what became of the people after its sudden abandonment (Birmingham and Goldstein 2005:101–102). While it may be something of a stretch, Lapham's recognition of wattle and daub fragments at Butte des Morts might point to a northerly route from Aztalan toward Green Bay and account for the whereabouts of the Aztalan people after about AD 1250. Neither lithic nor truly ceramic and requiring the accident of burning to be preserved, wattle and daub evidence of a migration route might easily have been obliterated or simply overlooked. According to Alanson Skinner, the Ioway tribe, closely related to the Ho-Chunk and still in regular contact with them in the seventeenth century, once lived in large, rectangular wattle and daub structures with sodded roofs, indicating the tribe's origin in the middle or lower Mississippi valley, while their use of bark-covered gabled houses and mat- and bark-covered wigwams reflected later woodland influences as they moved north (Skinner 1926: 270–276). Wattle and daub structures predominated at Aztalan but the description, "roofed with thatch or bark," may be a logical assumption in the absence of hard evidence (Birmingham and Goldstein 2005:59). Sod, of course, would be equally difficult to determine archaeologically, but its reported use among the Ioway is interesting and may be relevant to certain puzzling artifacts found at Aztalan: heavy chipped stone ovoids about a foot long identified as spades and chipped stone about the same length shaped like broad knife blades (Barrett 1933:269–272, 508–511, 546–547). We raise the possibility that they might have served to cut sod. They do not fit the usual pattern of tools for gardening or processing game and are much more substantial than would be needed to cut grass, hay, or rushes for thatching.

Radin made no mention of wattle and daub among the eight house types he listed for the Ho-Chunk that included various forms of wigwams and temporary shelters indicating the massive incorporation of material traits from neighboring Algonquian speakers by the eighteenth century. He noted, "According to the oldest informants, the earliest type of lodge used by the Winnebago was the ten-fire gable lodge, of which there were two types, rectangular in form, one built on a platform and the other on the ground." Such lodges had long gone out of use in Nebraska where Radin did most of his field research. It is not clear if Radin's informants meant they could be up to 10 fireplaces in length or if this was the norm. In another context he mentions such dwellings could hold up to 40 people. Radin was puzzled by his informants' descriptions: "As far as can be learned at the present time, the platform lodges were merely gable lodges on platforms. What purpose the platform served is now difficult to determine, but most Winnebago questioned said it was provided as a protection against the dampness of the ground and insects" (Radin 1923:104–105, 139).

Radin tried to be ethnographically thorough, but unlike Skinner, a museum collector and curator, he was not a visually oriented person and took little interest in material culture believing that, unlike nonmaterial data, it offered no analytical challenges to the observer's objectivity to describe (1933:4–5). Apart from photographs, mostly of museum specimens, he devoted a chapter of only 20 pages of his 500-plus–page opus to the subject and the text includes long citations from published sources (Radin 1923:104–124).

In this chapter he incorporates the gist of an argument regarding "the disappearance of the bark canoe" that he had presented in detail a decade earlier (Radin 1914). Apart from demonstrating how Radin underestimated the problems of dealing with material culture, his analysis requires correcting because it has bearing on the chapters to follow concerning precontact Ho-Chunk culture and the case for Nicolet's landfall in Menominee country. Radin believed that the Ho-Chunk originally made mostly bark canoes because of the great expenditure of time required to make dugouts, but with the European introduction of metal tools, bark canoes disappeared. He claimed that "Winnebago interrogated on the subject were almost unanimous" in this opinion (1914:144). The lack of total unanimity can be chalked up to people who knew better, probably visitors from Wisconsin who understood, among other things, that the most northerly Ho-Chunk villages barely touched the range of large birch suitable for canoes. Radin's 1914 publication opens with the observation, "There seems little doubt that the Winnebago originally came from the South" (p. 137). Accepting this place of origin, it would be strange if they made anything but dugouts from the start. In any event, it is pretty much a toss-up whether the technology of dugout construction by burning and scraping, even with stone tools, was more arduous and time-consuming than the gathering and processing of multiple materials required to construct bark canoes with stone tools. As soon as metal tools were available they replaced native items in the bark canoe makers' tool kits, too, which raises the question: why didn't the Ho-Chunk continue to make bark canoes, like the Ojibwa, for example, after they got metal implements rather than switching to dugouts?

Given Radin's poor showing in the treatment of material culture, the absence of information about wattle and daub construction does not necessarily indicate its actual absence at an earlier date in Winnebago history. It also is possible that when Radin inquired about lodges on platforms, his informants thought he meant the wooden racks that served as sitting and sleeping areas along the inside walls of dwellings. They are called by the same term, *haza'tc* in Radin's orthography, that applied to a higher platform at the rear of the lodge for the favorite child in the family to live while fasting as well as to wooden grills for roasting and drying meat and to large open-sided sunshades (Radin 1923:56–57; Lurie 1961:8 and field observations). Admitting to difficulty in envisioning gable lodges on platforms, Radin let it go at that in his major monograph on the Winnebago.

There is evidence, however, that his informants tried to tell him as well as other investigators about structures built on earthen mounds, but they were dismissed out of hand. In the late summer of 1911, Radin and two Nebraska men, his interpreter Oliver LaMere and John Rave who had introduced the peyote religion to the reservation, spent a month in Wisconsin. While they were in Madison, Charles E. Brown took them to see some effigy mounds. Rave, a Bear clan member, agreed that a mound in Vilas Park identified as a bear looked like a bear to him, too, and Brown simply assumed Rave made a clan connection, but when he asked Rave about the purpose of linear mounds associated with the effigy mound complex, the situation became embarrassing:

> [Rave] expressed himself as believing them to have been erected by the early Winnebago to serve as locations of their "long houses." It was then and on several occasions afterward pointed out to Mr. Rave that such an explanation of the use of this class of earthworks would hardly be accepted by local archaeologists as these linear mounds are of a length of 100 to 500 or more feet. This information did not, however, have the effect of making him change his information of their purpose. . . . He is not the only Winnebago Indian who has offered this explanation. (Brown 1911:125)

When asked why earthen structures were erected for house sites, Rave hazarded the guess that it was to shed rain, and particularly long mounds might support several houses (Brown 1911:125). It can at least be argued from such general insistence on the point that the Winnebago had some kind of persisting memory of platform mounds characteristic of the Middle Mississippian tradition, albeit applied to linear mounds in answer to Brown's question. It seems noteworthy that Rave, a Nebraska Winnebago whose cohort was long removed from the Wisconsin landscape, would make the same connection to linear mounds as the Wisconsin Winnebago with whom Brown worked. Unfortunately, but understandably given his preconceptions, Brown provides no clues as to exactly what his Wisconsin informants said about structures on mounds.

Radin and his party went on to the Wittenberg settlement where Radin wrote to Brown that he collected data on the "making of mounds, pottery, etc.," and "that the Winnebago were at one time builders of earth lodges," raising a tantalizing hint that he might have stumbled on information about wattle and daub or sodded roofs. Apparently unable to picture what his informants really meant, he played it safe and avoided the topic entirely as he makes no mention of earth lodges in any of his publications. La Mere wrote from Nebraska in response to Brown's request to seek further information about effigy mounds there, but all he had to report was, "An Indian told me that his father used to tell him that the totem mounds would be placed in their fields that they would plant" (Brown 1911:128–129). This sounds like much smaller animal representations than the effigy mounds or it might be a faint echo from a Woodland ancestor.

The Ho-Chunk Nation at present is taking an active and commendable role in the protection and preservation of Wisconsin's effigy mounds and other archaeological features. Some believe their ancestors made the mounds. Griffin recalled that, "When [Will C.] McKern of the Milwaukee Public Museum asked the people with whom Radin had worked how they knew their ancestors had built the Effigy Mounds, they replied that Radin had told them that was the case" (Griffin 1995:15–16). Some knowledgeable elders, at least, deny that the Ho-Chunk built the mounds, claiming they were built by earlier people for the Ho-Chunk as places where their spirits could appear as needed. They now are considered holy places that are the Ho-Chunks' particular responsibility to protect. For example, Ho-Chunk elders Lyle Greendeer and Tom Hopinkah, speaking English in documentary films, advert to this interpretation of the mounds (Erickson 1994, 1997; quoted in Tigerman 2006:47, 49).

Besides mounds representing clan and other sacred animals familiar to the Ho-Chunk (such as turtle, a culture hero, but not a clan figure), the linear mounds are also said to have been made for the Ho-Chunk to dodge behind in times of war, an explanation that Brown knew about and Radin collected at Wittenberg, and that one still hears today: "they are found in greatest abundance in those places where, according to the Indians, ferocious battles occurred" (Brown 1911:128).

Brown regretted he could show Rave only a few effigy mound groups and apparently never thought of taking his visitors to Aztalan or asking them about it. Since archaeologists agreed that the Winnebago made the effigy and related mounds, Radin quoted the available literature on the subject in his chapter on archaeology but raised the logical question why no such mounds were found in the vicinity of the tribe's traditional homeland at Red Banks, though they abounded elsewhere. In fact, Radin was not fully convinced of the effigy mound theory even in his first major publication, Griffin and McKern notwithstanding, and over the years became less convinced of it. Perhaps a certain prescience prompted him to include most of George A. West's description of Aztalan in his archaeology chapter, distinguishing it from the mounds as an "earthwork," without denying or claiming an association with the Winnebago (Radin 1923:40–42).

The historical and popular emphasis on the Winnebago in relation to Jean Nicolet and to the succession of calamities that occurred after his journey have tended to overshadow what the historical and ethnographic records tell us about the tribe's precontact culture and history. Now that we know Nicolet's "Chinese" robe was a mistranslation and not Chinese at all, as was the designation, "The People of the Sea," the long-held premise is demolished that Nicolet was sent because the French thought the tribe had some kind of connection to the Orient. A reevaluation of the old sources may shed light on what it was about the Puan to inspire Champlain to send Nicolet to meet with them.

There is reason to question the accepted scholarly interpretations of the narratives of Ho-Chunk elders Spoon Decorah and Walking Cloud that are routinely cited regarding the precontact and early-contact locations and activities of the Ho-Chunk. Their stories were collected by Reuben Gold Thwaites in the spring of 1887 with Moses Paquette interpreting (Decorah 1895; Walking Cloud 1895). Paquette, a professional interpreter, was a member of a prominent mixed-blood family (Waggoner 2002:5–6). Although competently conversant in Ho-Chunk, his cultural orientation was white, so he did not have a traditional knowledge of locations and their names and tended to mix up sequences of events (Lurie 1988:173–175).

Walking Cloud began with what might have been the start of a sacred story but quickly backed off into the historic era, perhaps because it was the wrong season to tell such stories, and goes on to a rather disjointed account of subsequent events that may reflect confusion in Paquette's translation. "The Winnebagoes came from the sky, the old Indians say. They settled first at the Red Banks. They first met the French, who came in large boats to trade with them, near Green Bay" (Walking Cloud 1895:466). It is clear that Walking Cloud's reference to the French and big boats does not fit Nicolet but later traders such as Perrot. Hall is doubtless correct that, "The [Ho-Chunk] tradition of an origin north of the Great Lakes relates not to an actual homeland but to a long-forgotten or transformed mythical origin in the northern night sky," held in common with many other Siouan groups (Hall 1993:29–30). On the other hand, the insistence on a literal interpretation of a northern origin by many Ho-Chunk people may have to do with origin stories of people whose ancestors were long resident in Wisconsin with whom the Ho-Chunk intermarried.

Spoon Decorah gives a more detailed and entirely secular account, pinpointing Red Banks as the place where the tribe first met the French, also indicating an encounter with more than one French visitor. According to Paquette's translation and punctuation, the Winnebago were hard up because they had nothing but bows and arrows to kill game, but the willingness of neighboring tribes to engage in trade when the Ho-Chunk spurned the Ottawa emissaries suggests the Winnebago finally were defeated by enemies who were better armed:

> It has been told me, by my father and my uncles, that the Winnebagoes first lived below the Red Banks, on the east shore of Green Bay. There was a high bluff there, which enclosed [overlooked?] a lake. They lived there a very long time. From there they moved to the Red Banks, and met at that place the first Frenchmen whom they ever saw. The Winnebagoes were in a very bad condition; they had nothing but bows and arrows with which to kill game. They gave them guns, powder, blankets, kettles and other goods. After that, my ancestors lived in better conditions and could kill all the game they needed. The Frenchmen were very good to our peo-

ple, and bought all the furs they could get from them, at a good price. The Winnebagoes lived a long time at the Red Banks, and then moved to Lake Winnebago. They afterwards spread along the Upper Fox and the Wisconsin Rivers and down to the Rock River in the Illinois country. (Decorah 1895:457–458)

Radin recognized a distinction in Ho-Chunk traditional stories: *worak* that are primarily secular and can be told at any time, and *waikan* that are primarily sacred and are supposed to be told only when there is snow on the ground (Radin 1926a:18–51). The tribal newspaper in Wisconsin, for example, is called *Ho-Chunk Worak*. There are *worak* stories that the Ho-Chunk occupied a large, stockaded village at Red Banks on Green Bay at the time of European contact. Sacred stories, *waikan*, that involve synecdoche, allegory, and mystical allusions, revere Red Banks as their spiritual place of origin without specific geographical identification, but some writers confuse them with *worak* as clues to the geographic site of Red Banks.

Hall's generally accepted explanation of Spoon Decorah's narrative combines his assumption that the historic Red Banks village was at the Speerschneider site and a *waikan* collected by Radin on the origin of the Thunder clan that, according to Radin, expanded into a general tribal origin story. As the four Thunder brothers flew around the earth and made a second transit on the ground, they reached a place called *derok*, "Within Lake," where the other clans began gathering (Radin 1923:216–217). Hall equates this earlier, pre-Red Banks site with the Point Sable area, a location near the lakeshore and slightly west of both the Speerschneider and Robinson/Neville sites, with evidence of successive occupations up to a presumed early historic Potawatomi village:

> There is a small bluff or elevation on the Green Bay shore at Red Banks that slopes gently down to the east, away from Green Bay. Early white settlers reported that there was a cedar swamp at this location, between Red Banks and the Ledge [escarpment?], and it was low and wet even today. This would have to be what Spoon Decorah was referring to, unless he was led to this description only by the name Within Lake itself. (Hall 1993:21)

Spoon Decorah never uses the term "Within Lake," as claimed by Hall who might have been misled by Paquette's word "enclosed." More seriously misleading is the widely held assumption that Spoon Decorah's term "below" refers to elevation, synonymous with under or beneath. It means *downstream* along the same lake current that Stambaugh referred to in 1831 when he described Red Banks as "twelve miles below" Fort Howard. Thanks to James Uhrinak, we became aware of this distinction and its importance to the possible location of Ho-Chunk settlement prior to their move to Red Banks. This lake current still figures in modern concerns with pollutants such as PCBs from paper companies on the Fox River that are carried along the Door Peninsula down to Sturgeon Bay and beyond (Karl 2000).

If we look downstream, that is, northeast along the lakeshore from Red Banks, a stunningly logical candidate for Spoon Decorah's lake is Sawyer Harbor on the west side of the entrance to Sturgeon Bay, as Uhrinak suggested. It conforms closely to his description, being in the right location and overlooked on the south shore by a very impressive bluff, Lookout Point, located in what is now Potawatomi State Park. It is nearly enclosed like other bays on Lake Superior and Lake Michigan that various writers have tried to associate with the lake on Champlain's maps of 1616 and 1632, and, like that enigmatic lake, it even has an island. It could well have been the location of the Ho-Chunk when they first came to Champlain's attention as he tried to make cartographic sense of Indian information about the lay of the land far to the west.

Frequent reference is made in Wisconsin history to the disasters the Ho-Chunk experienced some time after Nicolet's journey. Bringing the wrath of tribes allied with the Ottawa on themselves, their numbers were steadily reduced by defensive and offensive warfare forcing the 4,000 or 5,000 survivors to unite in one village where they experienced further loss to disease and finally famine. The Illinois who sent a delegation of 500 men with food to aid the Ho-Chunk ended up being eaten like the Ottawa traders, sacrificed by the Ho-Chunk to placate the spirits of their recent dead. More hostilities followed, and by the time Perrot met them, the Ho-Chunk were reduced to fewer than 1,000 people. Described as still arrogant and irascible and admitting their ancestors caused their problems for killing peaceful envoys in the chief's lodge, the Ho-Chunk had "become somewhat more tractable" and were intermarried with the Potawatomi, Sauk, and Fox.

Radin observed, "The Winnebago still tell of these events and in practically the same words as Perrot obtained them." In 1910, he collected additional incidents and details such as identifying the village where they united as Red Banks when all the other tribes leagued against them. Mountain Wolf Woman added to a story Radin recounted from this period, that she and her siblings were descendants of the infant boy whose mother saved his life by tying his penis back so he looked like a girl when enemies were even killing male children (Radin 1923:55–58; Lurie 1961:97).

The recency and devastating effects of these events tend to obscure other information provided by Perrot relating to the period prior to white contact that point to southeastern and Middle Mississippian affiliations. The case is strengthened by Radin's later work with texts he collected during his Nebraska fieldwork but did not deal with in his 1923 volume and by data still current among the Ho-Chunk people and their Chiwere-speaking relatives. The impression is that the Puan were not only a serious barrier to the extension of French trade and empire to the West because of their warlike proclivities but also these proclivities betokened tribes and customs unfamiliar to the French, thereby requiring a special diplomatic overture. It is certainly a more creditable reason for Nicolet's venture than the supposed lure of the riches of the Orient as will be evident in the discussion to follow of Ho-Chunk culture prior to European contact.

Chapter 6

Precontact Ho-Chunk Culture

*G*iven the fragments of wattle and daub at Lake Butte des Morts and the presence of Middle Mississippian copper artifacts and Aztalan-style pottery in Green Lake County, and accepting the geographic logic that the major pre-Red Banks settlement mentioned by Spoon Decorah was around Sawyer Harbor on Sturgeon Bay, we can at least entertain the possibility that the Ho-Chunk are descended from the population that had mysteriously vanished from Aztalan by AD 1300. Some 300 years or so later we find them established on the Door Peninsula. They might have migrated in stages or scouted out the destination in advance and beelined there from Aztalan. In any event, they would have left little impact on the landscape during brief stopovers en route.

Wherever the Ho-Chunk came from, the Door Peninsula offered much to entice them. We are indebted to James Uhrinak for sharing his broad and deep knowledge of the ecological history of the Door Peninsula that illuminates understanding of Ho-Chunk culture on the eve of contact. The Niagara escarpment forming the spine of the peninsula reaches from Canada to southeastern Wisconsin. Springs, so important to ritual as well as everyday use, are located along the escarpment. Geologically, the falls of Wequiock Creek are the structural equivalent, in miniature, of Niagara Falls. Deposits of blue clay for pottery that Radin's informants recalled from the time they lived on Green Bay are located along the escarpment and clearly exposed in the area of the falls (1923:119).

Fish abounded and major coastal fishing areas such as the estuary of Wequiock Creek are still known to the Ho-Chunk. Although currently the preferred translation of the homonym *Ho* in Ho-Chunk is "voice" or "speech" rather than "fish," some elders Lurie consulted in the 1940s and 1950s considered it an open question, noting the Ho-Chunks' proclivity to identify them-

95

Niagara escarpment at Wequiock Falls. (Photograph by James Uhrinak)

selves by descriptive place names. After 1865, for example, they created new terms to distinguish between the Wisconsin branch, as dwellers among the pines, *Wazija haci*, and the Nebraska branch as dwellers on the muddy (Missouri) river, *Nishocja haci*. One can only wonder whether there is any connection between the Ho-Chunk and a settlement at a place the whites later found reason to call Sturgeon Bay. Schoolcraft noted, "By the tribe itself they are called Hochungara, which is said to mean Trout nation, and sometimes Horoji, or Fish-eaters" (1860, vol. 3:277). *Ho* means neither sturgeon nor trout specifically but Ho-Chunk can mean big or primordial fish. A dual meaning certainly serves the fluent Ho-Chunk speakers' delight in puns (Susman 1941).

From an ecological and geographic perspective the greater Red Banks region was like no other area in the western Great Lakes. Many mini-environments, some of which one would not expect this far north, provided an easily accessible bounty of natural resources. Special types and forms of plant life were supported by alvar conditions where shallow soil rests atop dolomite or dolomite is exposed. Elsewhere, deep-soil anthropogenic oak–hickory savanna once covered much of the greater Red Banks region, giving evidence of purposeful land management through burning. If the Ho-Chunk did not initiate the practice they most certainly maintained it to encourage desirable ground flora and to plant extensive gardens (Dorney and Dorney 1989). It remained a traditional practice among the Wisconsin Ho-Chunk until prohibited by state authorities in the early twentieth century. The rich

Remnant on private property of once extensive area of oak-hickory savannah along the stream east of Red Banks Hill adjacent to Kish-ke-kwan-te-no subdivision; restoration thinning by James Uhrinak. (Photograph by James Uhrinak)

vegetation of the region offered a broad range of edible and medicinal plants and also supported an abundance and variety of large and small game.

Because the Door Peninsula is now drastically altered, it is important to remember its once manifold resources to understand how they could allow the Ho-Chunk to flourish as a population with a highly complex social organization. The reported thousands of acres of prehistoric garden furrows on the most productive soils have been virtually obliterated and the peninsular environment as a whole has been severely compromised since the early twentieth century and at an accelerating rate since the beginning of the twenty-first century by building, dredging, quarrying, highway construction, drawing down ground water, and cutting off the flow of streams. The Ho-Chunk Nation is actively involved with other institutions and organizations in efforts to protect and preserve what remains of this unique cultural and environmental heritage.

Although the landscape had not been significantly changed when Perrot encountered the Ho-Chunk in the late seventeenth century, the Ho-Chunk were greatly reduced in numbers and power by warfare, disease, and famine since they had first come to the attention of the French. His unflattering description of them when they still dominated the area was doubtless supplied by their enemies and then filtered through his value system of seventeenth-century Catholicism. It nevertheless offers clues about precontact Ho-Chunk culture.

In former times, the Puans were masters of this [Green] bay, and of a great extent of adjoining country. This nation was a populous one, very redoubtable, and spared no one; they violated all the laws of nature; they were sodomites, and even had intercourse with beasts. If any stranger came among them, he was cooked in their kettles. The Malhominis [Menominees] were the only tribe who maintained relations with them, (and) they did not even dare to complain of their tyranny. Those tribes believed themselves the most powerful in the universe; they declared war on all nations whom they could discover, although they had only stone knives and hatchets.

First, both the Ho-Chunk and Menominee agree that they have always been friends and allies. If the interpretation of Spoon Decorah's narrative is correct, that the Ho-Chunk stronghold on the Door Peninsula was initially in the Sturgeon Bay area, they would have had to work their way up there by subjugating or driving out any resident peoples. While the resource base is more concentrated toward the western, Red Banks end of the peninsula, major habitation farther east at about the midpoint of the Door Peninsula at the entrance to Sturgeon Bay would have had clear strategic advantages. With the Menominee stronghold directly across Green Bay to the northwest, the two tribes could have controlled the territory on both sides of the bay and ingress and egress by water.

Second, while the practice of bestiality among people without docile domesticated animals may be questioned, something more than general animosity toward the Ho-Chunk could account for the jeremiad on carnal sin. It is possible that the French observed for the first time and drew their own conclusions about what is referred to in the anthropological literature as the "berdache" institution, which entails certain men who dress as women, take on female roles, and may marry other men. They are considered holy and highly respected for special gifts such as prophesy, healing, artistry, and excelling at women's tasks. Customs varied from tribe to tribe, but the role often was assumed at the direction of a vision quest spirit—in the Ho-Chunk case, it was the moon, a female deity (Lurie 1953). Although once common among Siouan-speaking and other western tribes, berdaches have not been reported among the northeastern tribes the French were familiar with in Perrot's time. Even the few references from farther south among the Delaware, Tuscarora, Miami, and Illinois are equivocal and may concern hermaphrodites or simple transvestitism for special purposes (Goddard 2004:231; Boyce 2004:285; Callender 2004:685; Jackson et al. 2004:31). Only the now extinct Timucua of Florida appear to have had a fully developed berdache role and, interestingly, also might have been Siouan-speaking (Milanich 2004:219, 222). Since about the 1970s, we find the use of such terms as men-women, two-spirit or 2-spirit, or third gender instead of berdache. Certainly, a more neutral term would be appropriate since berdache is derived from a Turkish word for male prostitute, with derogatory implications that do not apply to the honorable role found among North American Indian groups.

Third, while Barrett was quite convinced by the quantity of human remains in refuse pits that cannibalism was practiced at Aztalan, later investigators attributed them to Mississippian custom of extensive processing of the dead with long bones gathered up and placed together and other bones placed in refuse and fire pits. However, the appearance of human bones cracked like discarded animal bones make cannibalism hard to explain away (Birmingham and Goldstein 2005:100–101). Whether or not Perrot's mention of cannibalism strengthens the argument for an Aztalan connection, it must have contributed further to the Puans' distinctiveness compared to neighboring tribes as far as the French were concerned. The Ho-Chunk admit to allegations of cannibalism from matter-of-fact acceptance to unabashed joking about it to condoning references to particular instances of famine or the worldwide occurrence of ritual cannibalism or the symbolism of the Eucharist, to claims that they didn't actually eat people but spread the rumor to frighten their enemies and are now stuck with the reputation. Radin observed that the Hawk or Warrior clan seemed to have had a special association with cannibalism (1923:219), a case in point being "Woank-shik-rootsh-kay" (*Wankshikrucka*), who signed the Winnebago treaty of 1829 where the name is glossed as "Man Eater" and was readily identified by elders in both Wisconsin and Nebraska as a Hawk clan name (Lurie 1966:61). Whatever the case, cannibalism is an old and persistent theme among the Ho-Chunk, although in fairness it should be noted that it was not exclusive to them and appears to have been a kind of ultimate affront to one's enemies if perhaps more metaphoric as a claim than a frequent practice (Radin 1933:35). During the period the Ho-Chunk were under attack, they supposedly turned two Menominees living among them over to the Fox to avoid hostilities with the Fox who then taunted the Menominee that they "drank Menominee soup" (Radin 1923:63).

Finally, the fact that Nicolet was sent expressly to make peace with the Puan is consistent with a cultural focus on warfare that was elaborated beyond French experience with even the notoriously warlike Iroquois. The essence of Radin's comment, "the greatest of all Winnebago passions, success on the warpath" (1933:233), is expressed repeatedly in his writings and those of other observers such as Leo Srole who, in 1939–1940, undertook a field study on behalf of the Anthropology Department of the University of Chicago as a follow-up to Radin's work. Srole concentrated on the then contemporary Winnebago in contrast to Radin's research that had concentrated on reconstructing the past. Srole conducted his study in Wisconsin; perhaps there were plans to continue work in Nebraska where Radin had done most of his research, but the project was interrupted by World War II and never resumed. Besides field notes archived at the University of Chicago, the only result was an unpublished paper Srole delivered at the 1940 annual meeting of the American Anthropological Association in Philadelphia, "The Winnebago and Modern War," by which Srole meant World War I. Although not aware of it at the time he collected his data, Srole was struck, on reviewing and organizing his notes, by the importance of warfare, the role of the warrior, and the persistence of such ceremonies as war bundle feasts stressing spirits associated with war. He found it remarkable that "the war complex had had nothing to feed upon, so to speak, for up to 1917 hardly a handful of Winnebago had ever been on the warpath, in several generations." Despite drastic and devastating cultural change, Srole concluded, "The Winnebago culture pattern has been left intact at its core, namely in the war complex." In the years following Srole's research, the complex has had much to feed on and flourishes (Lurie 1994 and ongoing field observations; Arndt 2008:34–39).

Consider, then, the following distillation of research regarding what some archaeologists refer to as the Mississippian influence sphere expressed at many sites including Cahokia and Aztalan:

> Warfare and violence seem to have been a part of Mississippian life from the beginning and increasingly so as time went on. Settlements were heavily fortified and warfare was a major theme of Mississippian art. Images in many media feature warriors dancing with stylized war clubs and the severed heads of enemies. One stone figurine is of a warrior in the act of decapitating a dead enemy [an effigy pipe bowl from the Spiro site in Oklahoma]. Warriors dressed and painted or tattooed themselves as falcons complete with the forked eye pattern and spotted breast found on the bird itself. The falcon became a war symbol because of its swiftness and aggressiveness. (Birmingham and Goldstein 2005:34–35)

The former practice of taking entire heads as trophies is reflected in the Ho-Chunk word for scalp, literally man's head, but the Ojibwa and other tribes have an equivalent term. The Ho-Chunk seem to be alone, however, in seeing the patterns on the full moon as depicting a vengeful warrior holding two severed heads although, as noted, the moon is a female deity and protector of women (Lurie 1961:xix). The Ho-Chunk Hawk clan is associated specifically with warfare and is identified as the peregrine falcon, known for its forceful "stoop" that often sunders its prey and sometimes causes its own death (Lurie 1988:181).

Radin collected much more data than he dealt with in his general ethnology and culled this vast store of myths, rituals, specific customs, and the statements of individuals over the years for internal evidence of historical chronologies. Convinced almost from the start that the Winnebago had entered Wisconsin from the south (Radin 1914:137), he became increasingly aware of unmistakable indications of Ho-Chunk roots in the complex cultures of the Southeast. He began to discern two major phases of cultural change: accommodation to a more northerly habitat and the culture of the largely Algonquian-speaking tribes of the western Great Lakes but with extensive retention of features from what might be termed the primal southern culture, and adaptations to the European presence from roughly the mid-seventeenth century until the early nineteenth century based on the cultural model offered by less sedentary Algonquian-speaking neighbors that was more or less pre-adapted to take advantage of the fur trade. Despite calamities and severe population loss earlier in the seventeenth century, this was the golden age Radin's informants hearkened back to as a matter of their own recollections or learned about directly from their forebears, and which he initially assumed represented all of aboriginal Ho-Chunk culture.

In his 1923 volume on the Ho-Chunk, Radin generally explained away discrepancies in his data as due to the destructive effects of white culture after American hegemony in the nineteenth century led to the loss of land and tribal autonomy. From Radin's perspective and that of his contemporaries at the turn of the twentieth century, the onset of the reservation period was the beginning of the end, not the start of a new phase of cultural adaptation as it is now viewed. Indian cultures and identifiable Indian societies were simply doomed (Radin, personal communication 1957). Radin's unquestioning acceptance of the idea of "the vanishing Indian" shows up as an aside in the course of his discussion of burial customs that included earlier southeastern affinities: "We must, accordingly, seek further, to see whether the myths, rituals, and customs do not give evidence of other changes. We find that they do in a most decisive manner, and the net result is a picture of Winnebago society different from, and in many ways at variance with, that of today." Footnoting this statement, he says, "Naturally I mean by 'today' the culture as it existed three or four generations ago" (Radin 1933:34).

In his general ethnology, Radin described Winnebago social organization as a moiety system that is patrilineal and exogamous, that is, a social division of the tribe into two halves with membership inherited through the father's line and marriage forbidden between members of the same half. The Winnebago distinguish the halves as those who are above and those who are below—roughly, totemic birds and animals. There were 12 exogamous clans—four in the upper division and eight in the lower, each with duties to the civil chief or tribe as a whole and with reciprocal duties between various pairs of clans, particularly in regard to burials (Radin 1923:181–192). Each clan has an inventory of personal names that distinguish its members and dog names that the members can choose to name particularly cherished dogs.

A dual chieftainship drew the peace or civil chief from the Thunderbird clan while the Bear clan chief was in charge of maintaining order, akin to a police force, as well as having responsibilities in matters having to do with land. These roles are associated today with major tribal powwows, particularly in Wisconsin, when, ideally, the entire tribe is gathered at one place as they once lived together or in close proximity to one another long ago (Arndt 2008:32). The Thunder chief has special responsibilities to address the gathered throng and lead the dancing in the Grand Entry, while Bear clan people ideally, if not always in fact, predominate in the security force. Among other clans whose special duties were remembered in Radin's time and still figure today are the Buffalo clan that provided town criers for the civil chief regarding internal affairs and are now favored as a source of powwow announcers when available, and the Snake clan in charge of village cleanliness and are now involved in keeping the powwow grounds neat. The Hawk clan had special duties and privileges regarding war that no long apply because the Ho-Chunk no longer have the prerogative of initiating war, but the role of the "warrior" and acts of heroism while serving in the armed forces in modern wars are glorified at every opportunity. The Elk clan, now consisting of only a few people, once provided orators to present the civil chief's position, reached by consensus of the clan heads, in external affairs.

Since World War II and particularly since the 1950s when the federal Indian Relocation Program took many Indian people off the reservations, tribal powwows nationwide have become particularly important as homecomings. In Wisconsin, the tribal groups have evolved a generally understood calendar that seeks to avoid overlap and that is centered around their particular interests. For example, the Ojibwa, who have six reservations in the state,

Vietnam War Air Force veteran, Staff Sergeant Elliot Littlejohn, beside the flag pole honoring his father, Corporal Edward Littlejohn, Sr., World War II Army veteran; Ho-Chunk Powwow, Black River Falls, WI, Memorial Day, 2007. (Photograph by Tom Jones)

tend to emphasize ricing and natural resources, and the Oneida, who take pride in having fought on the American side in the Revolutionary War, claim the Fourth of July holiday weekend for their big powwow. The Ho-Chunk begin and end the season with major powwows at Black River Falls over the Memorial Day and Labor Day weekends with special emphasis during the former on honoring veterans. Government-issued casket flags of deceased veterans are raised and lowered on poles set around the dance arena with ceremonies following American military protocol. The veteran's picture often is hung on the pole and a container holds packs of cigarettes and matches for anyone to smoke a cigarette, a tobacco offering in the veteran's honor. Even the Labor Day weekend powwow without the flag raising and lowering has the honor guard carrying the banners of the four military services at the Grand Entry, and the four services' songs are sung. Flag songs go back to World War I and new songs are composed to honor recent heroes. Some powwow songs are very old war songs, recalling expeditions against enemy tribes.

Radin knit incomplete and sometimes conflicting information about the clan and moiety system into a logical whole, believing it to be an accurate reconstruction of past practices, but as he delved more deeply into his data, his rigorous intellectual integrity prompted the admission that lacunae and inconsistencies were not necessarily lost or broken pieces but pieces yet to be created or acquired and regularized into a developing system, re-organizing and replacing an older one (Radin 1948:45).

In the course of analyzing the body of myths only adverted to or not dealt with at all in his BAE volume, Radin found not only strong hints of southeastern antecedents but reason to reassess some of the conclusions he had set forth in his first major publication. By this time, more was known about the archaeology of the Southeast, and Radin himself had done research on the oral literature of Middle America that he found relevant to Ho-Chunk mythology. For example, he had firmly rejected the suggestion promoted by the cultural evolutionists who maintained all human societies evolved through the same stages but at different rates, reflecting degrees of advancement among different peoples. They speculated that humankind began as "promiscuous hordes," and as they developed social systems, they began with matriliny—tracing descent through the mother's line. But as groups wised up to the role of the male in procreation, they evolved to a higher, patrilineal stage—tracing descent through the male line. Thus, they attributed the occasional bestowal of names from a person's mother's clan or transmission of a warbundle through a female ancestor among otherwise patrilineal groups like the Ho-Chunk to lingering survivals of the matrilineal stage. Radin, representative of a newer, objectively relativistic position in anthropology that did not see patriliny as inherently superior to matriliny, initially attributed the discrepancies in Ho-Chunk patriliny to cultural breakdown since the inception of the reservation system (Radin 1923:192–193). Although marriage within the same clan, endogamy, is disapproved but not unknown, disregard for moiety exogamy has been accepted for a long time, perhaps indicating its transitional status. Radin surely must have been aware, for example, that both parents of his main informants, Jasper and Sam Blowsnake, belonged to the upper division; they were reckoned as members of their father's Thunderbird clan but their mother belonged to the Eagle clan (Lurie 1961:4–5).

Later, he found that the cultural evolutionists were right, but for the wrong reason. The Winnebago had, indeed, been matrilineal: "Internal evidence, myth, tradition, custom, all point to a period in Winnebago history where descent was reckoned through the female line" (Radin 1948:45). The avunculate was among the customs Radin recorded early in his research, that is, the role of the mother's brother rather than the father as teacher and disciplinarian of her children. It is almost universal to matrilineal systems but is occasionally found among patrilineal groups. Its elaboration among the Ho-Chunk, however, with reciprocal rights and obligations is still in effect today, and admonitions that a man is closer to his sister's children than his own because the former are of his "same blood" (as glossed in English) all add significant weight to indications of matriliny in former times.

Furthermore, besides hints of matriliny, Radin found that the plots and behavior of the characters of "innumerable myths" revealed "a very old stratum of Winnebago history," including "the existence of a stratified society where chiefs occupy a position of unusual power and authority, where they and their children are, to all intents and purposes, 'nobles', and where an orphan is not only a person of no social importance but actually belongs to an inferior class" (Radin 1949:75). The Winnebago, he concluded, had been in the process of becoming patrilineal and leveling distinctions in social status as a result of European contact, not because of any universal laws of succession from simple to more complex stages as cultural evolutionary theory would have it. Rather than contributing to the breakdown of a fully defined and functioning system, American rule in the nineteenth century interrupted a work in progress.

The reasons for the shift can be traced to the tribe's loss of dominance in the region, the lack of people qualified to fill all the social roles of a complex system due to population loss, the effect of cultural borrowing through extensive intermarriage with neighboring patrilineal tribes, and especially the economics of the fur trade. The last favored male roles as hunters over the importance of female roles associated with food produced through gardening and gathering and diverted female energies (with loss of status) into increased processing of animal skins now obtained largely for commercial purposes. It also led to the breakup of large, stable concentrations of population surrounded by huge areas devoted to gardens into small village bands scattered over a wide territory to maximize opportunities to obtain peltry animals. To the outside observer of the late eighteenth or early nineteenth centuries, the Ho-Chunk appeared to differ little from other tribes of the western Great Lakes except in language and relatively greater dependence on gardens.

In discussing clan names and the moiety system in his general monograph, Radin noted that J. Owen Dorsey, in an unpublished manuscript, adverted to a claim by Thomas Foster that the two-part division of Winnebago society had been preceded by a fourfold division. He dismissed it as simply "a grouping of the clans according to fauna . . . [that] hardly was intended as an enumeration of the clans" (Radin 1923:191). If Radin had had access to Foster's account in its entirety, he might have seen it as further evidence of earlier southeastern affiliations where, along with upper and lower and north–south divisions, fourfold organizations predominate. Foster's description adds a special feature in the association of certain flora with his Land and Water Families that put one in mind of the rich plant resources of the Door Peninsula. Although neither Dorsey nor Foster mentioned matriliny, it is the prevailing form of descent in the Southeast, sometimes entailing convoluted complexities such as the Natchez system that still defies deciphering (Galloway and Jackson 2004:602–603). Foster's account hints at such complexity at an earlier period for the Winnebago:

> Originally, it would seem, the Tribe was divided into *Four* Grand Families, which were perpetuated continually by a *plan* of formally naming children, and assigning them their place in each grand Family, (upon a principle of selection and division not yet ascertained,) by which children of the same parents were assigned to different Totemic Families, the classification being based, probably, upon the original practice of selecting wives from a totem different from that of the husband, and that a certain portion of their off-spring *should* therefore belong to the Totemic Family from which the parent came. These Four Original Totems, amongst the Winnebago were:
>
> 1ST. THUNDER-BIRD FAMILY: being those who are named after the invisible inhabitants of the *firmament,* deemed to be Gigantic Birds, and also after their manifestations, powers or attributes, as the Clouds, Lightning, Fire, the Wind, &c., and—
>
> 2d. THE AIR FAMILY—or, the Second Thunder (or Sacred Bird) Family—being all those named after the Visible Birds of the Air, from the great War Eagle down to the smallest of the feathered race; which birds are held to have been created from quill feathers, or head feathers, or the down feathers, of the Invisible Thunder Birds, and the smaller and smallest from the *fuzz* blown off from the plumage of the Sacred Thunders.
>
> These two Thunder Families are peculiarly the Warrior Caste, Having the decision, principally, of War and Peace, and as the originators of Fire, (from the lightnings) are deemed to be, in a certain sense, the Superior Families.
>
> 3d. THE LAND FAMILY, which includes the Bear, Wolf, Dog, Fox: in fact all four-footed animals, except the *amphibii*, and includes also the Trees, and the products of the Earth generally.
>
> 4TH. THE WATER FAMILY, including those named from the Water and everything that lives in it or partially in it; and the Snakes (land and water,) and all Medicine Roots, etc.: the ruling Spirit of the Water, being an animal with human and preter-human attributes, called **Wähtchæhē'**. (Foster 1876–1877:4)

Foster had been a government physician to the Winnebago in 1850–1851 during their residence at the Long Prairie Reservation in Minnesota, and this led to his interest in ethnology. He eventually obtained some congressional financing for a proposed encyclopedia of the North American Indians. Seeking critical input from other scholars before committing himself to final publication, Foster hit on the idea of having preliminary drafts for limited distribution set in newsprint—cheaper and quicker than hand copying, the only alternative of his day, but highly perishable. He did not live to finish the project but produced extensive accounts of the Winnebago and Iowa and a miscellaneous scattering of information about other tribes, Indian place names, long quotations from Schoolcraft's work, and the like.

Although Foster had an excellent ear for linguistic transcription, his ethnological reporting lacked depth of detail but, taken together with Radin's and Lurie's research, a Middle Mississippian connection to the Ho-Chunk seems obvious in regard to the so-called Warrior clan. Its membership seemed to be dying out in Nebraska when Radin worked there, prompting Birmingham and Goldstein to conclude from his work, "In the past, the Ho-Chunk also had a Warrior clan," but the clan survives in Wisconsin where it is also known by its original name as the Hawk clan for its totem animal as well as its newer name based on its function. Foster designates his two "Thunder Families" as the "Warrior caste" and makes no specific reference to Hawks among the "visible birds of the air," but notes that these families together had to do with decisions regarding both war and peace, apparently as matters outside the purview of the other clans. Radin indicates that while the Warrior clan could undertake war parties without special blessings, the Thunder or Peace chief had the authority to stop ill-considered war parties.

Radin also saw that the Water Spirit—envisioned as a huge serpent, the word rendered in bold type in Foster's account—once played a much more significant role in Ho-Chunk cosmology. During his 1957 visit at Lurie's home, he mused with a smile that perhaps it was half of Quetzalcoatl, the Plumed Serpent, separated as it moved out of Middle America from its other half that became syncretized with the northern Thunderbird.

Radin also changed his mind about "the myth that speaks of a village that at one time was so long that those at one end did not know what was transpiring at the other" as containing "too many literary touches to justify its use as an historical document" (Radin 1923:184–185). As he became increasingly aware of the evidence of the precontact culture and its southeastern affiliations, the idea of the big village did not seem so far fetched, but entailed new problems of chronology that Radin was still trying to clarify right up to the time of his death. The name of Red Banks on Green Bay is popularly attributed to the presence of reddish clay there but appears to have been the last and perhaps least of a series of villages carrying that name. Some, if not all, were stockaded. Although there was near total consensus and detailed information among Radin's informants that the big village of Red Banks was on Green Bay, he collected a few brief references to various other locations named Red

Banks farther west, one even on the Mississippi. He was eventually convinced that old memories of a really large village were combined with those of later settlements housing most of the tribe's diminishing numbers until the eighteenth century when they split up into smaller units across southwestern Wisconsin and northwestern Illinois (Radin, personal communication 1957).

From the beginning of her fieldwork in 1944 and over the course of many years of association with the Ho-Chunk people, Lurie has heard references to a Big Village where all the Ho-Chunk once lived and had gardens that were several arrowshots in length and breadth. According to a Bear clan member, the well-defined police functions and powers of enforcement of his clan were necessary to maintain order when the tribe all lived together in a big village (Lurie 1960:796–797). Just as Radin collected accounts in Nebraska paralleling Perrot's discussion, Lurie found it was a matter of common knowledge, at least among older Ho-Chunk people who never read or even heard about Perrot, that the disasters he described were brought on because a few foolish hotheads at the Big Village, usually identified as Red Banks on Green Bay, killed envoys from another tribe in the chief's lodge, a sacred place of sanctuary. Caramanee (one of various spellings), the recognized paramount peace chief in the early nineteenth century, testified at a hearing where a number of young men "of the Winnebago or Hochungarah tribe" were accused of murdering a Frenchman, Francis Methode: "Long ago we all lived in one large town. Then our chiefs had influence and our young men behaved well. Now we are scattered like the animals of the forest & can scarce restrain our own children" (Boilvin 1826).

Henry R. Schoolcraft reported on information collected between 1832 and 1846 by Indian Agent Jonathan Fletcher from those Winnebago who were residing on the Turkey River or Neutral Ground Reservation in Iowa. He noted that the Winnebagos' "earliest traditions relate to their residence at Red Banks—an ancient location on the east shore of Green Bay—and to trade with the French. They have a tradition that they once built a fort; an event that appears to have made a general impression on the tribe." Apparently, neither Schoolcraft nor Fletcher actually visited Red Banks where there would have been still visible remains of a fort, or Schoolcraft had reason to believe, contrary to Fletcher, that the reference was to a period even earlier than the occupation at Red Banks on Green Bay. He says of this fort that it "may, without improbability, be connected with the finding of archaeological remains of an ancient work on Rock River [sic]," adding a sarcastic footnote: "Called with pedantry, and entire disregard of Indian history, Aztalan" (Schoolcraft 1860, vol. 3:278). Fletcher provided details of a fort that was described to him as "constructed of logs or pickets set in the ground" but it is uncertain whether this was at Green Bay or Doty Island, as Lawson maintained, as it was supposedly built as a defense against hostilities with the Sauk and Fox in the eighteenth century (Schoolcraft 1860, vol. 4:231).

According to Allouez and other sources, the protracted disasters, and subsequent defeat of the Puan occurred about 1650, after Nicolet's journey,

Composite photo of Sawyer Harbor on Sturgeon Bay as seen from Lookout Point in Potawatomi State Park. (Photograph by James Uhrinak)

but the hostilities probably began prior to 1634 at a time when the Ho-Chunk were still living "below" the Red Banks, presumably in the Sturgeon Bay area. It is a reasonable surmise that the Ottawa trading party might have had its fatal encounter there that set the tumultuous events in motion described by Perrot insofar as the only recorded reason for Nicolet's venture was to make peace between the Ho-Chunk and the Huron, a term that included their allies such as the Ottawa. While the exact source of Champlain's information for his 1616 map showing the earliest mention of "Puans" cannot be known, the Ottawa chief who drew a map of the country on bark for Champlain in 1615 is the most likely candidate (Champlain 1922–1956, vol. 3:43–44). Sagard indicates that the Ottawa traveled as far as the Puan by 1623 but makes no mention of hostilities at that time. Perhaps it was the persistence of the Ottawa peddlers that tried the patience of the Puan who finally took drastic measures against them. After all, Perrot observed, the Puan did not want to trade with the French but, "the Outaouks, notwithstanding, sent to them envoys." Champlain strongly hints that the Huron and Ottawa were at war with the Puan before 1634. As mentioned in chapter 3, the Huron stated in 1611 that they were at war with western Indians, and Champlain noted in 1615 that the Indians with whom the French had contact (the Huron and probably the Ottawa) were at war with tribes to the west (Champlain 1922–1956, vols. 2:191, 3:119).

Nicolet put in his brief appearance in 1634, but, as frequently noted, the French could not follow up on his diplomatic efforts and did not return to Green Bay until some three decades later. During this time, we know from Perrot and the Ho-Chunks' own traditional history collected by Radin that the tide turned against the Puan nation, and they began to have second thoughts about the desirability of trade goods and the inconvenience of being under constant threat of attack. Perrot says that they fell out among themselves in "civil wars," and were compelled to "unite all their forces in one village, where they numbered four or five thousand men." This suggests that they had a number of settlements stretched along the Door Peninsula, but that their major village where they all took temporary refuge at the start of the hostilities was probably in the area of Sawyer Harbor on Sturgeon Bay if our analysis of Spoon Decorah's narrative is correct.

It would have been at this village, rather than at Red Banks as is usually assumed, that they suffered further disasters of disease and famine, the former perhaps an epidemic affliction of European origin. It can be inferred it was there that the Illinois took pity on them and brought them supplies of food only to be slain and eaten by the Ho-Chunk seeking to placate the spirits of their people lost in earlier battles. It would also be the location of the remains of the "cabin" Perrot claimed to have seen where the unsuspecting Illinois were killed in the midst of feasting and dancing. The Ho-Chunk then took refuge on an island where they would be safe from the inevitable vengeance of the Illinois who supposedly did not use canoes. When the Illinois returned two years later in the winter to cross the ice, the Ho-Chunk had just left for their winter hunt. The island could not have been very large as Perrot said it had been carried away by ice floes. His account is ambiguous at this point insofar as he describes the Illinois following the hunters for six days when they "descried their village, to which they laid siege." This passage might mean that only some able-bodied men holed up at the island and meanwhile the Ho-Chunk as a whole had moved their main village to the more easily defended but geologically unstable site at Red Banks where they built a stockade.

A Ho-Chunk presence on Sawyer Harbor has yet to be proved or disproved unless development in this desirable suburban area to the city of Sturgeon Bay now precludes ever testing it archaeologically. If there was a major settlement at Sawyer Harbor, it might or might not have been stockaded. It is simply a general assumption that references to a fortified village are to the known but now obliterated stockade at Red Banks. If the scenario is correct that the Puan moved from another location "below Red Banks" to the more easily defended elevation of Red Banks and built a "fort" there, the question arises whether it was a case of learning through necessity or whether they had a historical model or tradition for such construction. They might have had recent experience with such construction at Sawyer Harbor or a remembered model at Aztalan and the series of stockaded settlements along the Mississippi that appear to be the course of migration of Middle Mississippian people north out of Cahokia (Birmingham and Goldstein 2005:45).

The little attention that has been given to the possibility of a Winnebago connection to Aztalan is dismissive. A Mr. J. C. Brayton who lived in the vicinity of Aztalan since it first came to white notice wrote to Lapham: "The Winnebagos, the last occupants of this interesting locality, always answer in the negative by a significant shake of the head, when asked if they can tell who erected the mounds" (Lapham 2001:47). This might have been a denial as Brayton assumed or the Winnebago might have known but were not disposed to answer his question as it would be too complicated to handle, given the Winnebago–English language barrier, or just deemed it none of Brayton's business.

A familiar Mississippian motif appears in thousand-year-old painted images in caves in Wisconsin and Missouri and have been identified with the culture hero Red Horn. His name and exploits are known through Ho-Chunk and Iowa mythology, but Birmingham and Goldstein are unwilling to accept a direct Mississippian ancestry for these tribes that would link them to sites like Cahokia and Aztalan. They only suggest that "the distant ancestors of these people [Ho-Chunk and Iowa] probably had direct contact with the Mississippians, sharing many cultural ideas, including the Red Horn stories" (2005:27). They attribute any stories the Ho-Chunk might have about Aztalan to their possibly speculating about "the once great town" when archaeological evidence indicates they camped at times amidst its ruins in the eighteenth and nineteenth centuries (2005:102).

However, the stories, though not widely known, have too much substance to be mere historic myth making. In the spring of 2002, Jack Monegar, a member of the Ho-Chunk Nation from Ringle, Wisconsin, read a newspaper account of work at Cahokia conducted by University of Wisconsin–Milwaukee (UWM) Professor Melvin Fowler and its relation to Aztalan. He was so struck by the similarities to his maternal grandfather's stories, that he contacted Fowler. Fowler and his colleague in the UWM Anthropology Department, John Richards, met with Monegar at Aztalan in late June and taped his comments as they moved around the area. The transcript of the recording came to Lurie's attention two years later. Since it was typed by a student unfamiliar with the Ho-Chunk words and there had been technical problems with the recorder that resulted in breaks in the narrative, Lurie contacted Monegar for further information. They met for about three hours on May 30, 2005, at Black River Falls at the time of the annual Memorial Day Powwow and have had subsequent discussions by mail and telephone. The following account includes materials from the Fowler recording and the 2005 interview.

Monegar, who was born in 1941, belongs to the Water Spirit clan, but since he was raised by his mother's parents from the time he was two or three years old, and his grandfather, Tom Brown, belonged to the Bear clan, most of his information is from that clan. The Browns lived at De Soto in western Wisconsin about 30 miles north of La Crosse on the Mississippi River. They were traditionalists and Tom Brown was highly respected as a very knowledgeable elder. Lurie met the Browns during her first fieldwork in 1944 when Jack was a little boy but had lost touch with him until 2005 (Lurie 1972). She has lightly edited and supplied phonetic spellings in the excerpts from the Fowler recording, below:

> When I was young my grandfather mentioned a lot of stories, and a lot of them are myth and legend. But this one story concerns this here [Aztalan] and possibly Cahokia Mounds. Where we come from, he said, a long time ago, we built pyramids and he said we built palaces. He said we were good at it. And somewhere along the line we got into a squabble and the tribe kinda split into bands. And he never said where all this took place. He said we followed the waters. And somehow I keep thinking he's talking about the Gulf of Mexico. He said as we went along the water, parts of the bands would break off and go inland. And they kept going and they lost contact with the main group. He said that happened and we

went all the way out to the east coast. We went way out there and he said we settled there for a while. And then those days, as part of the worship, we'd fast. They'd go without food or water for days and they'd take ashes from a fire and put it on their face to humble themselves to the creator in quest of a vision or a blessing. He said we had leaders that could talk to God; they were spiritual leaders besides the chief.

They all saw white faces [in the visions], Columbus, I guess. They predicted what would come in days ahead and they didn't want to be there when that happened so they went West and stayed at that place quite a while. Fowler's "lost city," the way he described Cahokia, it might be. Then they decided to go North where we're at now [Aztalan].

We were the first Indians here and covered the whole state at one time or another. Wherever there is a big lake where there is red earth there are Ho-Chunk graves. Mogashuc [Red Banks] is not just one place, there's Mogashuces all the way to Duluth.

When we were on the east coast they were accustomed to the Menominee, knew each other there. Then when they got here, they recognized each other, hikaragiwi. They joked, they'd hear a twig snap, it must be them. The Menominee, we knew each other from way back and teased the same way.

Now my grandfather could read a little, not real good, or his English wasn't real good. He mentioned we lived at that place one time, coinhabited with other tribes and were cannibals. He didn't say if they did it just at ceremonies or ate people regularly.

What surprised Monegar was that the information that he had read fairly recently about Aztalan in Fowler's article matched what he had learned as oral tradition from his grandfather many years earlier, including the matter of cannibalism. In answer to Lurie's question, he said that if his grandfather ever told him a name for "that place" he couldn't recall, but knew it must be Aztalan because when he asked where it was, his grandfather said it was in the middle of the state near Madison.

Besides the issue of cannibalism, Monegar was interested in the Mississippian emphasis on astronomy discussed by Fowler and mentioned that, according to his grandfather, June 21 was considered a very sacred day. People would go to a high place and cut a groove into a rock to line up with the sunrise and when the sunbeam hit the groove, "he said it's real pure. There's not a flaw, there's not a shadow. It's pure. That's why they made it sacred and they'd light their pipes with the tobacco and they'd pray to the creator." Monegar himself observes the solstice, getting up early on June 21 and facing east and praying with his pipe until the sun starts to cast a shadow, and then, "It's broken, it's not pure anymore."

Jonathan Fletcher dismissed the Ho-Chunks' astronomical knowledge as practically nonexistent until they were enlightened by teachers at the school at Turkey River, an inevitable conclusion since his inquiries were couched in terms of Schoolcraft's Eurocentric questionnaire (Schoolcraft 1860, vol. 4:238–239). Also, Fletcher might have found his presumably all-male informants unresponsive because certain star knowledge was traditionally the exclusive concern of women. Using the wigwam smoke hole to track the movement of the stars, women determined times for planting and other agricultural tasks, menstrual cycles, the course of pregnancies, and the like (Lurie, unpublished field data). Radin deals with astronomical information in a number of publications and contexts indicating southeastern features, particularly in the importance of the morning star and the sun as the primary deity of war (Radin 1923:286–287, 440). The sun, called grandfather, figures in songs and orations of war bundle feast ceremonies.

Lurie has collected many references regarding cannibalism and the big village that seem to point to Aztalan, including one account, like Monegar's, that definitely makes the association though lacks any further details. Gordon Thunder, a man now in his 70s, remembers that when he was about six years old, his grandfather Henry Thunder asked his son Frank, Gordon's father, to drive him to Aztalan and they took Gordon with them. Henry spoke virtually no English and was a thorough-going traditionalist, even declining invitations to join the Medicine Lodge as he knew it was a ceremony borrowed from the Algonquian speakers, albeit long ago. For him, Warbundle feasts and Victory Dances (so-called Scalp Dances) were the primary Ho-Chunk rituals among other observances such as the Night Spirit Dance. Even though Frank had embraced the peyote religion, Henry felt he should be informed about tribal history and arranged for the Aztalan visit where he identified various places on the site and what took place there. Gordon has no recollection of any precise details; he was just a child along for the ride. In answer to a question from Lurie as to the name for Aztalan, he said "*derok*," a name associated with the tribal origin story, as discussed earlier, and considered highly sacred by traditionalists.

Although no systematic effort has been made to collect oral history beyond the Ho-Chunk, we are grateful for permission to use information from two Ioway elders, Jimm Goodtracks and Pete Fee, who independently mentioned in chance conversations with Lurie that their tribal traditions included accounts of visiting the Ho-Chunk when they lived on Green Bay. This accords with the Jesuit Allouez's report of Ioway visitors among the Ho-Chunk he ministered to in the late seventeenth century, although the tribes had long been officially separated. Fee noted that he had heard that the reason for the separation was the Ioways' rejection of the Ho-Chunk practice of cannibalism.

Although contemporary accounts drawn from oral history may be fragmentary and enigmatic, the fact that they exist at all and show both consistency and concordance with written history seems to attest to direct Mississippian affiliations of precontact Ho-Chunk culture. Both Monegar and Thunder read and approved the accounts of their information as presented here; Goodtracks and Fee also graciously allowed citation of their information. It is possible that further information on the subject exists in other Ho-Chunk families' stories or is still embedded in Ho-Chunk ritual—songs and orations—that religiously qualified Ho-Chunk people might recognize.

Chapter 7

The Case for a Menominee Country Landfall

*A*bout the time controversy was heating up between Lawson and Neville as to whether Nicolet met the Winnebago at Red Banks on Green Bay or Doty Island in Lake Winnebago, James Mooney and Cyrus Thomas published their entry on the Menominee for the *Handbook of American Indians North of Mexico:* "The people of this tribe, so far as known, were first encountered by the whites when Nicolet visited them, probably in 1634, at the mouth of the Menominee r., Wis.-Mich." (Hodge 1907–1910, vol. 1:842). Although not acknowledged, this claim must have been based on Butterfield's biography of Nicolet (1881:55–57) that traces his route into Green Bay along the shore of Bay de Noc. Butterfield has Nicolet encountering small, unidentified Algonquian-speaking groups until he reaches the Menominee River and the resident tribe of that name. It was from there, as Butterfield interprets Vimont's account, that Nicolet sent a man ahead to alert the Winnebago of his imminent arrival. This messenger returned with several young men to escort him the rest of the way and carry his baggage to meet the Winnebago at the mouth of the Fox River.

Neither Neville nor Lawson nor the many writers who have argued subsequently for other landfalls advert to an initial stopover with the Menominee. The *Handbook* entry on the Winnebago by Dorsey and Radin takes no notice of the Menominee: "The Winnebago have been known to the whites since 1634, when the Frenchman Nicollet [sic] found them in Wisconsin, on Green Bay" (Hodge 1907–1910, vol. 2:958). Before and since Hodge's *Handbook* appeared, popular and professional histories concerning Nicolet have linked him exclusively with the Winnebago and take it for granted that the great conclave he addressed took place in Winnebago country, wherever it might have been. Even Butterfield did not consider the Menominee as the possible endpoint of Nicolet's journey but had him not only reaching the Winnebago for his famous conclave but going far beyond them. With no supporting evidence, Butterfield has Nicolet ascending the Fox River as far as Green Lake County, meeting the Mascoutins, and exploring as far south as the tribes of the Illinois Confederacy before returning home.

A close appraisal of long-available evidence, however, more than suggests that Nicolet did not get much farther than the large Menominee village reportedly located in the vicinity of modern Marinette, Wisconsin. Furthermore, he probably made his initial landfall at Little Bay de Noc to the north of Marinette and completed most of the last lap of his journey to the Menominee on foot.

The various artists' imagined depictions of Nicolet, quaintly dressed as a Chinaman and terrifying the cowering Indians with the "thunder" he carried in his hands as he strides boldly toward them, have done Nicolet an egregious disservice, to say nothing of the effect on the public of the artists' Eurocentric attitude of superiority toward the Indians. The fact is that Nicolet embarked on an exceedingly dangerous assignment with no guarantee of success and a safe return, and the Indians, even allies, held the upper hand in numbers and knowledge of the territory. The assignment called for wisdom, diplomacy, and endurance—and reliable guides.

The Jesuit records we rely on were written for seventeenth-century readers who could be expected to know details that are not self-evident today. However, reasonable inferences based on general knowledge of the history of the fur trade and the skills Nicolet had necessarily acquired through long experience with the peoples and environment of the northern frontier can help to flesh out the story. We have no information, for example, whether Nicolet and his seven, presumably Huron, companions traveled in one or more canoes. Timothy J. Kent points out in his definitive study, *Birchbark Canoes of the Fur Trade*:

> During the first half of the 17th century, the transport of furs and trade goods in the interior was carried out exclusively by Indians. Native traders paddled their own canoes to the French trading centers on the St. Lawrence, and then back to their home regions. The style and size of these native craft and the number of paddlers comprising the crew established the norms upon which the canoes, crews, and cargoes of later European traders were based. (Kent 1997, vol. 1:87)

Champlain was the first to record dimensions of bark canoes and is believed to be primarily responsible for their ready adoption by the French in Canada (Adney and Chapelle 1964:7–9). Nicolet may have traveled in a forerunner of the voyageur *canoë de nord*; approximately 26 feet long, it was designed to hold eight men and perhaps a ton of payload to carry trade goods going out and beaver and other peltry returning. Alternatively, the party might have traveled in two such canoes as a hedge against accidents, but eight paddlers together meant greater speed in the possible need for a fast getaway and strengthens the argument for a single canoe. Weighing about 200 pounds, it was easily portaged by two men but, sturdily constructed and sheathed in birch bark, its size helped it to withstand fierce waters, a fact that militates against the likelihood of the expedition using two smaller canoes. While canoe construction took only a few days, depending on size, the gathering and processing of its component materials for shell, ribs, gunwales, sewing, and caulking took much longer. Although minor repairs could be made readily en route with materials at hand, the large canoe was a precious, not easily replaced possession on which men's fate depended.

As noted in the discussion of the various purported landfalls, the chronology of events that Vimont presented out of sequence really begins with Nicolet sending one of his Indian companions ahead when he was two days from his "destination," clearly a precautionary measure to scout out the situation. Had the whole party appeared en masse where they would be greatly outnumbered if a hostile reception awaited them, they might have been attacked and killed, or if captured, they stood to lose their canoe(s)—their means of escape. Champlain's 1616 map and his writings concerning his 1615–1616 expedition indicate that the Ottawa had almost certainly visited the Puan by at least 1615 and probably were at war with them; moreover, Sagard's works support this conclusion. Also, the Hurons had told Champlain in 1611 that they were at war with tribes further to the west, and they, too, almost certainly meant the Ho-Chunk (Champlain 1616 Map; Champlain 1922–1956, vols. 2:186–191, 3:43–44, 97–98, 114–115, 119). Moreover, Perrot's retrospective account of the tribe's bellicose reputation, the fate of the Ottawa traders, and the state of unrest that existed undoubtedly forced Champlain to send a Frenchman as a peacemaker just as he had to the Iroquois in 1627 (La Potherie 1911–1912, vol. 1:293; Champlain 1922–1956, vol. 5:224–231, 308–313). Nicolet must have been apprehensive at the very least and proceeded rationally and cautiously.

Given the data from Perrot and other sources, including consistent oral tradition from both the Winnebago and Menominee that the two tribes were closely allied and together controlled the Green Bay region at the time of contact, it probably did not matter for Nicolet's purposes if he made his official appearance among the Menominee or went the extra distance to the Winnebago homeland. There also could have been an element of haste to get the business at hand accomplished as quickly as possible as summer was drawing to a close. Accepting the above scenario, his advance man doubtless traveled the 60 to 80 miles between Little Bay de Noc and Marinette on foot. Besides the fact that one can travel between almost any two places on Green Bay in less than two days by water, weather permitting, we believe the party would have wanted to stay with the canoe at a safe distance if the scout did not return. When he did, Nicolet must have then gone with his escorts on foot since Vimont says his baggage had to be carried—which would have entailed somehow crossing or fording two small rivers en route. Local watercraft was probably available and certainly must have been used at the mouth of the sizeable Menominee River to bring the visitors from the east bank to the Wisconsin side. Traditionally, the Menominee, like the Winnebago, used dugouts, although in later historic times, the Menominee also used birch bark canoes like their neighbors, the Ojibwa (Hoffman 1896:291–294). At this time, a large canoe probably could have outdistanced the smaller dugouts if circumstances called for a fast retreat.

Logic argues that the prudent course would have been for Nicolet to divide his party, leaving some members behind to guard the canoe and supplies, thereby maximizing the chance of survivors returning to report on the fate of the expedition if he failed to complete his mission. The persisting sense of peril is underscored by the fact that even on arrival at his unnamed destination, Nicolet and the Hurons accompanying him took customary ceremonial precautions. This included performing a calumet ceremony, "to relieve these tribes from the notion of mistaking them for enemies to be massacred."

The news of his coming then quickly "spread to the places round about" and attracted a gathering of 4,000 or 5,000 men where Nicolet was feasted by "each of the chief men." Presumably, these were leaders of the "tribes" comprising the formidable Winnebago–Menominee alliance and perhaps also of unnamed neighboring "nations" they had subjugated, as described by Perrot. The Winnebago would have played a major part at this gathering. After all, they were the people whom Nicolet sought. We might even entertain the notion that it was their chief who hosted the huge banquet, of which Vimont took special note, where "at least sixscore beaver" were served. We also can speculate whether some 120 beaver pelts went back with Nicolet in exchange for the "baggage" the young men helped lug to the meeting place. We can only guess about details Vimont and his contemporaries would have known as a matter of course. Nicolet certainly was the first European of record to penetrate as far west as Green Bay but obviously the Indians were not ignorant of Europeans, thanks to Ottawa middlemen traders, since his message of peace was "well received" because it was carried by a European.

That Nicolet delivered his message in Menominee country may have been more than a matter of geographic convenience insofar as it was on the way to Ho-Chunk country. By the time Nicolet set out, the French were aware that the Puans' language was unrelated to the Algonquian and Iroquoian languages they knew, but apparently they had no interpreters. Given the fact that bi- and even multilingualism was, and is, prized among Indian people, the chances are that Nicolet chose an emissary who had a working command of an Algonquian tongue, probably that of the Hurons' neighbors the Nippissings in whose language Nicolet also was fluent. Being able to speak fairly directly to the Menominee surely would have facilitated this initial overture. Vimont's claim that when Nicolet arrived he was greeted as *Manitouiriniou*, an obviously Algonquian term, has puzzled some scholars. As noted in the discussion of landfalls, it was central to Dever's argument that Nicolet never reached Lake Michigan or the Siouan-speaking Puan on Green Bay but a northerly Algonquian group also known as *Ouinepigou*. If the resident throng gathered to meet Nicolet were Menominee they could be expected to use a recognizably Algonquian name for him. Of special interest is that although the word *manito* generally means a spirit per se in most Algonquian languages, in Menominee it is associated with animals and is the root of various constructions connoting supernatural or spiritual ability such as "he does wonders" or "he is animal-like" (Bloomfield 1975:111). The term provided by Vimont thus seems particularly apt in a Menominee context: the "wonderful man or being."

The speculation that Nicolet stopped at Little Bay de Noc to take stock of his situation is supported by a number of factors. In contrast to another possibility, Big Bay de Noc, it is closer to the mouth of the Menominee River—about the right distance for two days' travel by foot. It also is a more sheltered stopping place, particularly its farthest extension, Upper Little Bay de Noc; Nicolet's Indian companions might even have known about it as a safe haven and planned to cache the canoe there until they could ascertain what kind of welcome was in store for them. This assertion is strengthened by the fact that the Ottawa certainly knew of both Big and Little Bay de Noc. Both of them appear directly below "Les puans" on Champlain's 1616 map, and he undoubtedly learned about them from the Ottawa in 1615 (Champlain 1616 Map; Champlain 1922–1956, vol. 3:43–44).

Bay de Noc, sometimes referred to as a single geographic feature including Little and Big Bay de Noc, was named for the Noquet, described briefly in the *Handbook* as a small, widely dispersed tribe of the Upper Peninsula that was absorbed by either the Ojibwa or Menominee (Hodge 1907–1910, vol. 2:82). Augustin Grignon, 1780–1860, a particularly reliable source who was associated through trade and marriage with the Menominee people, considered them part of the Menominee tribe and observed, "The earliest locality of the Menominees, at the first visits of the whites, was at Bay de Noque and the Menominee River; and those at Bay de Noque were called by the early French, *Des Noques* or *Des Noquia*" (Grignon 1857:265). Vimont's account makes no mention of Nicolet meeting any Indians when he stopped two days' distance from his destination, but Grignon's memoir indicates that the Bay de Noc area was Menominee territory. Grignon, of course, is talking about the eighteenth century when the fur trade was well established.

A final element of Nicolet's journey that must be examined is the fact that he told the Jesuit Paul Le Jeune that "if he had sailed three days' journey farther on a great river which issues from this lake, he would have found the sea." The context of Le Jeune's remark concerned a confused Englishman who had blundered into French territory with a party of 20 Abnaki Indians seeking a route "to the sea of the North," and was escorted on his way back toward the English settlements under armed guard. Le Jeune also speaks of this as a freshwater sea. As discussed earlier, Lawson, among others, thought Le Jeune had made reference to the Fox River and Lake Michigan while Hall equated it with the Illinois River with convoluted reasoning to account for a river said to issue from rather than into Lake Michigan. Moreover, this was an idea originally championed by Louise P. Kellogg in 1925, but in the end she hinted that the "great sea" was most likely the Mississippi River (1925:81–82, 82n).

However, the strongest possibility is one that the "great river" to which Nicolet referred was the St. Mary's River, and the "sea," identified by historians as Lake Michigan as the source of this river, was really Lake Superior. This requires some explanation, for if one reads Le Jeune's passage carefully, we see that it is a geographical impossibility. He stated that Nicolet told him that had he traveled three days on a "great river" that issues from the "second great lake of the Hurons [Lake Michigan]," Nicolet would have entered the freshwater sea. No river issues from Lake Michigan, much less a great river. However, if we assume that Le Jeune misconstrued what Nicolet told him, the story can be rationalized. Nicolet must have told him that the great river issues forth from this previously unknown sea, or Lake Superior, and it issues into the "the second great lake of the Hurons," or Lake Michigan.

This identification is bolstered by the fact that Paul Ragueneau, a later Jesuit, wrote in 1648 that the "Freshwater Sea," or Lake Huron, is connected by a rapids to another "superior Lake," or Lake Superior. He stated that Lake Superior is separated from another large, freshwater lake called the "Lake of the Puants" by a peninsula of land that is easily identified as the Upper Peninsula of Michigan. Ragueneau asserted that this lake is linked to Lake Huron "by a mouth on the other side of the Peninsula, about ten leagues [25 miles] farther West than the Sault [or rapids]." While the distance is actually closer to 40 miles, his geography is sound, for the mouth to which he refers is the Straits of Mackinac, and Lake of the Puants is Lake Michigan. Finally, Ragueneau states, "On its shores [Lake Michigan] dwell other nations . . . called Puants" (Thwaites 1896–1901, vol. 33:149–151). This is a very accurate description of the basic geography of the upper Great Lakes, particularly the confluences of Lakes Huron, Michigan, and Superior at the Straits of Mackinac and the Sault Ste. Marie Rapids.

As mentioned in chapter 4, Ronald Stiebe insists that Ragueneau came into possession of information concerning Lake Superior due to an unrecorded voyage there in 1647, but, as we have argued, his evidence is thin, at best. Nevertheless, Ragueneau definitely had access to better information than did Le Jeune. Between 1641 and 1645, the Jesuits and their assistants had gathered additional geographic data that finally corrected the mistaken notions of Champlain that had conflated Lakes Michigan and Superior into a single body of water. For example, an expedition to the Sault Ste. Marie Rapids in September 1641 led by the Jesuits Charles Raymbault and Isaac Jogues appears to have confirmed much of the geographical information gathered by Nicolet. Moreover, a letter written by Mother Marie de l'Incarnation in 1646 strongly suggests that the French, by 1645, clearly understood that there were two great lakes west of Lake Huron (Thwaites 1896–1901, vol. 23:221–227; Heidenreich 1980:92–93). Conrad Heidenreich asserts that Médart Chouart des Groseilliers may have gathered some of this information in unrecorded journeys into the upper Great Lakes region prior to 1645 (Heidenreich

1997:97, 100–101). While this may be speculative, there is little doubt that the French had perfected their understanding of upper Great Lakes by 1645. For this reason, Ragueneau communicated the true geography of this region in 1648. Le Jeune, on the other hand, possessed only information provided by Nicolet, and thus, his understanding of the upper Great Lakes was not as accurate as that of Ragueneau.

Moreover, the St. Mary's River is, truly, a great river. The Jesuits established a mission at the Sault Ste. Marie Rapids in 1660 (Tanner 1987:36–37), and the description of one of these Jesuit priests leaves little doubt that the seventeenth-century French believed the St. Mary's to be a "great river." Fr. Claude Dablon wrote in 1670:

> What is commonly called the Sault [Sault Ste. Marie Rapids] is not properly a Sault, or a very high waterfall, but a very violent current of waters from Lake Superior,—which, finding themselves checked by a great number of rocks that dispute their passage, form a dangerous cascade of half a league [one mile] in width, all these waters descending and plunging headlong together, as if by a flight of stairs, over the rocks which bar the whole river. It [the Sault Ste. Marie Rapids] is three leagues [about six and a half miles] below Lake Superior, and twelve leagues [25 miles] above the Lake of the Hurons [Lake Huron], this entire extent making a beautiful river, cut up by many Islands, which divide it and increase its width in some places so that the eye cannot reach across. It flows very gently through almost its entire course, being difficult of passage only at the Sault. (Thwaites 1896–1901, vol. 54:127–129)

Nicolet's journey actually becomes clearer if we consider his description of a three-day journey up a great river to be a description of the route to Lake Superior. As he and his companions paddled westward, his Indian guides, who were familiar with the route, informed him that they were traveling past the rapids of a great river, and that if one traveled three days up that river, it led to another freshwater body, not that they actually made this journey. Étienne Brûlé was undoubtedly given the same information about 11 years earlier. Nicolet's Indian guides also must have told him about the many other Indian groups they were passing along the way to meet the Ho-Chunk at Green Bay; indeed, Ragueneau mentioned specifically that he had received such information from Nicolet, and Vimont noted more generally that Nicolet "passed by many small nations, both going and returning." This would hardly have been surprising, for while Champlain's principal purpose in sending Nicolet westward was to make peace between the Ho-Chunk and their enemies, he always wanted to learn more about the geography and the people of northeastern North America, as did the Jesuits. When one considers the writings of Le Jeune, Vimont, and Ragueneau, it would seem that Nicolet did an admirable job in this regard.

It is difficult to know the starting point that Nicolet had in mind when he told Le Jeune that it was a three-day journey by canoe up the St. Mary's River to Lake Superior. What has thrown previous scholars off has been that they thought he was talking about a body of water three days distant from his final destination where he met the Ho-Chunk and the Menominee (Kellogg 1925:81–82). We believe Nicolet referred instead to a point along the route that he and his guides traveled from Lake Huron to Green Bay. Whether Nicolet skirted the southern shore of Lake Huron north of Manitoulin, Cockburn, and Drummond Islands, or the southern shores of these islands, he eventually would have ended up at about the same place: the strait between Drummond Island and the eastern tip of the Upper Peninsula of Michigan. This is sometimes referred to as the Straits of St. Mary (Schoolcraft 1821:126). It was almost certainly at this point, where the St. Mary's River enters Lake Huron, that Nicolet reckoned a three-day journey to Lake Superior.

This conclusion is supported by a journal kept by Henry Rowe Schoolcraft, who accompanied Lewis Cass, the governor of Michigan Territory, on a canoe voyage from Mackinac Island to Lake Superior in 1820. The party of 42 persons and four canoes was camped at the Straits of St. Mary on the morning of June 14, 1820. The members of the party traveled north from there and stayed two days (June 15–16) at the village at Sault Ste. Marie to hold a council with the local Indians. They resumed their journey on the morning of June 17. Because they had to negotiate the main rapids, their canoes carried only half-loads over the churning waters while the soldiers who accompanied the party carried the remaining baggage by land over the half-mile portage. This task consumed an entire day. The next day, June 18, they traveled the remaining length of the river into Lake Superior. Thus, Cass's party required three days of travel to go from the Straits of St. Mary to the entrance of Lake Superior (Schoolcraft 1821:125–142).

When Cass made his journey, the historians had not yet "discovered" Nicolet in the Jesuits' records and, as far as we know, neither Winnebago nor Menominee oral tradition preserved recollections of his brief appearance. The "first" Frenchmen they remembered were probably the trader-diplomat Perrot and the Jesuit father Allouez who arrived more than 30 years later and heralded the beginning of continuous European contact. Whatever promise of peace Nicolet achieved was short-lived, and Nicolet was forgotten by Indians and whites. Perrot makes no mention of him and claimed to be the first white man the Indians around Green Bay had ever seen. Meanwhile, the Puan had suffered defeats and disasters and during the eighteenth century began their migration south and west, establishing regular villages in their old seasonal hunting grounds. For all that, as late as the 1820s when the New York tribes approached the Menominee, by then firmly ensconced on both sides of Green Bay, for land to settle on, the Menominee respected the Ho-Chunks' prior claims of occupancy and considered it necessary for them to participate in the decision (Lurie 2002:19).

It also is possible that the first Frenchmen the Ho-Chunk recall meeting were actually Pierre-Esprit Radisson and his brother-in-law, known as des Groseilliers, who were in the Green Bay area about 1654 (Radisson 1961:239–

258). Radisson makes no mention of the Ho-Chunk by name or location apart from the term "Lake of the Stinkings," his delightfully Gallicized version of the usual English translation of Puan as "Stinkard." These adventurers appear to have arrived during a hiatus in the hostilities after Nicolet's visit if the Ho-Chunk were among the tribes on Green Bay included in Radisson's passing comment: "We meet with several nations, all sedentary, amazed to see us, and were very civil" (Radisson 1961:91).

If the first Frenchmen the Ho-Chunk recall meeting were Radisson and des Groseilliers, according to their traditions it would have been at Red Banks. This location has been invested with historical importance almost entirely because of its alleged association with Nicolet, a European, to the neglect of preservation and systematic study of the Ho-Chunk heritage there and in the region at large. The fort at Red Banks occupied but a small area and, it seems, relatively late at that, of the vast and varied resource base needed to support what by all accounts was a large Ho-Chunk population before contact.

The duration and possible stages of Nicolet's return journey are as open to debate as the location of his landfall, although not of as much interest to most Nicolet scholars. Sulte figured that the journey between Quebec and Wisconsin took 10 weeks each way, a calculation that does not take into account that a good part of the return journey would be downstream, helped by prevailing westerly winds, and perhaps faster. He established Nicolet's departure from Quebec as early July 1634 on the basis of the Indians' usual time of returning to their homelands after trading their furs with the French, but he admits it is only his "supposition" that Nicolet spent the winter in Wisconsin and "return[ed] to Canada with the trading parties the following summer," that is, July 1635 (1908:192). Butterfield simply uses Sulte's dates in his biography of Nicolet (1881:72). Henri Jouan, believing Nicolet explored far beyond the Puan, ignored Sulte's departure date and has Nicolet setting out in June 1634 and not returning to Quebec until December 1635, a period of about 20 months (Jouan 1888:15). As editor of *The Jesuit Relations*, Thwaites accepted Jouan's dates, evidently also figuring in time to explore, since he also accepted Le Jeune's erroneous belief that Nicolet actually visited all the tribes whose names he learned about during his travels (Thwaites 1896–1901, vol. 8:295).

Hall uses Jouan's June departure date but, like Sulte, recognizes that December is simply the first recorded mention of Nicolet after his journey, not necessarily the time he arrived in Three Rivers. The return journey is particularly germane to Hall's choice of a landfall as he is obliged to give Nicolet time to get all the way to Illinois and poke around the presumed Winnebago villages there before starting back in the summer of 1635. He concludes that Nicolet was away "from June of 1634 until the beginning of autumn of 1635; maybe fifteen or sixteen months" (Hall 1993:12). The opinion that Nicolet did not set out for home until 1635 rests, of course, on the problems of travel in the winter when Nicolet and his companions would have had to hole up somewhere.

Vimont's terse entry seems to offer the best clue as to Nicolet's return trip: "The peace was concluded; he returned to the Hurons, and some time later to the Three Rivers [Trois Rivières]." If Sulte's calculation of 10 weeks is correct, Nicolet would have arrived in Wisconsin by the beginning of September or somewhat earlier as he started from Trois Rivières. He would have arrived considerably earlier if he started out in June as Jouan believed. If Nicolet went no farther than some location on Green Bay, even as far as Red Banks as is popularly believed, and did not tarry after completing his mission as Vimont seems to say, he would have needed only a couple weeks to return to Huron country on Georgian Bay, considerably less than half the distance to Quebec or even Trois Rivières.

It is worth considering the importance of the role of Nicolet's Huron guides in trying to determine his itinerary. Unless they were very atypical Great Lakes Indians in the seventeenth century, they would have wanted to get back to their own country before "freeze-up" in 1634 so they could trap for trade peltry and hunt for their own families' winter subsistence. Following this logic, Nicolet reached Huronia about the end of September 1634 and wintered there. The next spring he made his way to Trois Rivières with the fur flotillas and then, on some unrecorded date, wound up again at Quebec. We know he was in Quebec when Champlain died there on Christmas Day of 1635, but there is no information to indicate that he ever had the opportunity to report on his journey to Champlain. It really didn't matter because the French were unable to capitalize on his mission and it was forgotten until Shea's passing observation that Nicolet was the first European to reach Lake Michigan. Interest in Nicolet was further stimulated by Sulte's reappraisal of the data, establishing the date of Nicolet's departure from Quebec as 1634 rather than 1639 as Shea had believed.

C. W. Butterfield, who considered Nicolet responsible for opening the Northwest to European discovery and expansion, was determined to rescue him from obscurity. While Butterfield let his imagination fill in many of the gaps in the record of Nicolet's journey, he found reasonably complete and reliable documentation of his life prior to and after the journey. His biography of Nicolet reveals not only a man of admirable character and considerable accomplishments, but it also sheds light on the larger picture of opportunities for personal advancement that commercial enterprises overseas offered to members of the educated, rising middle class during the Renaissance. Nicolet was about 20 years old when he left his home in Cherbourg in 1618 to work as one of Champlain's "young men" in establishing a French foothold in Canada. He spent extended periods with the Huron and Nipissing, becoming fluent in their languages and learning to survive as an Indian among Indians while promoting their trade and allegiance with the French. He showed special aptitude in mediating disputes among the tribes. Champlain recognized his talents and diligence in entrusting him with the task of contacting the formidable Puan people in 1634.

In 1636, Nicolet was appointed interpreter and superintendent (*commissaire*) at the important trading center of Trois Rivières, upstream of Quebec where, besides carrying out his official duties as an employee of the Company of One Hundred Associates, he took personal interest in furthering the work of the Jesuit missionaries. According to Butterfield, citing Jesuit sources, Nicolet led an exemplary life, "His official labors were performed to the great satisfaction of both French and Indians by whom he was equally and sincerely loved" (1881:77–78). In 1637 he married Marguerite Couillard, Champlain's godchild; they had one child, a daughter. He never again ventured forth as an explorer, but even domestic life in New France was not without its perils, including skirmishes with marauding Iroquois and surviving the hazards of his job. During spring "breakup" in 1637, Nicolet had a narrow escape on one of his regular visits to Quebec when he was compelled to abandon his canoe to grinding slabs of ice and make his way to shore across the moving floes.

In early October 1642, he was promoted to general superintendent of the Company's affairs in Quebec, but did not long enjoy the benefits of his new position. On the 27th he was headed to Trois Rivières, characteristically on a mission of mercy outside his regular duties to seek the release of an Indian prisoner being tortured by the Algonquins. According to Vimont, he took passage on a launch or shallop (*chaloupe*) of a M. de Savigny, identified by Gagnon as François Berchereau de Chavigny (1996:100) who, with three of his men, was taking a large load of trade goods to Trois Rivières. Hardly underway, they encountered freezing weather and a fierce northeast squall that capsized their boat. The men clung to it until it was swamped by the raging waters. Pushed against the rocks, the boat sank near Sillery, just upstream from Quebec. Only de Savigny survived, barely reaching the shore and the nearby Jesuit mission where "he could only manifest his thoughts for some time by motions . . . until, recovering his speech, he explained what happened," and that Nicolet had time to say to him, "Save yourself, sir; you can swim; I can not; I am going to God. I recommend to you my wife and daughter" (Butterfield 1881:82–83, 104). This report from Vimont, in slightly varying translations, is a favorite of Nicolet scholars for its tragic irony that a man who had made an epic journey by canoe from Quebec to the distant shores of Lake Michigan and spent much of his working life traveling by water didn't know how to swim.

But think about it. Three other men drowned with Nicolet. Were they all nonswimmers? What did they say to their boss as the sinking shallop slipped from their stiffening fingers? How far could a voice be heard above the noise of the storm and rushing waters?

From being clad in a fictitious robe to visit an imagined "People of the Sea" on the contrived premise that they pointed the way to a passage to the Orient, even Nicolet's death is the stuff of myth, memorialized as an exercise in "Christian courage" by the pious Jesuits. In the grip of hypothermia, even the most powerful swimmer "cannot swim." If Nicolet could gasp out anything and be heard above the roar of the river, would a man in de Savigny's condition remember it in such poetic detail?

Although Nicolet enjoys a measure of fame for largely mistaken reasons, he had shown great promise, rising to prominence in the work of the Company of One Hundred Associates. But for his early death at age 44, the knowledge he acquired on his journey of what lay beyond Lake Huron and his new authority might have significantly affected the course of history in New France. Or not?

On July 7, 1934, a first-class postage stamp was issued at Green Bay, Wisconsin, in honor of the Tercentenary of Nicolet's alleged landfall there, featuring E. W. Demming's 1904 painting. (Courtesy of Milwaukee Public Museum)

Documents Relating to the Puan/Winnebago

Document 1:

Gabriel Sagard. *Le grand voyage du pays des Hurons.* **Paris: Denys Moreav, 1632.**

The passages below are taken from the English translation of the book cited above; see Gabriel Sagard, The Long Journey to the Country of the Hurons, *edited and translated by George M. Wrong and H. H. Langton, Toronto, Canada: The Champlain Society, 1939, p. 9. The pagination below is from the original French edition published in 1632.*

Page xix
Likewise those who, following a holy

Page xx
inspiration, may desire to go to that land to take part in the conversion of the savages, or to make a home and live there like Christians, will learn also the nature of the country in which they will have to dwell, and the people with whom they will have to deal, and what they will need in that land, so as to provide themselves before setting out on their journey. Then, our Dictionary will teach them, first, all the chief and essential things they will have to say among the Hurons, and in the other provinces and tribes by whom this language is used, such as the Tobacco tribe, the Neutral nation, the province of Fire [Mascouten], that of the Stinkards [Puan or Ho-Chunk], the Forest nation, that of the Coppermines, the Iroquois, the province of the High-Hairs [Ottawa], and several others.

Document 2:

Gabriel Sagard. *Histoire du Canada*. **Paris: Claude Sunnivs, 1636.**

The passages below are from two sources. Pages 200 and 201 are translated into English for the first time by Leslie Weidensee. The translation of page 644 is taken from Olga Jurgens, "Étienne Brûlé," in George W. Brown, editor, Dictionary of Canadian Biography, vol. 1, Toronto, Canada: University of Toronto Press, 1966, p. 132. The pagination below is from the original French edition published in 1636.

Page 200

This nation [the Ottawa] is a great people

Page 201

and most of the men are great warriors, hunters or fishermen. Here I see many young women skillfully weave braids of reeds into fine cloth and embellish it with diverse colors that they later trade for other merchandise with Indians of other nations who approach their village. . . . They live a long way from the ones we hold with, nine or ten days journey by canoe, which is about two hundred leagues or more from here: they travel in groups to several regions and lands, farther away than five hundred leagues [1050 miles] . . . and then from there transport themselves to the tribes all the way to those of the Puants [Ho-Chunk], who make up one way or the other more than five hundred leagues of country, where they trade their merchandise, in exchange for fur pelts, paintings, pottery, and other trivial items they are very interested in acquiring. . . .

Page 644

The interpreter Bruslé [sic] and a number of Indians have assured us that beyond the *mer douce* [the Freshwater Sea or Lake Huron], there is another very large lake, which empties into the former by a waterfall, nearly two leagues [four miles] across, which has been called the Gaston Falls [Sault Ste. Marie Rapids]; this lake [Lake Superior] with the freshwater sea [Lake Huron], represents about a 30-day trip by canoe according to the Indians' statement, and according to the interpreter [Brûlé] is 400 leagues [840 miles] long.

Document 3:

Jean de Brébeuf. "Relation of What Occurred in the Country of the Hurons in the Year 1636." In *The Jesuit Relations and Allied Documents: Travels and Explorations of the Jesuit Missionaries in New France, 1610–1791*. Edited by Reuben Gold Thwaites. Vol. 10. Cleveland: Burrows Brothers. 1897.

Page 83

On the eighth of June, the Captain of the Naiz percez, or Nation of the Beaver, which is three days journey from us, came to request one of our Frenchmen to spend the Summer with them, in a fort they had made from fear of the *Aweatsiwaenrrhonon*, or stinking tribe, who have broken the treaty of peace, and have killed two of their men, of whom they made a feast.

Document 4:

Jerome Lalemant. **"Relation of the Occupations of the Fathers of the Society of Jesus, Who Are in the Huron Land, A Country of New France. From the Month of June, 1638, to the Month of June, 1639."** In *The Jesuit Relations and Allied Documents: Travels and Explorations of the Jesuit Missionaries in New France, 1610–1791.* **Edited by Reuben Gold Thwaites. Vol. 16. Cleveland: Burrows Brothers. 1898.**

Page 253

We have also thought of setting apart some for the study of new languages. We were considering three other languages, of Peoples that are nearest to us,—that of the Algonquains, scattered on all sides, both to the South and to the North of our great Lake; that of the neutral Nation, which is a main gateway for the Southern tribes; that of the Nation of the Stinkards, which is one of the most important openings for the Western tribes, and somewhat more for the Northern. But we have not yet found ourselves strong enough to keep our acquisitions, and at the same time to dream of so many new conquests; so we have judged it wiser to defer the execution of this plan for some time longer, and to content ourselves, meanwhile, with seizing the opportunity that God has sent to our doors,—that of entering a nation of the Neutral language through the arrival in this country of the Weanohronons, who have taken refuge here, as we shall relate hereafter, and who formed one of the Nations allied with the neutral Nation.

Document 5:

François du Peron. **"Letter of Father François du Peron of the Society of Jesus, to Father Joseph Imbert du Peron, his Brother, Religious of the Same Society . . . 27th of April, 1639."** In *The Jesuit Relations and Allied Documents: Travels and Explorations of the Jesuit Missionaries in New France, 1610–1791.* **Edited by Reuben Gold Thwaites. Vol. 15. Cleveland: Burrows Brothers. 1898.**

Page 153

So much for the cultivation of the land, which is the occupation and employment of the Huron women; that of the men is fishing, hunting, trading with the French and other neighboring tribes, such as the tobacco nation, the Neutral nation, that of the Sault, that of the "raised hair," that of the "stinking people," etc.

Document 6:

Paul Le Jeune. "Relation of What Occurred in New France, in the Year 1640." In *The Jesuit Relations and Allied Documents: Travels and Explorations of the Jesuit Missionaries in New France, 1610–1791*. Edited by Reuben Gold Thwaites. Vol. 18. Cleveland: Burrows Brothers. 1898.

Page 231

To the South of these is an Island in this fresh-water sea about thirty leagues [sixty-three miles] long, inhabited by the Outaouan; these are people who have come from the nation of the raised hair. After the Amikouai, upon the same shores of the great lake, are the Oumisagai, whom we pass while proceeding to Baouichtigouian,—that is to say, to the nation of the people of the Sault, for, in fact, there is a Rapid, which rushes at this point into the fresh-water sea. Beyond this rapid we find the little lake, upon the shores of which, to the North, are the Roquai. To the North of these are the Mantoue, people who navigate very little, living upon the fruits of the earth. Passing this smaller lake, we enter the second fresh-water sea, upon the shores of which are the Maroumine; and still farther, upon the same banks, dwell the Ouinipigou, a sedentary people, who are very numerous; some of the French call them the "Nation of Stinkards," because the Algonquin word "ouinipeg" signifies "bad-smelling water," and they apply this name to the water of the salt sea,—so that these peoples are called Ouinipigou because they come from the shores of a sea about which we have no knowledge; and hence they ought not to be called the nation of Stinkards, but the nation of the sea. In the neighborhood of this nation are the Naduesiu, the Assinipour, the Eriniouai, the Rasaouakoueton, and the Pouutouatami. These are the names of a part of the nations which are beyond the shores of the great river saint Lawrence and of the great lakes of

Page 233

the Hurons on the North. I will now visit the Southern shores. I will say, by the way, that sieur Nicolet, interpreter of the Algonquin and Huron languages for the Gentlemen of new France, has given me the names of these nations, which he himself has visited, for the most part in their own country. All these peoples understand Algonquin, except the Hurons, who have a language of their own, as also have the Ouinipigou, or people of the sea. . . .

Page 235

On the twenty-fourth day of June, an Englishman arrived here with one of his servants, brought in canoes by twenty Abnaquiois Savages. He departed from the lake or river Quinibequi in Lacadie, where the English have a settlement, to search for some route through these countries to the sea of the North. Monsieur the Governor, having learned of this, did not permit him to come to Kebec; he sent him away, guarded by some soldiers, enjoining him to hasten his return. He set about doing so, but some of the principal Savages who had brought him having fallen sick, and the streams or brooks by which he had journeyed having dried up, he came and threw himself into the hands of the French to avoid the death that he could scarcely escape on his return, so horrible and frightful are the roads. Monsieur de Montmagny had him taken to Tadoussac, that he might return to England by way of France.

This good man related some wonderful things to

Page 237

us about new Mexico. "I have learned," said he, "that one can sail to that country through seas that are North of it. For two years I have ranged the whole Southern coast, from Virginia to Quinebiqui, seeking to find some great river or great lake that might lead me to peoples who had some knowledge of this sea which is to the North of Mexico. Not having found any, I came to this country to enter the Saguené, and penetrate, if I could, with the Savages of the country, to the North sea." This poor man would have lost fifty lives, if he had had so many, before reaching this North sea by the way he described; and, if he had found this sea, he would have discovered nothing new, nor found any passage to new Mexico. One need not be a great Geographer to recognize this fact.

But I will say, in passing, that it is highly probable one can descend through the second great lake of the Hurons, and through the tribes that we have named, into this sea that he was seeking. Sieur Nicolet, who has advanced farthest into these so distant countries, has assured me that, if he had sailed three days' journey farther upon a great river which issues from this lake, he would have found the sea. Now I have strong suspicions that this is the sea which answers to that North of new Mexico, and that from this sea there would be an outlet towards Japan and China. Nevertheless, as we do not know whither this great lake tends, or this fresh-water sea, it would be a bold undertaking to go and explore those countries. Our Fathers who are among the Hurons, invited by some Algonquins, are about to extend their labors to the people of the other sea, of which I have spoken above.

Document 7:

Barthelemy Vimont. "Relation of Occurrences in New France in the Year 1642 and 1643." In *The Jesuit Relations and Allied Documents: Travels and Explorations of the Jesuit Missionaries in New France, 1610–1791*. Edited by Reuben Gold Thwaites. Vol. 23. Cleveland: Burrows Brothers. 1898.

Page 275

I will now speak of the life and death of Monsieur Nicollet, Interpreter and Agent for the Gentlemen of the Company of New France. He died ten days after the Father [Raymbault], and had lived in this region twenty-five years. What I shall say of him will aid to a better understanding of the country. He came to New France in the year sixteen hundred and eighteen; and forasmuch as his nature and excellent memory inspired good hopes of him, he was sent to winter with the Island Algonquins, in order to learn their language. He tarried with them two years, alone of the French, and always joined the Barbarians in their excursions and journeys,—undergoing

Page 277

such fatigues as none but eyewitnesses can conceive; he often passed seven or eight days without food, and once, full seven weeks with no other nourishment than a little bark from the trees. He accompanied four hundred Algonquins, who went during that time to make peace with the Hyroquois, which he successfully accomplished; and would to God that it had never been broken, for then we would not now be suffering the calamities which move us to groans, and which must be an extraordinary impediment in the way of converting these tribes. After this treaty of peace, he went to live eight or nine years with the Algonquin Nipissiriniens, where he passed for one of that nation, taking part in the very frequent councils of those tribes, having his own separate cabin and household, and fishing and trading for himself. He was finally recalled, and appointed Agent and Interpreter. While in the exercise of this office, he was delegated to make a journey to the nation called People of the sea, and arrange peace between them and the Hurons, from whom they are distant about three hundred leagues [630 miles] Westward. He embarked in the Huron country, with seven Savages; and they passed by many small nations, both going and returning. When they arrived at their destination, they fastened two sticks in the earth, and hung gifts thereon, so as to relieve these tribes from the notion of mistaking them for enemies to be massacred. When he was two days' journey from that nation, he sent one of those Savages to bear tidings of the peace, which word was especially well received when they heard that it was a European who carried the message; they despatched several young men to meet the Manitoui-

Page 279

riniou,—that is to say, "the wonderful man." They meet him; they escort him, and carry all his baggage. He wore a grand robe of China damask, all strewn with flowers and birds of many colors. No sooner did they perceive him than the women and children fled, at the sight of a man who carried thunder in both hands,—for thus they called the two pistols that he held. The news of his coming quickly spread to the places round about, and there assembled four or five thousand men. Each of the chief men made a feast for him, and at one of these banquets they served at least sixscore Beavers. The peace was concluded; he returned to the Hurons, and some time later to the three Rivers, where he continued his employment as Agent and Interpreter, to the great satisfaction of both the French and the Savages, by whom he was equally and singularly loved. In so far as his office allowed, he vigorously coöperated with our Fathers for the conversion of those peoples, whom he could shape and bend howsoever he would, with a skill that can hardly be matched. Monsieur Olivier, Chief Agent of the Gentlemen of the Company, having gone to France last year, sieur Nicollet came down to Quebec in his place, with joy and lively consolation at sight of the peace and devotion at Quebec: but his joy was not long. A month or two after his arrival, he made a journey to the three Rivers for the deliverance of a Savage prisoner; which zeal cost him his life, in a shipwreck. He sailed from Quebec, toward seven o'clock in the evening, in the shallop of Monsieur de Savigny, bound for the three Rivers. Before they reached Sillery, a gust of wind from the Northeast, which had raised a horrible storm upon the great

Page 281

river, filled the shallop with water and caused it to sink, after two or three turns in the waves. The passengers did not immediately sink, but clung for some time to the shallop. Monsieur Nicollet had leisure to say to Monsieur de Savigny, "Sir, save yourself; you can swim. I cannot; as for me, I depart to God. I commend to you my wife and my daughter." One by one, the waves tore them all from the shallop, which was floating overturned against a rock. Monsieur de Savigny alone plunged into the water, and swam amid the billows and waves, which were like small mountains. The shallop was not very far from shore, but it was now black night, and there prevailed a sharp frost, which had already frozen the borders of the stream; so that the sieur de Savigny, perceiving his heart and strength fail, made a vow to God, and, soon afterward striking with his foot, he felt the ground. Drawing himself out of the water, he came to our house at Sillery, half dead, and remained a long time without strength to speak; then at last he told us of the woeful mischance, which, besides the death of Monsieur Nicollet, so grievous for all the country, had lost him three of his best men, and a great part of his furniture and stores. He and Mademoiselle his wife endured this notable affliction in a barbarous country with great patience and resignation to the will of God, and without abating a jot of their courage. The Savages of Sillery, at the noise of Monsieur Nicollet's shipwreck, ran to the spot, and manifested unspeakable grief to see him appear no more. This was not the first time that this man had exposed himself to the peril of death for the weal and salvation of the Savages,—he did so very often, and left us

Page 283

examples beyond one's expectations from a married man, which recall Apostolic times, and inspire even the most fervent Religious with a desire to imitate him.

Document 8:

Paul Ragueneau. "Relation of What Occurred in the Country of the Hurons, a Country of New France, in the Years 1647 and 1648." In *The Jesuit Relations and Allied Documents: Travels and Explorations of the Jesuit Missionaries in New France, 1610–1791*. Edited by Reuben Gold Thwaites. Vol. 33. Cleveland: Burrows Brothers. 1898.

Page 149

The great Lake of the Hurons, which we call "the fresh-water Sea," four hundred leagues [840 miles] in circumference, one end of which beats against our house of Sainte Marie, extends from East to West, and thus its width is from North to South although it is very irregular in form.

The Eastern and Northern shores of this Lake are inhabited by various Algonquin Tribes,—Outaouakamigouek, Sakahiganiriouik, Aouasanik, Atchougue, Amikouek, Achirigouans, Nikikouek, Michisaguek, Paouita-goung,—with all of which we have a considerable acquaintance.

The last-named are those whom we call the Nation of the Sault, who are distant from us a little over one hundred leagues [about 210 miles], by means of whom we would have to obtain a passage, if we wished to go further and communicate with numerous other Algonquin Tribes, still further away, who dwell on the shores of another lake larger than the fresh-water sea, into which it discharges by a very large and very rapid river; the latter, before mingling its waters with those of our fresh-water sea, rolls over a fall that gives its name to these peoples, who come there during the fishing season. This superior Lake extends toward the Northwest,— that is, between the West and the North.

A Peninsula, or a rather narrow strip of land,

Page 151

separates that superior Lake from a third Lake, which we call the Lake of the Puants, which also flows into our fresh-water sea by a mouth on the other side of the Peninsula, about ten leagues [about 21 miles, although the real distance is closer to 40 miles] farther West than the Sault. This third Lake extends between the West and Southwest,—that is to say, between the South and the West, but more toward the West,—and is almost equal in size to our fresh-water sea. On its shores dwell other nations whose language is unknown,—that is, it is neither Algonquin nor Huron. These peoples are called Puants, not because of any bad odor that is peculiar to them; but, because they say that they come from the shores of a far distant sea toward the North, the water of which is salt, they are called "the people of the stinking water."

But let us return to our fresh-water sea. On the South shore of this fresh-water sea, or Lake of the Hurons, dwell the following Algonquin Tribes: Oua-chaskesouek, Nigouaouichirinik, Outaouasinagouek, Kichkagoneiak, and Ontaanak, who are all allies of our Hurons. With these we have considerable intercourse, but not with the following, who dwell on the shores of the same Lake farther toward the West, namely: the Ouchaouanag, who form part of the Nation of fire; the Ondatouatandy and the Ouinipegong, who are part of the Nation of the Puants.

Document 9:

Jean de Quen. "Relation of What Occurred in the Missions of the Fathers of the Society of Jesus, In the Country of New France, In the Years 1655, and 1656." In *The Jesuit Relations and Allied Documents: Travels and Explorations of the Jesuit Missionaries in New France, 1610–1791.* Edited by Reuben Gold Thwaites. Vol. 42. Cleveland: Burrows Brothers. 1899.

Page 221

In the second place, there are in the Northern regions many Lakes which might well be called freshwater Seas, the great Lake of the Hurons, and another near it, being as large as the Caspian Sea.

In the third place, we were told of many Nations surrounding the Nation of the Sea which some have called "the Stinkards," because its people formerly lived on the shores of the Sea, which they call *Ouinipeg*, that is, "stinking water." The *Liniouek*, their neighbors, comprise about sixty Villages; the *Nadouesiouek* have fully forty; the *Pouarak*, at least thirty; and the *Kiristinons* surpass all the above in extent, reaching as far as the North Sea. The Country of the Hurons, which had only seventeen Villages, extending over about as many leagues, maintained fully thirty thousand people.

Page 223

A Frenchman once told me that he had seen, in the Country of the people of the Sea, three thousand men in an assembly held to form a treaty of peace. All those Tribes make war on other more distant Nations,—so true is it that men are Wolves toward men, and that the number of fools is infinite.

Document 10:

Claude Charles Le Roy, Bacqueville de la Potherie, "History of the Savages Peoples Who Are Allies of New France." In Emma Blair, ed. and trans. *The Indian Tribes of the Upper Mississippi Valley and Region of the Great Lakes.* **2 Vols. Cleveland: Arthur H. Clark Company, 1911–1912. Volume 1, page 293.**

Page 293

In former times, the Puans were the masters of this bay [Green Bay], and of a great extent of adjoining country. This nation was a populous one, very redoubtable, and spared no one; they violated all the laws of nature; they were sodomites, and even had intercourse with beasts. If any stranger came among them, he was cooked in their kettles. The Malhominis [Menominees] were the only tribe who maintained relations with them, and they did not dare even to complain of their tyranny. Those tribes [the Ho-Chunk and the Menominees] believed themselves the most powerful in the universe; they declared war on all the nations they could discover, although they had only stone knives and hatchets. They did not desire to have commerce with the

French. The Outaouaks [the Ottawas], notwithstanding, sent to them envoys, whom they had the cruelty to eat. This crime incensed all the nations [Indian tribes], who formed a union with the Outaouaks, on account of the protection accorded to them by the latter under the auspices of the French, from whom they received weapons and all sorts of merchandise. They made frequent expeditions against the Puans, who were giving them much trouble; and then followed civil wars among the Puans—who reproached one another for their ill-fortune, brought upon them by the perfidy of those who had slain the envoys, since the latter had brought them knives, bodkins, and many other useful articles, of which they had no previous knowledge. When they found that they were being vigorously attacked, they were compelled to unite all their forces in one village, where they numbered four or five thousand men; but maladies wrought among them more devastation than even the war did, and the exhalations from the rotting corpses caused great mortality. They could not bury the dead, and soon were reduced to fifteen hundred men. Despite all these misfortunes, they sent a party of five

Page 294
Hundred warriors against the Outagamis, who dwelt on the other shore of the lake; but all those men perished,

Page 295
while making that journey, by a tempest which arose. Their enemies were moved by this disaster, and said that the gods ought to be satisfied with so many punishments; so they ceased making war on those who remained. All these scourges, which ought to have gone home to their consciences, seemed only to increase their iniquities. All savages who have not yet embraced the Christian faith have the notion that the souls of the departed, especially of those who have been slain, can not rest in peace unless their relatives avenge their death; it is necessary, therefore, to sacrifice victims to their shades, if their friends wish to solace them. This belief, which animated those barbarians, inspired in them an ardent desire to satisfy the manes of the ancestors, or perish utterly; but, seeing that this was impossible for them, they were obliged to check their resentment—they felt too humiliated in the sight of all the nations to dare undertake any such enterprise. The despair, the cruel memory of their losses, and the destitution to which they were reduced, made it still more difficult for them to find favorable opportunities for providing their subsistence; the frequent raids of their enemies had even dispersed the game; and famine was the last scourge that attacked them.

Then the Islinois [Illinois], touched with compassion for

Page 296
these unfortunates, sent five hundred men, among whom were fifty of the most prominent persons in their nation, to carry them a liberal supply of provisions. Those man-eaters received them at first with utmost gratitude; but at the same time they meditated taking revenge for their loss by the sacrifice

which they meant to make the Islinois to the shades of their dead. Accordingly, they erected a great cabin in which to lodge these new guests. As it is a custom among the savages to provide dances and public games on splendid occasions, the Puans made ready for a dance expressly for their guests. While the Islinois were engaged in dancing, the Puans cut their bow strings, and immediately flung themselves upon the Islinois, massacred them, not sparing one man, and made a feast of their flesh; the enclosure of

Page 299

that cabin, and the melancholy remains of the victims may still be seen. The Puans rightly judged that the nations would league themselves together to take vengeance for the massacre of the Islinois and for their own cruel ingratitude toward that people, and resolved to abandon that place which they were occupying. But, before they took that final step, each reproached himself for that crime; some dreamed at night that their families were being carried away, and others thought that they saw on every side frightful spectres, who threatened them. They took refuge on an island, which has since been swept away by the ice-floes.

The Islinois, finding that their people did not return, sent out some men to bring news of them. They arrived at the Puan village, which they found abandoned; but from it they descried the smoke from the one which had just been established in that island. The Islinois saw only ruins of the cabins, and the bones of many human beings which, they concluded, were those of their own people. When they carried back to their country this sad news, only weeping and lamentation were heard; they sent word of their loss to their allies, who offered to assist them. The Puans, who knew that the Islinois did not use canoes, were sure that in that island there were safe from all affronts. The Islinois were every day consoled by those who had learned of their disaster; and from every side they received presents which wiped away their tears. They consulted together whether they should immediately attempt hostilities against their enemies. Their wisest men said that they ought, in accordance with the custom of their ancestors, to spend one year, or even more, in mourning, to move the Great Spirit; that he had chastised them because they had not offered enough sacrifices to him; that

Page 300

he would, nothwithstanding, have pity on them if they were not impatient; and that he would chastise the Puans for so black a deed. They deferred hostilities until the second year, when they assembled a large body of men from all the nations who were interested in the undertaking; and they set out in the winter season, in order not fail therein. Having reached the island over the ice, they found only the cabins, in which there still remained some fire; the Puans had gone to their hunt the day before, and were traveling in a body, that they might not, in an emergency, be surprised by the Islinois. The army of the latter followed these hunters, and on the sixth day descried their village, to which they laid siege. So vigorous was their attack that they killed, wounded, or made prisoners all the Puans, except for a few who escaped, and who reached the Malhomini's village, but severely wounded by arrows.

The Islinois returned to their country, well avenged; they had, however, generosity to spare the lives of many women and children, part of whom remained among them, while others had the liberty to go whither they pleased. A few years ago, they [the Puans] numbered possibly one hundred and fifty warriors. These savages have no mutual fellow-feeling; they have caused their own ruin, and have been obliged to divide their forces. They are naturally very impatient of control, and very irascible; a little matter excites them; and they are great braggarts. They are, however, well built, and are brave soldiers, who do not know what danger is; and they are subtle and crafty in war. Although they are convinced that their ancestors drew upon themselves the enmity of all the surrounding nations, they cannot be humble; on the contrary, they are the first to affront those who are with them. The women are extremely

Page 301

laborious; they are neat in their houses, but very disgusting about their food. These people are very fond of the French, who always protect them; without that support, they would have been long ago utterly destroyed, for none of their neighbors could endure them on account of their behavior and their insupportable haughtiness. Some years ago, the Outagamis, Maskoutechs, Kikabous, Sakis, and Miamis were almost defeated by them; they have now become somewhat more tractable. Some of the Pouteouatemis, Sakis, and Outagamis have taken wives among them, and have given them their own daughters.

Appendix B

Documents Relating to Samuel de Champlain

Document 1:

Samuel de Champlain, Petition to King Louis XIII, 1630. In *The Works of Samuel de Champlain*. Edited by H. P. Biggard. Vol. 6. Toronto: The Champlain Society, 1936.

The original French text of the English translation below can be found in the source above. The original pagination from this source has been used below. The French text has been translated into English for the first time thanks to the efforts of Martine Meyer, Leslie Weidensee, Helen Johnson, and Gabrielle Verdier.

Page 362

I can tell you also that the country of your New France is a new world and not a kingdom, beautiful in its complete perfection, with very useful geographical features, as much as on the banks of the mighty river Saint Lawrence, the crown jewel of the country, as in other rivers, lakes, ponds, and streams, an infinity of pretty islands accompanied by very pleasant and agreeable prairies and thickets where in spring and summer one sees a great number of birds that come there in their time and season, very fertile land for all sorts of grains, pastures in abundant supply, the communication of large rivers and lakes which are like oceans crossing the regions and which greatly facilitate discoveries in the most remote of the lands from which one could go to the oceans of the West, of the East, of the North, and stretch to the South. The country is filled with wide and tall forests of all the same kinds of wood that we have in France. The salubrious air and the excellent water are on the same latitudes of your France. And moreover, if the way to China which so desired could be found, either through the rivers and lakes, some of which are three hundred leagues [630 miles] long, and if the reports of the people of the

137

country are to be believed, some of these lakes empty into the southern and northern seas, there would be through this a great and

Page 363

admirable outcome, with a shortening of the way of more than three thousand leagues [6,300 miles]. That's why the Portuguese, Spanish, English, and Flemish have tried their luck through glacial seas, of Nova Zembla [Novaya Zemlya] as well as on the side of the Davis Strait; all these attempts with great expenses were in vain and fruitless, because the ice stopped them in the middle of their voyage; all these dangers cannot be feared in your New France where the temperature is very mild in comparison to the others.

Document 2:

Samuel de Champlain to Cardinal Richelieu, 15 August 1633. In *The Works of Samuel de Champlain*. Edited by H. P. Biggard. Vol. 6. Toronto: The Champlain Society, 1936.

The original French text of the English translation below can be found in the source above. The original pagination from this source has been used below. The French text has been translated into English for the first time by Leslie Weidensee and Gabrielle Verdier.

Page 375

My Lord,

The honor of the commands I received from your nobleness, have so lifted my courage to render you any service you require with such fidelity and affection as one could wish from a faithful servant. I will spare neither my blood, nor my life in the opportunities that may present themselves. There are enough matters in these parts, if your nobleness desires to contribute his authority, which to consider, if it pleases, the state of this land which is such, that the expanse is more than fifteen hundred leagues in longitude, accompanied by one of the most beautiful rivers in the world, on the same parallel as those of our France, where numerous streams, and lakes of more than four hundred leagues discharge, which embellish these lands, that are inhabited by an infinite number of people, those who are sedentary in towns and villages, although constructed of wood, in the fashion of the Moscovites [Russians], those who are nomadic, hunters, fishers, all who want but a number of Franciscans and clergy in order to be instructed in our faith. The beauty of these lands cannot be too prized or praised, as for the bounty of the land, prairies, the diversity of forest, as those we have in France, as for the hunt of animals, game, and of the fish in an abundance of a monstrous size, all offered into your arms, my Lord, and seem that God has reserved for you and

Page 376

created for the advantage of your predecessors, in order to make a progress pleasing to God, more than any other has done, since the thirty years I have frequented these lands, which have given me a perfect understanding, as much by experience as by the reports made to me by the inhabitants of these lands. My Lord, please pardon my zeal and if I say to you that, after your renown will be extended to the East, as you have made completely known in the West, as it [Richelieu's renown] has very prudently begun to chase the English from Quebec, who nevertheless since the peace treaties, made between the crowns come again to deal with and to trouble in this river your interests, as far as Tadoussac, one hundred leagues upstream of this said river, saying they had been enjoined to leave from there, but not to return, and for this dismissed their king, for thirty years. But when your Eminence would like, it [Richelieu's renown] could make itself felt were you to extend your authority further if it pleases, to a situation that presents itself in these parts by making a general peace amongst the people who are at war with a nation called the Iroquois, who hold more than four hundred leagues in subjugation, not allowing the streams and the roads to be free. If this peace is made we will possess all, and easily; claiming the rights of the lands, we will chase away and constrain our enemies, whether English or Flemish, making them retreat to the coasts, in preventing them from trade with the said Iroquois, they will be compelled to abandon everything. It will only require one hundred twenty men armored lightly in order to avoid arrows, with this there will be two or three thousand savage warriors allied with us, in a year this will allow us to be the absolute master of all these people in bringing to them the order required, and this will augment religious worship and unbelievable trade. The country is rich in mines of copper, iron, steel, pewter, silver and other minerals which can be found here. My Lord, the cost of six twenty [120] men is little for His Majesty, the enterprise honorable, more than can be imagined; all for the glory of God, to whom I pray with all my heart will give

Page 377
increase in prosperity all your days, and me to be always in my life,
    My Lord,
    Your very humble, very faithful and obedient servant.
In Quebec, in New France,
    This 15 day of August 1633

Document 3:

Samuel de Champlain to Cardinal Richelieu, 15 August 1633. In *The Works of Samuel de Champlain*. **Edited by H. P. Biggard. Vol. 6. Toronto: The Champlain Society, 1936.**

The original French text of the English translation below can be found in the source above. The original pagination from this source has been used below. The French text has been translated into English for the first time by Leslie Weidensee.

Page 378

My Lord,

Last year I informed your nobleness that we have retaken possession of these lands in the name of his Majesty and of your Eminence, protector of such a sanctified and laudable design. I would also like to make it known that I have found these parts in a pitiful state made ruined by the English. This is to assure your nobleness that I have rebuilt from the demolished ruins, increased the fortifications, augmented the buildings, erected two new habitations of which one, fifteen leagues [31.5 miles] above Quebec, holds the entire river in check, it is impossible for a boat to go upstream or downstream without being halted by the fort that I have placed on an island that my duty has obliged me to give your name, and from here on it is called the island of Richelieu, in order to designate it under the protection of your nobleness, these parts will be inhabited and the people converted to our sanctified faith. The other is found in one of the most beautiful areas of this country, fifteen leagues [31.5 miles] beyond the island of Richelieu, where the temperature of the air is much more moderate, the territory more fertile, the fishing and the hunting more abundant than in Quebec. There it is the work that has occupied us this year, which has been strongly encouraged by the care and vigilance of Monsieur de Lauzon, without whom this affair [business arrangement] conforming to your design could not have succeeded. The confidence that I also observed in our associates has greatly guided me and given me new courage

Page 379

seeing so many artisans and families who they sent this year and that they project to send the following years for these said habitations, with war munitions and sufficient canons. And as every year the French colony grows, it also augments the habitations that terrorize the enemies of the savages, those who try us a great deal by coming to spy from afar on our people while they work and kill them in treachery. In order to vanquish and subjugate them into obedience of his majesty six twenty [120] well-equipped men from France with our savage allies would suffice to exterminate or bring them to reason. I know their strengths and way of making war which gives me such an advantage over them that with the grace of God, if I were to receive the assistance that I described above, I would subjugate them easily as a duty. The experience I have acquired in all the years I have frequented this land with this help, promises me certain victory. If I dare I would ask it of you, My Lord, as from one who can do all and who manages the most important affairs in France. If there are certain considerations that will not allow my request to be entertained, at least I beg of your nobleness if it pleases to do me the honor of keeping me in your favor, which obliges me to not only pray God for your health and prosperity but also for your life and death.

Of your nobleness, My Lord,

The very humble and very obedient servant

Champlain

From Quebec the 19 of August 1634

Appendix C

Recollections of Paul Radin, by Nancy Oestreich Lurie

*I*nformation from Paul Radin cited as personal communications was obtained in 1957, two years before his death. I feel an obligation to make clear that because the information was obtained under such unstructured circumstances I did not always recognize its significance or record it until years later. I am not sure where I first met Radin, but our paths crossed at an anthropology meeting where he mentioned that he was about to move from California to Massachusetts where he had just been offered a faculty position at Brandeis University. Since he was afraid to fly because of a heart condition, I suggested that he and his wife take a short break from their long train trip at my home near Ann Arbor, Michigan. When I mentioned this "brief visit" to Prof. James Griffin at the University of Michigan, his response was, "Ha! You mean the rest of the summer!" As Griffin predicted, the Radins settled in for well over a month until Paul was due at Brandeis.

Doris Radin was an amateur botanist and set out happily each day on our six wooded acres collecting specimens that she processed in my study in the evening. Paul spent his time reading, writing, and napping so he was well primed for socializing when my husband and I returned at the end of the day from our summer teaching jobs at the university. Paul was gracious about my work with what many people considered "his" tribe and he enjoyed hearing about mutual friends in Nebraska.

It did not occur to me to take notes on our dinner table conversations; Winnebago discussions were interspersed among other interesting topics— the Radins' recent residence in Switzerland, Paul's boyhood in New York City, academic life, politics. Over the years, however, certain comments would come to mind as my Winnebago research took me in new directions. A few of these recollections are in print (Lurie 1972:162–163; Hall 1993:33).

Others lay dormant in my memory until awakened by some of the discoveries contained in the present study.

Radin's monograph, *The Winnebago Tribe*, published in 1923 as the 37th Annual Report, 1915–1916, of the Smithsonian Institution's Bureau of American Ethnology (BAE), remains the primary ethnographic reference work on the Winnebago. Radin was the right person at the right time and place to collect an unprecedented body of oral tradition from an American Indian tribe. He made a conscious effort to separate his "raw" field data, much of it in his informants' own words and language, from his analyses. He reasoned correctly that while the former would always stand on their own, the latter, as well as information from other scholars that he cited, might require revision (Radin 1923:xv). His Winnebago field studies, conducted largely in Nebraska during the years 1908–1913, generated a great deal more data than he could deal with in his major opus, particularly myths, and were the basis of many articles and monographs. Over the years, he gained new insights and reached new conclusions regarding his field studies.

As a graduate student of Franz Boas at Columbia University he rejected the speculative theorizing about cultural evolution that had dominated anthropological thought in the nineteenth century and embraced his mentor's concept of "historical particularism," that each society must be studied and understood in its own historical context. Thus, there was an urgent need to assemble as complete a record as possible from preliterate societies before it was lost forever. To Radin, anthropology was synonymous with ethnology, assisted by archaeology and linguistics, but completely divorced from biology. He was especially opposed to anthropology seeking scientific generalizations or cultural laws, accepting the dictum of British historian F. W. Maitland who died in 1906 when anthropology was in its formative stage, that eventually the discipline would have to choose "between being history or nothing." To Radin that meant reconstructing the distinctive histories of aboriginal cultures for their own sake, mainly on the basis of evidence internal to their own traditional knowledge. He took vehement issue with his teacher, Boas, and his "school" when they strayed into the search for universal cultural "processes" based on wresting cultural elements from their contexts for comparative purposes (Radin 1933). In 1957, I did not understand his passing comment that anthropology would disappear as a discipline with the last "primitive society."

Radin chose to work in Nebraska believing that the concentration of population on the reservation enjoying relative prosperity would be more conducive to the preservation of traditional lore than would be the case among the widely dispersed Winnebago people scrabbling for a living in Wisconsin (Radin 1949:1). In fact, the Wisconsin people had maintained more traditional knowledge and practices but were far less accessible physically and socially. The reservation was established in 1865, the culmination of a succession of removals, beginning in 1832, from northern Illinois and southern Wisconsin to Iowa, two locations in Minnesota, and South Dakota whence the people fled. They finally had rebelled when forced out of Minnesota, innocent victims of retribution for the Sioux uprising there in 1862, and ended up in Nebraska where they procured a reservation on part of the Omahas' land. Most of these people originally came from the area along the Rock and Lower Wisconsin Rivers that was ceded by treaties in 1829 and 1832. This land, prime for lead mining and farming, was already filling with settlers, and the Winnebago residents, then known to the Bureau of Indian Affairs (BIA) as the "treaty abiding faction," had little choice but to move west. By the time Radin began his research they had experienced more than 60 years of forced relocations and acculturation, including the removal of numbers of children for long periods in distant boarding schools. The southern villagers also included a higher percentage of old mixed-blood families, descendants of fur traders reflected in Nebraska Winnebago surnames though now found in Wisconsin, too, because of marriages between the two enclaves—St. Cyr, La Mere, Tebo (Thibaux), Armel—whose ancestors' names appear on treaties and other documents as interpreters.

The name Decorah (variously spelled, including French variations such as De Kaury) occurs in both Wisconsin and Nebraska. The two sons of a French officer at Green Bay and "Glory of the Morning," daughter of a prominent chief, had many descendants, but Decorah also became a generic surname simply denoting a French forebear. In Wisconsin, however, the original Decorah offspring and their immediate descendants identified fully as Winnebago in language and culture.

The Wisconsin people, known as the "disaffected bands" because they resisted removal, were mostly from the north central part of the state. They believed, with reason, that the treaty by which their land had been ceded in 1837 had been fraudulent. Largely cutover tracts and wetlands known as the "barren heart of Wisconsin" with few white settlers, the area afforded a relatively safe haven even after its cession. The government made several attempts to remove these Winnebago but those who actually got caught soon lit out for their Wisconsin homes from whatever reservation the tribe occupied at the time. In 1875, they finally were allowed to take up family homesteads, and the BIA created separately administered Nebraska and Wisconsin Winnebago "tribes."

The Winnebago Tribe of Nebraska retains its original designation, but in 1994 the Wisconsin Winnebago changed their name to the Ho-Chunk Nation. This is somewhat ironic insofar as the idea was to lose them among Wisconsin's white farmers, but they scattered their homesteads around some half dozen old communities from Wittenberg in the eastern part of the state to Black River Falls in the west and, contrary to Radin's expectations, not only retained a strong sense of identity as a people but finally succeeded in getting official recognition of their own traditional name, Ho-Chunk. Its etymology is discussed in detail in the chapter on Nicolet's purported landfalls.

The Wisconsin people supported themselves by means of a seasonal itinerary of harvesting crops for white growers, trapping, selling baskets and beadwork, and returning periodically to their homesteads to plant, tend, and harvest their gardens. Unlike the reservation situation, large groups could congregate for ceremonial purposes at remote homesteads without attracting attention or BIA opposition. Children were encouraged but not forced to attend one-room rural schools when families were not on the move to pick up some English, literacy, and ciphering as useful skills. When BIA and missionary boarding schools were established in Wisconsin in the late nineteenth century, some parents enrolled children to see them through hard winters but where they could visit them regularly (Lurie 1978). Only exceptional circumstances caused children to be sent to school far away from Wisconsin.

In the preface to his BAE monograph, Radin expresses his gratitude to the Winnebago people in general but singles out four individuals whose help had been absolutely essential to his work: Oliver LaMere, his main interpreter, and his primary informants John Rave and, significantly, two brothers from Black River Falls, Wisconsin, living in Nebraska at the time, Jasper Blowsnake, and Sam Carly (aka Blowsnake). While Radin benefited from the Blowsnakes' impressive knowledge and their philosophical and intellectual comprehension to analyze traditional information, he recognized that Nebraska offered "exceptionally propitious conditions" to collect such information (Radin 1923:xv).

He arrived on the reservation not long after John Rave had introduced the religious use of peyote from Oklahoma with its pan-Indian paraphernalia of drums, rattles, and tipis, and Albert Hensley, a convert, was in process of synthesizing it with Christianity and the Bible. The new religion, soon to be chartered on a national basis as the Native American Church, appealed to many Indians whose forced attendance at boarding schools had deprived them of a traditional upbringing but left them feeling unwelcome or spiritually unfulfilled in white churches. As a revitalization movement, it also attracted people like the Blowsnakes who had been fully indoctrinated in their own tribal ways but had become disillusioned in finding no guidance in managing their lives in a white world. The zeal of some converts to the peyote religion had even led them to destroy religious objects, and Radin cashed in on their willingness to reveal sacred information.

Edison's cylinder recorder was on the market when Radin began his research and he experimented with it, recognizing its special usefulness in recording music, but it would be many years before mechanical recording was a practical field tool. Yet, he was able to collect huge amounts of data in the native language because a few years before his arrival the Winnebago had enthusiastically embraced a form of syllabic writing. According to Radin, "It was a comparatively easy task to induce them to write down their mythology and, at times, their ceremonies, and then have an interpreter translate them" (Radin 1923:xv; 1924). Finally, while Radin was linguistically gifted, the presence of fully literate, professional interpreters such as La Mere greatly expedited his work.

There is record of only one short field trip Radin made to Wisconsin. In the late summer of 1911 he spent several weeks in the company of La Mere and

Rave at Wittenberg where enthusiasm for the peyote religion assured a warm welcome in contrast to religiously conservative communities such as Black River Falls where it was strenuously opposed (Brown 1911; Lurie 1961:46).

I was still an undergraduate when I began fieldwork with the Winnebago in 1944 at a camp for harvesters at a cherry orchard in Door County, Wisconsin (Lurie 1972). I also did research for my M.A. thesis and part of my Ph.D. dissertation in Wisconsin. Although proselytizing by peyote people from Nebraska since 1907 had made some inroads in all the Wisconsin communities, the old religion flourished, as it still does, at Black River Falls and the other western communities. Radin is not held in high esteem there. Because of his publications of sacred knowledge, even some fairly neutral information was not readily divulged in Wisconsin. His idea that the Nebraska people were in a better position to preserve traditional knowledge also made him no friends in Wisconsin.

I spent the summer of 1950 at the reservation collecting data for my Ph.D. dissertation comparing the Wisconsin and Nebraska communities. By then, anthropology had not become history but something Maitland had not anticipated. Radin was resigned to but not participatory in the four-field biocultural approach, promoted by Boas, with ethnology (variously called social or cultural anthropology) dominated by functionalism, culture contact studies, and the scientific search for predictable processes he scorned as sociology, not anthropology. He considered Margaret Mead's work journalism—very good journalism, but not anthropology (Radin 1933:168–182). Even a modified cultural evolutionism had regained respectability in some quarters by the 1950s.

In Nebraska, the elders remembered Radin fondly. Many had worked with him when they all were young men and appreciated his preserving their elders' knowledge. The traditional religion had all but disappeared. I think I witnessed the last Warbundle ceremony held on the reservation. In response to the separation of the tribe, some of the warbundle groups divided the contents of their bundles in order to hold rituals in both Nebraska and Wisconsin. Several bundles have now been reunited in Wisconsin. The Nebraska community is divided religiously among the Native American Church and the Roman Catholic and various protestant denominations. The few people with continuing traditional leanings sometimes journey to Wisconsin to attend ceremonies.

Radin's bibliography reveals an astounding record of research and publication in many parts of the world, but the Winnebago always held a special and continuing interest throughout his life (Werbner 1960; Du Bois 1960). As the only other anthropologist in the world who had spent time with the Winnebago in both Wisconsin and Nebraska, I was a somewhat informed and certainly avid audience for Radin's reminiscences, but also a disappointment. His continuing concern with his Winnebago data had raised questions on details he wanted to pursue but he felt that his age and health precluded fieldwork. Since I made fairly regular trips to Wisconsin where the traditionalists lived, he thought I could obtain information he desired. As a young woman my age and sex were a disadvantage in pursuing sacred information and I simply did not have the capability for such research, just as Radin was unable to conjure up much enthusiasm or aptitude for studying material culture. I did not explain that even if I were a man with his special ethnographic talents, I knew that the Wisconsin Winnebago would not give up their secrets as the Nebraska people had done.

I also sat silent as Radin told how he got specialized information from old men who would not talk to him by paying their nephews to activate the prescribed kinship behavior that requires uncles (one's mother's brothers and their male descendants) to give nephews what they request. As fond as Radin was of his Winnebago associates, he saw his first obligation as a scholar to get the data, and honestly thought he was doing the Winnebago a kindness in preserving an accurate account of their "vanishing" culture for their descendants.

He returned alone to my home for a few days the next year while I was taping the life story of Stella Stacy, Jasper and Sam Blowsnake's youngest sister (Lurie 1961). Radin, of course, was particularly interested in this sequel to his groundbreaking publication, Sam's autobiography titled with his brother's Indian name, *Crashing Thunder* (Radin 1926b). He had been instrumental in obtaining funds from the Bollingen Foundation to help support the project and planned to write a preface comparing the two narratives. Sadly, his death in 1959 deprived the scholarly world of the benefit of what would have been a perceptive discussion of a unique ethnographic and literary situation.

Works Cited

Abbass, K. Kathleen
  1980   American Indian Ribbonwork: The Visual Characteristics. *In* Native American Ribbonwork: A Rainbow Tradition. 4th Annual Plains Indian Seminar. George P. Horse Capture, ed. Pp. 31–43. Cody, WY: Buffalo Bill Historical Center.
Adney, Edwin Tappan, and Howard I. Chapelle
  1964   The Bark Canoes and Skin Boats of North America. Washington, DC: Smithsonian Institution.
Allen, John L.
  1992   From Cabot to Cartier: The Early Exploration of Eastern North America, 1497–1543. Annals of the Association of American Geographers 82 (3):500–521.
Anonymous
  1924   The Development of Various Decorative and Upholstery Fabrics. New York: F. Schumacher & Co.
Arndt, Grant
  2008   Ho-Chunk Powwows: Innovation and Tradition in a Changing World. Wisconsin Magazine of History 91(3):28–41.
Baraga, Frederic
  1966[1878]   A Dictionary of the Otchipwe Language Explained in English. Minneapolis: Ross & Haines, Inc.
Barrett, Samuel A.
  1933   Ancient Aztalan. Bulletin of the Public Museum of the City of Milwaukee, vol. 13. Milwaukee: Milwaukee Public Museum.
Beaumont, William
  1827   Fort Howard Quarterly Weather Return, January–March, 1827. Climatological Records, 1819–1892   Microfilm Publication T-907, Reel 546. Record Group 27, Records of the United States Weather Bureau. National Archives, Washington, DC.
Benchley, Elizabeth D., Gathel Weston, and Carrie A. Koster
  1995   Preliminary Report of 1995 Archaeological Investigations State Highway 57 Improvement Project, Brown, Kewaunee, and Door Counties, Wisconsin. Archaeological Research Laboratory Report of Investigation, No. 126. Milwaukee: University of Wisconsin–Milwaukee.

Bieder, Robert E.
   1986   Science Encounters the Indian, 1820–1880. Norman: University of Oklahoma Press.
Birmingham, Robert A., and Leslie E. Eisenberg
   2000   Indian Mounds of Wisconsin. Madison: University of Wisconsin Press.
Birmingham, Robert A.
   2001[1855]   Foreword. *In* The Antiquities of Wisconsin as Surveyed and Described, by Increase A. Lapham. Pp. vii–ix. Madison: University of Wisconsin Press.
Birmingham, Robert A. and Lynne G. Goldstein
   2005   Aztalan: Mysteries of an Ancient Indian Town. Madison: Wisconsin Historical Society Press.
Bishop, Morris
   1948   Champlain: The Life of Fortitude. New York: Alfred A. Knopf, 1948.
Bloomfield, Leonard
   1975   Menominee Lexicon. Charles F. Hocket, ed. Publications in Anthropology and History, No. 3. Milwaukee: Milwaukee Public Museum.
Boilvin, Nicolas
   1826   Depositions in the Methode Murder, 18 July–4 August 1826. Crawford and Iowa County Criminal Case Files for the Additional Circuit Court of Michigan Territory, 1824– 1836, Iowa Series 20, Box 1, Folder 84. Records of the Iowa County Clerk of Court. University of Wisconsin–Platteville Area Research Center, Platteville, Wisconsin.
Boucher, François
   1996   20,000 Years of Fashion. New York: Harry N. Abrams, Inc.
Boyce, Douglas W.
   2004   Iroquoian Tribes of the Virginia–North Carolina Coastal Plain. *In* Handbook of North American Indians, vol. 14. Raymond Fogelson, ed. Pp. 282–289. Washington, DC: Southeast.
Bradley, Carolyn G.
   1954   Western World Costume: An Outline of History. New York: Appleton-Century-Crofts.
Braudel, Fernand
   1982[1979]   Civilization and Capitalism, 15th–18th Century, vol. 2: The Wheels of Commerce. New York: Harper and Rowe, Publishers.
Brown, Charles E.
   1906   A Record of Wisconsin Antiquities. Wisconsin Archeologist o.s. 5(3-4):289–429.
   1909   [Notes on Archaeology at Speerschneider Farm, Red Banks area]. Charles E. Brown Papers. Wisconsin Historical Society Archives, Box 17, Folder 1879–1944.
   1911   The Winnebago as Builders of Wisconsin Earthworks. Wisconsin Archeologist o.s. 10(3):124–129.
Bruhn, Wolfgang, and Max Tilke
   1955   A Pictorial History of Costume. London: A. Zwemmer.
Butterfield, Consul W.
   1881   History of the Discovery of the Northwest by John Nicolet in 1634 With a Sketch of His Life. Cincinnati: Robert Clarke & Co.

Cabot, Edward C.
   1946   Dual Drainage Anomalies in the Far North. Geographic Review 36(3):474–482.
Callender, Charles
   2004   Illinois. *In* Handbook of North American Indians, vol. 14. Raymond Fogelson, ed. Pp. 673–680. Washington, DC: Southeast.
Campeau, Lucien
   1987   La mission des Jésuites chez les Hurons, 1634–1650. Montreal: Éditions Bellarmin.
Chaiklin, Martha
   2006   Silk. *In* The Encyclopedia of Western Colonialism since 1450, vol. 3. Thomas Benjamin, ed. Farmington Hills, MI: Macmillan Reference.
Champlain, Samuel de
   1880[1567–1635]   Voyages of Samuel de Champlain, vol. 1. Edmund F. Slafter, ed., Charles P. Otis, trans. Boston: The Prince Society.
   1922–1956[1599–1632]   The Works of Samuel De Champlain. 7 Vols. H. P. Biggar, ed., H. H. Langton and W. F. Gangon, trans. Toronto: The Champlain Society.
Clifton, James
   1977   The Prairie People: Continuity and Change in Potawatomi Indian Culture, 1665–1965. Lawrence: Regents Press of Kansas.
Conn, Richard G.
   1980   Native American Cloth Applique and Ribbonwork. *In* Native American Ribbonwork: A Rainbow Tradition, 4th Annual Plains Indian Seminar. George P. Horse Capture, ed. Pp. 9–22. Cody, WY: Buffalo Bill Historical Center.
Contini, Mila
   1965   Fashion From Ancient Egypt to the Present Day. New York: Odyssey Press.
Crouse, Nellis M.
   1924   Contributions of the Canadian Jesuits to the Geographical Knowledge of New France, 1632–1675. Ithaca, NY: Cornell Publications and Printing Company.
   1928   In Quest of the Western Ocean. New York: William Morrow and Company.
Decorah, Spoon.
   1895   Narrative of Spoon Decorah. *In* Collections of the State Historical Society of Wisconsin, vol. 13. Rueben G. Thwaites, ed. Pp. 448–62. Madison: State Historical Society of Wisconsin.
Dever, Harry
   1966   The Nicolet Myth. Michigan History 50(4):318–322.
Dionne, N. E.
   1891   Samuel de Champlain: Foundateur de Québec et Père de Nouvelle-France, vol. 2. Quebec: A. Coté et cie Imprimeurs-Éditeurs.
Dix, Edwin A.
   1903   Champlain: The Founder of New France. New York: D. Appleton and Co.
Dorney, Cheryl H. and John B. Dorney
   1989   An Unusual Oak Savanna in Northeastern Wisconsin: The Effect of Indian-Caused Fire. The American Midland Naturalist 122:103–113.
Douglas, James
   1897   The Consolidation of the Iroquois Confederacy: Or, What Happened on the St. Lawrence Between the Times of Cartier and Champlain. Journal of the American Geographical Society of New York 29 (1):41–54.
Du Bois, Cora
   1960   Paul Radin: An Appreciation. *In* Culture in History: Essays in Honor of Paul Radin. Stanley Diamond, ed. Pp. ix–xviii. New York: Columbia University Press.

Eccles, W. J.
  1969 The Canadian Frontier, 1534–1760. New York: Holt, Rhinehart and Winston.
Erickson, David, dir.
  1994 Gather Like the Waters. Lone Rock, WI: Ootek Productions.
  1997 Ho-Chunk Stories. Lone Rock, WI: Ootek Productions.
Feltwell, John
  1991 The Story of Silk. New York: St. Martins Press.
Foster, Thomas
  1876–1877 Foster's Indian Record and Historical Data. Bladensburg, MD (Newsprint).
Fritze, Ronald H.
  2002 New Worlds: The Great Voyages of Discovery, 1400–1600. Phoenix Mill, UK: Sutton Publishing.
Gagnon, Jacques
  1996 Jean Nicolet au lac Michigan: historie d'une erreur historique. Revue D'histoire de l'Amérique française 50(1):95–101.
Galloway, Patricia, and Jason Baird Jackson
  2004 Natchez and Neighboring Groups. *In* Handbook of North American Indians, vol. 14, Northeast. Fogelson, Raymond D., ed. Pp. 598–615. Washington, DC: Smithsonian Institution.
Giafferri, Paul Louis de
  [1927] The History of French Masculine Costume, vol. IV [portfolio in ten parts called volumes]. New York: Foreign Publications.
Goddard, Ives
  2004 Delaware. *In* Handbook of North American Indians, vol. 14. Raymond Fogelson, ed. Pp. 213–239. Washington, DC. Southeast.
Goldstein, Lynne and Sannie K. Osborn
  1988 A Guide to Common Prehistoric Projectile Points in Wisconsin. Milwaukee: Milwaukee Public Museum.
Gorsline, Douglas
  1952 What People Wore: A Visual History of Dress from Ancient Times to Twentieth Century America. New York: Bonanza Books.
Green Bay Press Gazette
  1934 Historical Painting In Courthouse Caused Furor, July 18: A34.
  1951 Jean Nicolet Memorial, June 4: A 1.
  1976 Green Bay Has Many Historical Sites, July 4: A 4
Green, William, ed.
  1995 Oneota Archaeology: Past, Present, and Future. Iowa City: University of Iowa Press.
Griffin, James B.
  1960 A Hypothesis for the Prehistory of the Winnebago. *In* Culture in History: Essays in Honor of Paul Radin. Stanley Diamond, ed. Pp. 809–869. New York: Columbia University Press.
  1995 The Search for Oneota Cultural Origins: A Personal Retrospective Account. *In* Oneota Archaeology: Past Present, and Future. William Green, ed. Pp. 9–18. Iowa City: University of Iowa Press.

Grignon, Augustin
    1857   Seventy-two Years' Recollections of Wisconsin. Collections of the State
        Historical Society of Wisconsin, vol. 3. Lyman C. Draper, ed. Pp. 197–296.
        Madison: State Historical Society of Wisconsin.
Hall, Robert L.
    1962   Archaeology of Carcajou Point. 2 Vols. Madison: University of Wisconsin
        Press.
    1993   Red Banks, Oneota, and the Winnebago: Views from a Distant Rock. The
        Wisconsin Archeologist 74(1-4):10–79.
    1995   Relating the Big Fish and the Big Stone: Reconsidering the Archaeological
        Identity and Habitat of the Winnebago in 1634. *In* Oneota Archaeology, Past,
        Present, and Future. William Green, ed. Pp. 19–32. Office of the State
        Archaeologist, Report 20. Iowa City: University of Iowa Press.
    2003   Rethinking Jean Nicolet's Route to the Ho-Chunks in 1634. *In* Theory,
        Method, and Practice in Modern Archaeology. Robert J. Teske and Douglas
        K. Charles, eds. Pp. 238– 251. Westport, CT: Praeger.
Hamelin, Jean
    1966   Jean de Belleborne Nicollet. *In* Dictionary of Canadian Biography, vol. 1.
        George W. Brown, ed. Pp. 516–518. Toronto: University of Toronto Press.
Hayes, Paul G.
    1995   Increase A. Lapham: A Useful and Honored Life. Wisconsin Academy
        Review 44(2):10–15.
Heidenreich, Conrad E.
    1976   Explorations and Mapping of Samuel de Champlain, 1603–1632. Toronto:
        University of Toronto Press.
    1980   Analysis of the 17th-Century Map "Nouvelle France." Cartographica
        25(3):67–111.
    1997   Early French Exploration in the North American Interior. *In* North Ameri-
        can Exploration, vol. 2. John Logan Allen, ed. Pp. 65–148. Lincoln: Univer-
        sity of Nebraska Press.
Hill, Margot Hamilton, and Pete A. Bucknell
    1967   The Evolution of Fashion: Pattern and Cut from 1066 to 1930. London:
        B.T. Batsford, Ltd.
Hodge, Frederick Webb
    1907–1910   Handbook of American Indians North of Mexico. 2 Vols. Bureau of
        American Ethnology Bulletin 30. Washington, DC: Smithsonian Institution.
Hoffman, Walter J.
    1896   The Menomini Indians. 14th Annual Report of the Bureau of American
        Ethnology for the years 1892–1893, Pt. 1, Washington, DC.
Holmes, William H.
    1901   Aboriginal Copper Mines of Isle Royale, Lake Superior. American Anthro-
        pologist 3(4): 684–696.
Horse Capture, George P., ed.
    1980   Native American Ribbonwork: A Rainbow Tradition. 4th Annual Plains
        Indian Seminar. Cody, WY: Buffalo Bill Historical Center.
Hunt, George T.
    1940   The Wars of the Iroquois: A Study in Intertribal Trade Relations. Madison:
        University of Wisconsin Press.

Jackson, Jason Baird, Raymond D. Fogelson, and William C. Sturtevant
  2004   History of Ethnological and Linguistic Research. *In* Handbook of North American Indians, vol. 14. Raymond D. Fogelson, ed. Pp. 31–47. Washington, DC: Smithsonian Institution.

Jouan, Henri
  1888   Jean Nicolet, Interpreter and Voyageur in Canada—1618–1642. Collections of the State Historical Society of Wisconsin, vol. 11. Reuben G. Thwaites, ed. Pp. 1–22. Madison: State Historical Society of Wisconsin.

Jung, Patrick J.
  1997   Forge, Destroy, and Preserve the Bonds of Empire: Euro-Americans, Native Americans, and Métis on the Wisconsin Frontier, 1634–1856. Ph.D. dissertation, Marquette University, Milwaukee, Wisconsin.

Jurgens, Olga
  1966   Étienne Brûlé. *In* Dictionary of Canadian Biography, vol. 1. George W. Brown, ed. Pp. 130–133. Toronto: University of Toronto Press.

Karl, John R.
  2000   PCBs In Green Bay: Locations, Amounts, and Clean-up Scenarios. Madison: Sea Grant, University of Wisconsin.

Karpinski, Louis C.
  1931   Bibliography of the Printed Maps of Michigan, 1804–1880. Lansing: Michigan Historical Commission.

Kehoe, Alice Beck
  2007   Osage Texts and Cahokia Data. *In* Ancient Objects and Sacred Realms. F. Kent Reilly and James Garber, eds. Pp. 246–261. Austin: University of Texas Press.

Kellogg, Louise Phelps
  1925   The French Regime in Wisconsin and the Northwest. Madison: State Historical Society of Wisconsin.

Kelly, Francis M., and Randolph Schwabe
  1925   Historic Costume, A Chronicle of Fashion in Western Europe, 1490–1790. New York: Charles Scribner's Sons.

Kent, Timothy J.
  1997   Birchbark Canoes of the Fur Trade, vol. 1. Ossineke, MI: Silver Fox Enterprises.

Kinzie, Juliette A.
  1930[1856]   Waubun: The Early Day in the Northwest. Menasha, WI: George Banta Publishing Co.

Kuhm, Herbert W.
  1952   Indian Place Names in Wisconsin. Wisconsin Archeologist 33(1&2):1–157.

Lapham, Increase A.
  2001[1855]   The Antiquities of Wisconsin as Surveyed and Described. Madison: University of Wisconsin Press (facsimile edition with Foreword by Robert A. Birmingham and Introduction by Robert P. Nurre).

La Potherie, Claude Charles Le Roy, Bacqueville de
  1911–1912[1722]   History of the Savage Peoples Who are the Allies of New France. *In* The Indian Tribes of the Upper Mississippi Valley and Region of the Great Lakes, vols. 1 and 2. Emma H. Blair, ed. Pp. vol. 1:273–372, vol. 2:13–136. Cleveland: Arthur H. Clark.

Laver, James
  1963   Costume Through the Ages. New York: Simon and Schuster.

Lawson, Publius V.
    1900a   The Outagamie Village at West Menasha. *In* Proceedings of the State His-
        torical Society of Wisconsin, 1899. Pp. 204–211. Madison: State Historical
        Society of Wisconsin.
    1900b   Winnebago Village on Doty Island. Menasha, WI: n.p. (5-page pamphlet,
        reprinted from article in Milwaukee Sentinel, Sept. 11, 1900).
    1907a   Habitat of the Winnebago, 1632–1832. *In* Proceedings of the State Histor-
        ical Society of Wisconsin, 1906. Pp. 144–166. Madison: State Historical Soci-
        ety of Wisconsin.
    1907b   The Winnebago Tribe. Wisconsin Archeologist 6(3):78–162.
Legget, William F.
    1949   The Story of Silk. New York: Little Ives & Co.
Le Jeune, Paul
    1636   Relation de ce qui s'est passé en la nouvelle France ou Canada. *In* Le Mer-
        cure François 19:771–867.
Lescarbot, Marc
    1911[1618]   The History of New France, vol. 2. W. L. Grant and H.P. Biggar, ed.
        and trans. Toronto: The Champlain Society.
Lurie, Nancy Oestreich
    1953   Winnebago Berdache. American Anthropologist 55(5):708–712.
    1960   Winnebago Protohistory. *In* Culture in History: Essays in Honor of Paul
        Radin. Stanley Diamond, ed. Pp. 790–808. New York: Columbia University
        Press.
    1961   Ed. Mountain Wolf Woman: Sister of Crashing Thunder. Ann Arbor: Uni-
        versity of Michigan Press.
    1966   A Check List of Treaty Signers by Clan Affiliation. Journal of the Wiscon-
        sin Indians Research Institute 2(1):50–73.
    1972   Two Dollars. *In* Crossing Cultural Boundaries: The Anthropological Expe-
        rience. Solon T. Kimball and James B. Watson, eds. Pp. 151–163. San Fran-
        cisco: Chandler Publishing Company.
    1973   An Aztalan-Winnebago Hypothesis. In author's possession.
    1978   Winnebago. *In* Handbook of North American Indians, vol. 15. Bruce Trig-
        ger, ed. Pp., 690–707. Smithsonian Institution, Washington, DC.
    1988   In Search of Chaetar: New Findings on Black Hawk's Surrender. Wiscon-
        sin Magazine of History 71(3):162–183.
    1994   Winnebago Veterans and the Warrior Tradition. Ho-Chunk Wo-Lduk
        8(17):3–4.
    2002   Wisconsin Indians. Madison: Wisconsin Historical Society Press.
Lyford, Carrie A.
    1943   Ojibwa Crafts. Washington, DC: Bureau of Indian Affairs, U.S. Depart-
        ment of the Interior.
MacBeath, George
    1966   Pierre du Gua de Monts. *In* Dictionary of Canadian Biography, vol. 1.
        George W. Brown, ed. Pp. 291–295. Toronto: University of Toronto Press.
Marriott, Alice, and Carol Rachlin
    1980   Southern Plains Ribbonwork Development and Diffusion. *In* Native American
        Ribbonwork: A Rainbow Tradition. 4th Annual Plains Indian Seminar. George
        P. Horse Capture, ed. Pp. 22–30. Cody, WY: Buffalo Bill Historical Center.

Martin, Morgan Lewis
    1851   Address Delivered Before the State Historical Society of Wisconsin at Madison, Jan. 21, 1851   Green Bay: Robinson & Brother, Printers.
Mason, Carol L.
    1994   Where Did Nicolet Land? Fox Valley Archeology 23(April): 38–45.
Mason, Ronald J.
    1997   Archaeoethnicity and the Elusive Menominis. Midcontinental Journal of Archaeology 22(1): 69–94.
McCafferty, Michael
    2004   Where did Jean Nicollet Meet the Winnebago in 1634?: A Critique of Robert L. Hall's "Rethinking Jean Nicollet's Route to the Ho-Chunks in 1634." Ontario History 46(2):170–182.
McKern, Will C.
    1939   The Midwestern Taxonomic Method as an Aid to Archaeological Study. American Antiquity 4(4):301–313.
Mercator, Gerard
    1613   L'atlas mediations cosmographique du monde et figure diceluy. Amsterdam: Iudoci Hondij.
Milanich, Jerald P.
    2004   Timucua. *In* Handbook of North American Indians, vol. 14. Raymond D. Fogelson, ed. Pp. 219–228. Washington, DC: Smithsonian Institution.
Milwaukee Journal Sentinel
    1996   Archaeologists Uncover Artifacts of Early Encampment at Park, October 7, B1.
Moir, John S.
    1966   David Kirke. *In* Dictionary of Canadian Biography, vol. 1. George W. Brown, ed. Pp. 404–407. Toronto: University of Toronto Press.
Morison, Samuel Eliot
    1971   The European Discovery of America: The Northern Voyages, A.D. 500–1600. New York: Oxford University Press.
    1972   Samuel de Champlain: Father of New France. Boston: Little, Brown and Company.
Neatby, L. H.
    1966   Henry Hudson. *In* Dictionary of Canadian Biography, vol. 1. George W. Brown, ed. Pp. 374–379. Toronto: University of Toronto Press.
Neville, Arthur Courtenay
    1906   Some Historic Sites Around Green Bay. *In* Proceedings of the State Historical Society of Wisconsin, 1905. Pp. 143–156. Madison: State Historical Society of Wisconsin.
    1926   Historic Sites About Green Bay. Green Bay Historical Bulletin 2(4):1–16.
Overstreet, David F., principal investigator and ed.
    1980   Archaeological Survey of the Green Bay Coastal Corridor, vol. 1 Survey Results. Reports of Investigation, No. 87. Milwaukee: Great Lakes Archaeological Research Center, Inc.
    1993   Ed. Exploring the Oneota-Winnebago Direct Historical Connection. The Wisconsin Archaeologist 74(1–4).
    1995   The Eastern Wisconsin Oneota Regional Continuity. *In* Oneota Archaeology Past, Present, and Future, Report 20. William Green, ed. Pp. 33–64. Iowa City: Office of the State Archaeologist of Iowa.

2005   Data Recovery at the Boss Tavern Locality, Fabry Farm Site Complex (47 Dr 107), Door County, Wisconsin. Milwaukee: Center for Archaeological Research at Marquette University.

Parkman, Francis
1879[1869]   La Salle and the Discovery of the Great West. Boston: Little, Brown, and Company.

Pasco, George L., and W. C. McKern
1947   A Unique Copper Specimen. Wisconsin Archeologist 28(4):72–75.

Pasco, George L., and Robert E. Ritzenthaler
1949   Copper Discs in Wisconsin. Wisconsin Archeologist 30(4):63–64.

Payne, Blanche
1965   History of Costume: From the Ancient Egyptians to the Twentieth Century. New York: Harper and Row.

Perrot, Nicolas
1911[1864]   Memoir on the Manners, Customs, and Religion of the Savages of North America. In The Indian Tribes of the Upper Mississippi Valley and Region of the Great Lakes, vol. 1. Emma H. Blair, ed. Pp. 25–272. Cleveland: Arthur H. Clark.

Petersen, William J.
1960   Nicolet and the Winnebagoes. Palimpsest 41(7):325–356.

Pluvinel, Antoine de
1625   L'instruction du roy en l'exercice de monter à cheval. Paris: Chez Michel.

Purchas, Samuel
1617   Purchas His Pilgrimage, Or Relations of the World and the Religions. London: William Stanley.
1625   Purchas His Pilgrimes, vol. 3. London: William Stanley.
1626   Purchas His Pilgrimage, Or Relations of the World and the Religions. London: William Stanley.

Radin, Paul
1914   The Influence of Whites on Winnebago Culture. In Proceedings of the State Historical Society of Wisconsin, 1913. Pp. 137–145. Madison: State Historical Society of Wisconsin.
1923   The Winnebago Tribe. In 37th Annual Report of the Bureau of American Ethnology, 1915–1916. Washington, DC: Bureau of American Ethnology.
1924   The Adoption of an Alphabet by an Aboriginal People. Cambridge University Reporter (Proceedings of Cambridge Philosophical Society), Nov. 25:24–31.
1926a   Literary Aspects of Winnebago Mythology. Journal of American Folklore 39(1):18–52.
1926b   Crashing Thunder: The Autobiography of an American Indian. New York: Appleton and Company.
1933   The Method and Theory of Ethnology. New York: McGraw-Hill.
1945   The Road of Life and Death: A Ritual Drama of the American Indians. Bolligen Series No. 5. New York: Pantheon Books.
1948   Winnebago Hero Cycles: A Study in Aboriginal Literature. Indiana University Publications in Anthropology and Linguistics, Memoir 1 (also issued as International Journal of American Linguistics, Memoir 1). Supplement to International Journal of American Linguistics 14(3).
1949   The Culture of the Winnebago: As Described by Themselves. Special Publications of Bolligen Foundation, No. 1 (also issued as Memoir 2 of the International Journal of American Linguistics).

Radisson, Pierre-Esprit
  1961 The Explorations of Pierre-Esprit Radisson: From the Original Manuscript in the Bodleian Library and the British Museum. Arthur T. Adams, ed. Minneapolis: Ross & Haines, Inc.
Richards, Patricia B., and John D. Richards, eds.
  2003 Transportation Archaeology on the Door Peninsula: Progress and Prospect 1992–2004. Archaeological Research Laboratory Report of Investigations No. 157. Historic Resource Management Services. Milwaukee: University of Wisconsin–Milwaukee.
Rioux, Jean de la Croix
  1966 Gabriel Sagard. *In* Dictionary of Canadian Biography, vol. 1. George W. Brown, ed. Pp. 590–592. Toronto: University of Toronto Press.
Risjord, Norman K.
  2001 Jean Nicolet's Search for the South Sea. Wisconsin Magazine of History 84 (3):34–43.
Ritzenthaler, Robert E.
  1985 Prehistoric Indians of Wisconsin. 3rd Edition. Revised by Lynne G. Goldstein. Milwaukee: Milwaukee Public Museum.
Roberts, William J.
  2004 France: A Reference Guide from the Renaissance to the Present. New York: Facts on File.
Robinson, Charles D.
  1856 Legend of Red Banks. Collections of the State Historical Society of Wisconsin, vol. 2. Pp. 491–494. Madison: State Historical Society of Wisconsin.
Rodesch, Jerrold
  1984 Jean Nicolet. Voyageur: Northeast Wisconsin's Historical Review 1(1):4–8.
Ross, John
  1835 Narrative of a Second Voyage in Search of a Northwest Passage. London: A.W. Webster.
Royce, Charles C., and Cyrus Thomas
  1899 Indian Land Cessions in the United States. 18th Annual Report of the Bureau of American Ethnology for the Years 1896–1897. Washington, DC: Smithsonian Institution.
Sagard, Gabriel
  1632 Le grand voyage du pays des Hurons. Paris: Denys Moreau.
  1939[1632] The Long Journey to the Country of the Hurons. George M. Wrong and H. H. Langton, ed. and trans. Toronto: Champlain Society.
  1636 Histoire du Canada. Paris: Claude Sunnivs.
Salisbury, Neal
  1996 Native People and European Settlers in Eastern North America, 1600–1783. *In* The Cambridge History of the Native Peoples of the Americas, vol. 1, North America, Part 1. Bruce G. Trigger and Wilcomb E. Washburn, eds. Pp. 399–460. New York: Cambridge University Press.
Schoolcraft, Henry R.
  1821 Narrative Journal of Travels from Detroit Northwest through the Great Chain of American Lakes to the Sources of the Mississippi River in the Year 1820. Albany: E. E. Hosford.
  1860 Archives of Aboriginal Knowledge . . . of the Indian Tribes of the United States. 7 Vols. Philadelphia: J. B. Lippincott & Co.

Shea, John Gilmary
   1852   Discovery and Exploration of the Mississippi Valley. New York: Redfield.
Shirley, Rodney W.
   1984   The Mapping of the World: Early Printed World Maps, 1472–1700. London: Holland Press.
Skinner, Alanson
   1926   Ethnology of the Ioway Indians. Bulletin of the Public Museum of the City of Milwaukee 5(4):181–354.
Speth, Janet
   2000   Site Complex at Red Banks (47-Br-4/Br-31), Brown County, WI, as Seen through Collections at the Neville Public Museum of Brown County. Report on file, Neville Public Museum, Green Bay, WI.
   2001   Update on Red Banks Gunflints. Report on file, Neville Public Museum, Green Bay, WI.
   2007   Town of Scott Escarpment to Bay Project—Archeology. Report on file, Neville Public Museum, Green Bay, WI.
Speth, Janet and Seth A. Schneider
   2004   Testing at the Brown County Historical Society Gazebo and Parking Lot, Red Banks, Brown County, WI. Report on file, Neville Public Museum, Green Bay, WI.
Spindler, Louise S.
   1978   Menominee. *In* Handbook of North American Indians, vol. 15 Northeast. Bruce Trigger, ed. Pp.: 708–724. Washington, DC: Smithsonian Institution.
Squier, Ephraim G., and Edgar H. Davis
   1848   Ancient Monuments of the Mississippi Valley. Smithsonian Contributions to Knowledge, vol. 1. Washington, DC: Smithsonian Institution.
Squier, George H.
   1905   Certain Archeological Features of Western Wisconsin. Wisconsin Archeologist o.s. 4(2):24–34.
Stambaugh, Samuel
   1900[1831]   Report on the Quality and Condition of the Wisconsin Territory, 1831. *In* Collections of the State Historical Society of Wisconsin, vol. 15. Pp. 399–438. Madison: State Historical Society of Wisconsin.
Steuer, Mark
   1984   The Mapping of the Great Lakes in the Seventeenth Century. Voyageur: Northeastern Wisconsin's Historical Review 1 (1):32–42.
Stiebe, Ronald
   1999   Mystery People of the Cove: A History of the Lake Superior Ouinipegou. Marquette, MI: Lake Superior Press.
Sulte, Benjamin
   1876   Melanges D'Histoire et de Litterature. Ottawa: Imprimerie Joseph Bureau.
   1908   Notes on Jean Nicolet. *In* Collections of the State Historical Society of Wisconsin, vol. 8. Lyman C. Draper, ed. Pp. 188–194. Madison: State Historical Society of Wisconsin.
Susman, Amelia
   1941   Word Play in Winnebago. Language 17(4):342–344.
Tanner, Helen Hornbeck, ed.
   1987   Atlas of Great Lakes Indian History. Norman: University of Oklahoma Press.

Tanner, Herbert Battles
　　1900　Early Days at Kaukauna. *In* Proceedings of the State Historical Society of Wisconsin, 1899. Pp. 212–217. Madison: State Historical Society of Wisconsin.

Tapié, Victor
　　1975　France in the Age of Louis XIII and Richelieu. New York: Praeger.

Thwaites, Reuben G., ed.
　　1896–1901　The Jesuit Relations and Allied Documents: Travels and Explorations of the Jesuit Missionaries in New France, 1610–1791. 73 Vols. Cleveland: The Burrows Brothers.

Tigerman, Kathleen, ed.
　　2006　Wisconsin Indian Literature: Anthology of Native Voices. Madison: University of Wisconsin Press.

Trigger, Bruce G., and James F. Pendergast
　　1978　St. Lawrence Iroquoians. *In* Handbook of North American Indians, vol. 15, Northeast. Bruce G. Trigger, ed. Pp. 357–361.

Trigger, Bruce G., and William R. Swagerty
　　1996　Entertaining Strangers: North America in the Sixteenth Century. *In* The Cambridge History of the Native Peoples of the Americas, vol. 1, North America, Part 1. Bruce G. Trigger and Wilcomb E. Washburn, eds. Pp. 325–398. New York: Cambridge University Press.

Trudel, Marcel
　　1966a　Jacques Cartier. *In* Dictionary of Canadian Biography, vol. 1. George W. Brown, ed. Pp. 165–172. Toronto: University of Toronto Press.
　　1966b　New France. *In* Dictionary of Canadian Biography, vol. 1. George W. Brown, ed. Pp. 26–37. Toronto: University of Toronto Press.
　　1966c　Samuel de Champlain. *In* Dictionary of Canadian Biography, vol. 1. George W. Brown, ed. Pp. 186–199. Toronto: University of Toronto Press.
　　1980　Jean Nicolet dans le lac Supérieur non dans le lac Michigan. Revue D'histoire de l'Amérique française 34(2):183–196.

Tucker, Sara Jones, comp.
　　1942　Indian Villages of the Illinois Country, Scientific Papers, Part I, Atlas. Springfield: Illinois State Museum.

Varron, A.
　　1938　Silks of Lyons. Basel, Switzerland: Ciba, Ltd.

Vennum, Thomas, Jr.
　　1988　Wild Rice and the Ojibway People. St. Paul: Minnesota Historical Society Press.

Waggoner, Linda M., ed.
　　2000　"Neither White Men Nor Indians": Affidavits from the Winnebago Mixed-Blood Claims Commissions, Prairie du Chien, Wisconsin, 1838–1839. Roseville, MN: Park Genealogical Books.

Walking Cloud
　　1895　Narrative of Walking Cloud. *In* Collections of the State Historical Society of Wisconsin, vol. 13. Pp. 463–467. Madison: State Historical Society of Wisconsin.

Waugh, Norah
　　1964　The Cut of Men's Clothes 1600–1900. New York: Theatre Art Books.

Weibel, Adele Coulin
　　1972[1952]　Two Thousand Years of Textiles. New York: Hacker Art Books.

Werbner, Richard
1960   A Bibliography of the Writings of Paul Radin. *In* Culture in History: Essays in Honor of Paul Radin. Stanley Diamond, ed. Pp. 1001–1010. New York: Columbia University Press.

Whitehead, Alfred North
1929   Process and Reality. New York: Harper.

Wilson, Clifford P.
1946   Where Did Nicolet Go? Minnesota History 27(3):216–220.

Wingate, Isabel B., ed.
1979   Fairchild's Dictionary of Textiles. 6th ed. New York: Fairchild Publications.

Winship, George P.
1904   The Journey of Coronado, 1540–1542. New York: A.S. Barnes.

Winsor, Justin
1894   Cartier to Frontenac: Geographical Discovery in the Interior of North America in Its Historical Relations, 1534–1700. Boston: Houghton Mifflin.

Wroth, Lawrence C.
1954   An Unknown Champlain Map of 1616. Imago Mundi 11:85–94.

Index